America in Fiction

America in Fiction

An Annotated List of Novels
That Interpret Aspects of Life in the
United States, Canada, and Mexico

FIFTH EDITION

Otis W. Coan

Richard G. Lillard

1967
Pacific Books, Publishers
Palo Alto, California

First four editions published by Stanford University
Press, Stanford, California. © 1941, 1945, 1949,
and 1956 by the Board of Trustees of the
Leland Stanford Junior University

FIFTH EDITION

Published by

PACIFIC BOOKS, PUBLISHERS, Palo Alto, California 94302

Copyright © 1967 by Otis W. Coan and Richard G. Lillard

Printed and bound in the United States of America

Library of Congress Catalog Card Number 66-28118

PREFACE

America in Fiction is designed to help a whole range of readers interested in the complex and colorful civilizations of three countries on
the North American continent—Canada, the United States, and Mexico.
This volume, the authors hope, will be useful to students of American
life and civilizations whether they be adults using public libraries, college undergraduates, or young people in the eleventh and twelfth grades.
Through the imaginative writings listed here—novels, volumes of short
stories, and collections of folklore—the lives of human beings in num-
berless phases of American life, on many levels of society, and in many
stages of civilization are illuminated. Indeed, the book might have been
entitled *North Americans in Fiction*.

The United States and Canadian titles are listed in groups corres-
ponding to the phases and aspects of life that have been most frequently
treated by writers of fiction. The first three main lists and their subdivisions indicate the major integrated patterns of culture through
which the countries have passed. They are the frontier (forest, plain,
and Far West), farm and village (in five regions), and the Machine Age
(industry, labor, business and finance, city, high society and modern war).
The remaining three lists overlap the foregoing and yet stand alone as
elements that merit special attention. They are politics, religion, and
ethnic minorities (especially the Indian, the Negro, and the European immigrant). Since life in Mexico does not fit well into categories for the
nations to the north, we have made a separate list of novels that deal with
the human experience in Mexico. All novels included were written in
English or have been translated from other languages.

Several major subjects may seem to the reader to be missing until
he sees that they have become minor parts in the general scheme. The
Colonial Period, for instance, does not appear as such. Books laid in
pre-Revolutionary days are distributed among several categories such
as "Pioneering" and "Religion." And war, which has certainly been a
topic much favored by writers, appears under other headings. The novels of the Revolution and the Civil War are under "Politics," and those
of the World Wars appear under "Industrial America." Novels about
Americans abroad, once to be found mostly under "Leisure Class," now
appear in increasing numbers, as the United States imitates imperial
Rome, under "Modern War," "Politics and Institutions" in the twentieth
century, and in novels about industry and business.

Many novels important in literary history are omitted because they
are of interest only to specialists. A number of "big-name" authors are
missing; either they wrote nothing, however artistic, that fits into the
scheme of the book list, or they wrote nothing that can be classified,
however loosely, as prose fiction. The lists are representative rather

than exhaustive. In general, popular but unenduring writers like G. A. Henty, F. Marion Crawford, Joseph Altsheler, Harold Bell Wright, Frank Yerby, and Mickey Spillane do not appear; but a number of writers popular or propagandistic to the point of being pulpish are included because they are the only writers to deal with certain important subjects or because they illustrate characteristic approaches to given material such as the Old West of railroad building, the Populist reform movement, the proletarian crusade of the 1930's, or the contemporary pro-sex anti-novel campaign. By and large, novels in the list are more than routine love tales, thin satires, or cliché-ridden sex naturalism and possess at least a minimum of excellence in both form and content.

We have listed the books alphabetically by author under the various topics, giving the author's dates (when available), the date of first publication, and the publisher's name if the book was first published after 1919. With rare exceptions we have not made note of later editions, though many of the books we list are now readily available in paperback. We have briefly annotated each title so as to suggest the subject matter and the treatment given it. We have tended to favor substantial, realistic books over those that are romantic or sentimental or melodramatic or that merely broke ground.

We thank the correspondents who have sent us criticisms and suggestions during the years since the fourth edition appeared.

Otis W. Coan
Richard G. Lillard

CONTENTS

AMERICA IN FICTION

PIONEERING

Pioneering has long been considered one of the major molding influences of American life. Noteworthy books make the claim that it has been the most important single influence in American history and literature. We divide novels dealing with pioneering into three sections in accordance with the three distinctive types of frontier life. There was a type of life, mainly in the East, in which the forest was dominant. In another era, and particularly in the Great Plains, grassland and the absence of trees determined the way of life. In the Far West, from the eastern foothills of the Rockies to the Pacific, the mountains and the deserts caused men to fashion ways of living different from anything that they had known farther east.

A fourth section is devoted to wars of the westward movement, since the various wars with the French, the struggle between the United States and the British for the possession of the Northwest Territory, the Mexican War, and the Indian wars were all parts of pioneering—and since they all involved activities other than those of everyday life on the frontier.

1. TREES

Novels about the wooded frontier, from Maine to the Great Plains, and from Nova Scotia to Manitoba in Canada, have been numerous ever since Cooper first gave the tradition a popular start. These novels have shown colorful characters leading lives of unremitting toil and constant danger in a picturesque setting of log settlements, long rifles, wild game, domestic handicrafts, and Indian warfare.

The stories vary from the picaresque and romantic historical novels, such as those of Hervey Allen, to the more carefully realistic tone of James Boyd, Esther Forbes, and Vilhelm Moberg. Among other new writers of the 1950's, William Donohue Ellis and Mrs. Janice (Holt) Giles have produced several noteworthy works with settings in early Ohio and Kentucky.

ADAMS, SAMUEL HOPKINS, 1871-1958
Canal Town (Random, 1944). A robust tale of vigorous, colorful folk in a semi-frontier community in upstate New York during boom days on the Erie Canal.

ALLEN, HERVEY, 1899-1949
The Forest and the Fort (Farrar, 1943). A story of frontier life among Indians and colonists in the Shawnee country of western

Pennsylvania. Romantic, picaresque, the book gives an epic-like treatment to the interplay of early Americans and their forest environment.

Bedford Village (Farrar, 1944). Story of a small village east of the present Pittsburgh in 1763-1764.

ALLIS, MARGUERITE, 1886-

Not Without Peril (Putnam, 1941). This shows the customs, language, excitement, and hardship of pioneers in Vermont.

Now We Are Free (Putnam, 1952). The story follows Moses Cleaveland, General Rufus Putnam, and a variety of fictional characters who emigrate from Connecticut to lands of the Ohio Company in order to seize material opportunities and to realize freedom of conscience in religion and politics.

To Keep Us Free (Putnam, 1953). Continues *Now We Are Free* from 1797 to 1815, in Marietta, Chillicothe, and the settlement called Cleveland. Attention to the problems of changing from a territory to a state. The Blennerhassets appear, on their island, and William Henry Harrison helps during the war with Britain. Some of the research shows through.

ALTROCCHI, JULIA, 1893-

Wolves Against the Moon (Macmillan, 1940). America of the Great Lakes region and Mississippi Valley, 1794-1834. The hero is a fur trader who marries a French-Indian girl and builds up a fortune.

BEST, HERBERT, 1894-

Young'un (Macmillan, 1944). A portrait of a pioneer girl, schooled in the life of forest and field, developing from childhood to maturity. Shows a New York community on Lake Champlain changing from woods to farms in the late eighteenth century. Re-creates the ways of thought and action of the common people.

BOYD, JAMES, 1888-1944

The Long Hunt (Scribner's, 1931). One of the best stories of the frontier. A realistic story of a trapper who could not adjust himself to permanent settlement of the country. A vivid portrayal of land speculators, squatters, Indians, and frontier individualists. The main character goes on the "long hunt" from North Carolina into Tennessee.

CANNON, LeGRAND, 1899-

Look to the Mountain (Holt, 1942). A fresh, detailed story of home-making in the New England forest between the Saco River and Lake Winnipesaukee. The transformation of frontier individualism into community spirit. A sincere, clear transcript from the American past.

CARMER, CARL, 1893-

Genesee Fever (Farrar, 1941). Depicts land promotion and town building in the Genesee Valley, New York, in the 1790's, and the consequent moving in of settlers.

CARUTHERS, WILLIAM ALEXANDER, 1800-1846
The Cavaliers of Virginia (1834-35). About Bacon's Rebellion and about Indian fights. The author shows sympathy for the more democratic elements.

CHENEY, BRAINARD
River Rogue (Houghton, 1942). A picture of logging and rafting in the East Georgia back country. An illegitimate child whose past catches up with him struggles to adjust himself to a hard, turbulent world of raftsmen, squatters, and small farmers.

COLBY, MERLE ESTES, 1902-
All Ye People (Viking, 1931). Presents the panorama of settlers crossing from Vermont to the Northwest Territory.

COOPER, JAMES FENIMORE, 1789-1851
The Pioneers (1823). Pictures the "Deerslayer" as an old man in New York, feeling cramped by civilization.
Deerslayer (1841). A classic story of the woodsman of the dense Eastern forests. Forerunner of hundreds of stories.
The Oak Openings (1848). A story of a family's flight from Indians in Michigan about 1812. Cooper's last frontier story.

DERLETH, AUGUST, 1909-
Bright Journey (Scribner's, 1940). Growth of the small villages near the Mississippi River. Describes the subjection of the Wisconsin Indians and the retirement of the French-Canadian trapper.

DOWNES, ANNE MILLER
The Pilgrim Soul (Lippincott, 1952). A fictionalized biography of Hayes and Dolly Copp, who pioneered around 1830 at the foot of Mount Madison, New Hampshire. A quiet, detailed, charming picture of self-subsistence and of social change over a fifty-year period.

DYKEMAN, WILMA
The Tall Woman (Holt, 1962). Story of a pioneer woman in North Carolina. An emphasis on folkways and on the courage of those who battled for life in a difficult environment. Covers approximately the years 1864 to 1896.

EGGLESTON, EDWARD, 1837-1902
The Hoosier Schoolmaster (1871). An account of the life and love of a Hoosier schoolmaster in the backwoods of Indiana. Presents a "spelling bee," children's pranks, etc. Describes the activities of both school teacher and pupils. An American classic. Sentimental.
The Graysons (1887). Realistic portraiture of the habits of people, including the shiftless, unprogressive poor whites in Illinois about 1850.

EHLE, JOHN, 1925-
The Land Breakers (Harper, 1964).   Pioneering in the Southern mountains, perhaps North Carolina. Emphasis on the hardships of pioneer life.

ELLIS, WILLIAM DONOHUE
The Bounty Lands (World, 1952). A careful historical novel laid in Ohio before and after 1800. The author treats basic matters such as land surveying, land titles, land values and money values, and legal and Indian problems.
Jonathan Blair: Bounty Lands Lawyer (World, 1954). Stimulating account with ample action, of how a frontier lawyer helped put a big tract of Ohio lands on a sound financial basis. Fresh and vigorous depiction of land and money problems, banking hazards, and the settlers' struggle against the United States Bank.
The Brooks Legend (Crowell, 1958). Well-told story of pioneering days in Ohio. The central character is a successful doctor who never had time to work for an M.D. degree.

FORBES, ESTHER, 1894?-
Paradise (Harcourt, 1937). A kaleidoscopic view of seventeenth-century English Puritans being hardened and democratized by the Massachusetts frontier.

FRIERMOOD, ELISABETH HAMILTON
Hoosier Heritage (Doubleday, 1954). A local color and love story, designed for older girls, about a pioneer Indiana girl who becomes a school-ma'am in the Ozarks.

GEBLER, ERNEST, 1915-
The Plymouth Adventure: A Chronicle Novel of the Voyage of the Mayflower (Doubleday, 1950). Inventing dialog and sensuous detail, the author has carefully and conscientiously reconstructed the ocean voyage and the first winter in Massachusetts.

GILES, JANICE (HOLT), 1905-
Hannah Fowler (Houghton, 1956). Good solid treatment of pioneers in Kentucky in the 1770's. Full of folkways, convincing.
Land Beyond the Mountains (Houghton, 1959). Appealing story of men with large landholdings in Kentucky in the late 1780's. Detail on the struggle to get help from Congress to fight the Indians and to open the Mississippi River to trade.

GORDON, CAROLINE, 1895-
Green Centuries (Scribner's, 1941). Laid on the southern frontier just before the American Revolution, this gives an account of Cherokee life and of a group of settlers who moved across the mountains into Tennessee.

HAVIGHURST, WALTER, 1901-
The Winds of Spring (Macmillan, 1940). Pioneer days in Wisconsin from the early 1840's to about 1870. The main character is a naturalist-pioneer.

HÉMON, LOUIS, 1880-1913
Maria Chapdelaine: A Tale of the Lake St. John Country (translated by W. H. Blake; Macmillan, 1921). A tender, moving story of French Catholic pioneers on the Canadian forest frontier. Dramatizes the role of church and family mores.

JOHNSTON, MARY, 1870-1936
The Great Valley (Little, 1926). Set in the Shenandoah Valley in 1735. Deals with the strong faith of the daughter of a Scotch-Presbyterian minister who endured the hardships of the French and Indian War. Gives a version of Braddock's defeat.

KIRKLAND, JOSEPH, 1830-1894
Zury, the Meanest Man in Spring County (1887). An unsparing picture of an Illinois pioneer greedily acquiring property. Shows what the struggle against nature and against fellow profit-makers can do to a potentially fine man.

KROLL, HARRY H., 1888-
Rogue's Companion: A Novel of John Murrell (Bobbs, 1943). A romantic historical tale, based on research, of the dangerous and debonair ruffian of the area near Natchez, Mississippi. A fast-moving yarn of a horse stealer and slave snatcher, the founder of Murrell's Mystic Clan.
Fury in the Earth (Bobbs, 1945). An account of the effect of the earthquake of 1811-1812 on various inhabitants of New Madrid, Missouri Territory. Lively, humorous, and satisfying.

KROLL, HARRY H., 1888-   , and SUBLETTE, C. M., 1887-1939
Perilous Journey (Bobbs, 1943). A lusty, lurid novel of the Natchez Trace and the Mississippi River, this dramatizes life in the days of flat-boats and pirogues, backwoods cutthroats, boastful keelboatmen, and Hoosier railsplitters. Much social history is worked in.

LAIRD, CHARLTON, 1901-
West of the River (Little, 1953). Pictures events in 1837, when the fur trade was declining, in the region around the junction of the Mississippi and the Wisconsin. Concerned with the relations of whites and Indians, of the fur company and the government. Written with historical integrity.

LANCASTER, BRUCE, 1896-1963
For Us the Living (Stokes, 1940). A story of pioneer days in Indiana and Kentucky. Deals with a settler's son, and also with the adolescence of Abe Lincoln.

MATSCHAT, CECILE (HULSE)
Preacher on Horseback (Farrar, 1940). A novel of the struggle for existence on the Michigan frontier after the Civil War. The main characters are a Hungarian immigrant, who later became a minister, and his wife.

MEINE, FRANKLIN JULIUS, 1896-
Tall Tales of the Southwest (Knopf, 1930). Realistic stories of a varied assortment of forest and river frontiersmen, including bear hunters, levee woodcutters, county politicians, horse traders, backwoods doctors, homespun lovers, and hard-shell preachers. The tales exploit the humor in the lives and speech of non-slave-holding common men. They give an enjoyable and yet revealing picture of certain aspects of Alabama, Mississippi, Arkansas, and neighboring states when they were the Western frontier rather than the South.

MEINE, FRANKLIN JULIUS, 1896-   , and BLAIR, WALTER, 1900-
Mike Fink, King of Mississippi Keelboatmen (Holt, 1933). A biography based on legends and folklore, this is a full account of the man who became a symbol of the prowess of the rivermen.

MILLER, CAROLINE, 1903-
Lamb in His Bosom (Harper, 1933). A vivid, realistic account of pioneers in Georgia in the early nineteenth century. One of our finest novels. Shows the traits developed by frontier life.

MOBERG, VILHELM, 1898-
Unto a Good Land (translated by Gustaf Lannestock; Simon, 1954). This details the experiences of a party of Swedish immigrants as they travel from New York City to forested land in Minnesota Territory, where they establish homes and spend the first winter. A substantial novel, documentary in flavor.

MOODIE, SUSANNA, 1803-1885
Roughing It in the Bush (1852). Autobiographical sketches of English immigrants in their day-to-day struggle for existence in the backwoods of Ontario near Port Hope and in the Kawartha Lakes district during the period 1832-1840.

MOORE, IDA L.
Like a River Flowing (Doubleday, 1941). Pioneer life in one community in North Carolina from the earliest settlement up to the coming of industrialism. Author evidences a solid knowledge of her background.

NORTH, JESSICA NELSON, 1906-
Morning in the Land (Greystone, 1941). A novel of English immigrants who settle in Milwaukee in 1840. Gives a good picture of the times-- the forcing of the Indian out of the Wisconsin Territory, the 1857 depression, the coming of better highways and railways, etc. A picture of the many Norwegians, Indians, and British who lived in the territory.

O'MEARA, WALTER
The Trees Went Forth (Crown, 1947). A quiet, convincing story of life in a logging camp as seen by a young college student working as a clerk. Good detail about Americans of Irish, French, and Finnish descent.

PAGE, ELIZABETH, 1889-
Wilderness Adventure (Rinehart, 1946). Story of an expedition from western Virginia to New Orleans, led by Captain Howard of the Virginia Rangers, in the early eighteenth century.

PAULDING, JAMES KIRKE, 1779-1860
The Dutchman's Fireside (1831). A leisurely romantic novel, with several dramatic episodes, laid in and around Albany in the early 1750's. Introduces Dutch, Negro, Indian, urban, military, and frontier types. Gives interesting portraits of Indians as drunkards and woods fighters.

PINCKNEY, JOSEPHINE, 1895-
Hilton Head (Farrar, 1941). Based on the actual adventures of a young surgeon who went to Carolina from England by way of Barbados. Time, 1665-1686.

POUND, ARTHUR, 1884-
Hawk of Detroit (Reynal, 1939). Story of the founding of Detroit by the French under the leadership of Sieur Antoine de la Mothe Cadillac. Gives a good picture of the political and social background of French expansion in America.

POWELL, RICHARD PITTS
I Take This Land (Scribner's, 1962). A novel of pioneering in the Everglades of Florida, covering the years 1895-1946. The author succeeds in making major characters of a hunter, a cattleman, a farmer, and a railroad builder. Local color well portrayed. Some incidents verge on the tall-tale tradition.

RAWLINGS, MARJORIE KINNAN, 1896-1953
South Moon Under (Scribner's, 1933). Unusual story of backwoodsmen of the swamp regions of Florida. Emphasizes the development of the animal senses of man. Vivid.
The Yearling (Scribner's, 1938). Sentimental but effective portrayal of a family living in the Florida scrublands under pioneer conditions requiring constant struggle.

RICHTER, CONRAD, 1890-
The Trees (Knopf, 1940). Tells the story of the transition of American pioneers from the ways of the wilderness to the ways of civilization. Pictures a normal frontier family and their daily struggle for security.

The Fields (Knopf, 1946). Continues story of the family in *The Trees*. The settlement grows into a town.

Light in the Forest (Knopf, 1953). Briefly and adroitly this tale sets forth the points of view of settlers and Indians in Pennsylvania and Ohio, at the time of Bouquet's expedition in 1765 to free the captives of Indians. Excellent style.

ROBERTS, ELIZABETH MADOX, 1886-1941
The Great Meadow (Viking, 1930). Combination of poetry and prose in the setting of the heroic life of early pioneers. A significant portrayal of the mental and spiritual reactions of these settlers to their environment. Also a dramatic presentation of a love triangle.

ROBERTS, KENNETH LEWIS, 1885-1957
Northwest Passage (Doubleday, 1937). A stirring re-creation of events in the life of Robert Rogers. Details of the expedition of Rogers' rangers against the St. Francis Indian village and of the fur trade in the Great Lakes region. Gives detailed accounts of the life of an Indian scout and of the politics of fur trading. Deservedly popular.

ROURKE, CONSTANCE M., 1885-1942
Davy Crockett (Harcourt, 1934). One of the most delightful retellings of a choice bit of American folklore. A biography not afraid to make use of legend.

SCHLYTTER, LESLIE, 1896-
Tall Brothers (Appleton, 1941). Story of lumbering in Wisconsin. Contrasts the attitudes of loggers and a Swedish couple who have come to Wisconsin to make a permanent home.

SEIFERT, SHIRLEY, 1889-
Land of Tomorrow (M. S. Mill, 1937). Virginians carrying on pioneering activities in central Kentucky. The story chronicles three generations of one family.

SINGMASTER, ELSIE (MRS. HAROLD LEWARS), 1879-1958
A High Wind Rising (Houghton, 1942). Dealing with the relationships of Mohawks and whites, this novel depicts German immigrants in Pennsylvania and the "high wind" of Indian discontent, 1728-1755.

SWANSON, NEIL H., 1896-
The Phantom Emperor (Putnam, 1934). The fictional re-creation of an obscure incident in history concerning one James Dickson, who in the 1830's attempted to form, with Indian backing from the Great Lakes area, a vast empire in the Southwest.

VAN EVERY, DALE, 1896-
The Voyagers (Holt, 1957). A long, rambling story of pioneer adventurers who went down the Ohio and back to the Monongahela Valley in 1788. Realistic details. Perhaps overplays the hard, callous qualities of pioneers.

VACZEK, LOUIS
River and Empty Sea (Houghton, 1950). Canada in 1671-1678 during uneasy co-operation of royal officials, the fur company, and the Jesuits. Good on the hardships of winter journeys to Hudson's Bay, on political problems raised by the traffic in brandy, and on men caught between civilizations.

WILLIAMS, BEN AMES, 1889-1953
Come Spring (Houghton, 1940). Tale of pioneering in Maine during the time of the Revolution. Much detail on hardships and on folkways.

WILSON, WILLIAM EDWARD, 1906-
Abe Lincoln of Pigeon Creek (Whittlesey, 1949). Based on Lincoln's life from 1816 to 1830, from the arrival of his Kentucky stepmother to his return from his trip to New Orleans. A credible, detailed, and sometimes amusing account.

ZARA, LOUIS, 1910-
This Land Is Ours (Houghton, 1940). From Braddock's defeat in 1775 to the withdrawal of the Indians across the Mississippi in 1835. A novel of the Northwest Territory.

2. GRASS: THE PLAINS COUNTRY

Novels depicting pioneer life on the grassy prairies and plains have been abundant since about 1890, when first-generation pioneers began to look back and reminisce. These novels recount a grim epic of life on bleak homesteads where survival is threatened by blizzards, drought, and grasshoppers, and existence is blighted by loneliness and isolation. They show pioneers used to forests and ample wood painfully adjusting themselves to a woodless, semi-arid region which called for dry farming, windmills, and barbed wire. The very fact that pioneering was so difficult in the region west of "the great bend of the Missouri" and west of Lake Winnipeg in Canada contributed to the development of a more realistic treatment of the frontier.

ADAMS, ANDY, 1859-1935
Log of a Cowboy (Houghton, 1903). A classic account of a cattle drive from Texas north to the railroad. Realistic, rich in detail.

ALDRICH, BESS STREETER, 1881-1954
A Lantern in Her Hand (Appleton, 1928). Intimate story of the life of a pioneer woman in Nebraska who brought up her family with true courage and faith. Sentimental, but skillful enough to move the reader. Makes the farmer heroic and important.

AYDELOTTE, DORA, 1878-
Trumpets Calling (Appleton, 1938). A story of the land rush in

Oklahoma, followed by detail about life on an Oklahoma homestead. Sentimental, but fairly good in detail, as are her other books.

BOATRIGHT, MODY COGGIN, 1896-
Tall Tales from Texas (Southwest, 1934). A collection of wild yarns about many matters, especially Pecos Bill.

BOJER, JOHAN, 1872-1959
The Emigrants (Century, 1924). A solid, informative account of Norwegians under a medieval land system who come to North Dakota to get good soil and greater wealth.

BURGESS, JACKSON
Pillar of Cloud (Putnam, 1957). Factually told story of a small band of pioneers who left the Santa Fe Trail and struck out across Kansas to explore a direct route to the Cherry Creek area of Colorado in 1858.

BUSCH, NIVEN, 1903-
Duel in the Sun (Morrow, 1944). Superior to the standard Texas ranch-and-border novel. An exciting tale of the ranch and town on the Staked Plains after the Civil War.

CATHER, WILLA SIBERT, 1876-1947
O Pioneers! (1913). A somewhat realistic story of a Norwegian girl running a large farm in Nebraska. It contains melodramatic incidents of the life of what may be termed "the younger set" among the pioneers.
My Antonia (Houghton, 1918). Story of the life of a young Bohemian girl on the prairie of Nebraska and her adjustment to its conditions. She works in the fields with the men and does not attend school. She works as a hired girl in town but gains her greatest happiness as a farm wife, mother of many children.

DAVIS, CLYDE BRION, 1894-1962
Nebraska Coast (Farrar, 1939). Story of a "York state" farmer who went west to a Nebraska frontier town with his family because he found his antiwar sentiments making him unpopular at the outbreak of the Civil War.

DRAGO, HARRY SINCLAIR, 1888-
Montana Road (Morrow, 1935). A story of hectic years in the Dakota Territory. Brings in the activities of General George Custer, the rush to the Black Hills, and the great wrong done to the Indians of the Dakota country. Shows the part played by the railroad magnates in this wrong.

DRISCOLL, CHARLES B., 1885-
Kansas Irish (Macmillan, 1943). An understanding account of an intemperate Irish immigrant who settled in Wichita. Much rich anecdote and a record of pioneer life. Can be taken as either humorous or thoroughly unhappy.

ERDMAN, LOULA GRACE
The Edge of Time (Dodd, 1950). A quiet tale of sodbusters with their "sort of stubborn courage"—the women particularly—in the Texas Panhandle wheat country of the 1880's.

FERBER, EDNA, 1887-
Cimarron (Doubleday, 1930). A romantic story of the Oklahoma land rush and the gradual establishment of permanent civilization. The main character is a sort of superman.

GARLAND, HAMLIN, 1861-1940
Rose of Dutcher's Coolly (Harper, 1896). Story of a country girl who goes to the city. The thesis is that the hard life of the farm destroys the finer things of life.

GILES, JANICE (HOLT), 1905-
Voyage to Santa Fe (Houghton, 1962). Capable story of the wife of a trader on a long hard trek from Indian Territory to Santa Fe. Nice handling of various characters, a Mexican, a Negro, an Indian, and others.

HARRIS, JOHN, 1911-   , and HARRIS, MARGARET, 1912-
Arrow in the Moon (Morrow, 1954). A good, carefully researched Western and love story that tells of a man's building up a cattle ranch in Nebraska and facing the moral problem of displacing the Cheyennes under Dull Knife.

HAVILL, EDWARD, 1907-
Big Ember (Harper, 1947). Story of daily life in southern Minnesota from 1863 on. Emphasizes the hardihood of the pioneers and their will to go on even after a terrible Indian massacre.

HOUGH, EMERSON, 1857-1923
The Covered Wagon (Appleton, 1922). Popular fiction, treating the westward emigration. Melodrama and heroic action.

LANE, ROSE WILDER, 1887-
Free Land (Longmans, 1938). Deals with the struggles of a young couple homesteading in South Dakota. Describes the cold, hunger, and crop failures.

LANHAM, EDWIN M., 1904-
The Wind Blew West (Longmans, 1935). Of the booming of a new town west of Fort Worth by the settlers' advertising their adventures. A story of hardships, Indian fights, etc. Realistic.

LAURENCE, MARGARET, 1926-
The Stone Angel (Knopf, 1964). The story of a pioneer woman in Manitoba. As a woman of ninety, she recalls episodes of her life, her marriage to a middle-aged farmer, her later life as a housekeeper for an elderly man on the West Coast after she leaves her husband, her

return to the ranch, her life as an old woman with her married son and his wife. Starkly realistic.

MANFRED, FREDERICK FEIKEMA (originally FEIKE FEIKEMA), 1912-
Lord Grizzly (McGraw, 1954). A vigorous retelling of the story of Hugh Glass. Built around his wrestle with a grizzly bear, his long crawl, and his vengeful chase—during the period 1822-1833.

O'MEARA, WALTER
The Grand Portage (Bobbs, 1951). A carefully documented novel, free of cliché but also slim on story, based on the life of Daniel Harmon of the North West Company during the great days of the fur business in central Canada. Readable history for the period 1800-1819.

OSKISON, JOHN M., 1874-
Black Jack Davy (Appleton, 1926). Life among Indian Territory pioneers and the Oklahoma land rush of 1889. A quarrelsome neighbor makes trouble for the settlement Indians and for Black Jack Davy's foster parents, who are newcomers.

PORTER, WILLIAM SYDNEY (O. HENRY, pseud.), 1867-1910
The Heart of the West (1907). Stories of Texas cow country, in O. Henry style.

QUICK, HERBERT, 1861-1925
Vandemark's Folly (Bobbs, 1922). A well-rounded picture of immigrants to Iowa and their establishment of permanent homes. Some realistic details; a romantic plot reminiscent of *Lorna Doone*.
Hawkeye (Bobbs, 1923). Sequel to *Vandemark's Folly;* same community, but not the same main characters.

REID, MAYNE, 1818-1883
Boy Hunters of the Mississippi (1852). Adventures of boys who go from Louisiana to Texas to hunt for a white buffalo. Much data about flora and fauna. Adventures in hunting various animals.

RHODES, EUGENE MANLOVE, 1869-1940
Good Men and True (1910). A tale of cowboy ingenuity. Debunks some of the cowboy legend.

RICHTER, CONRAD, 1890-
The Sea of Grass (Knopf, 1937). Story of the struggles of the nesters to till the dry country. Shows the cattleman as knowing the uses to which the country could be put, also the waste involved in plowing this land. Pictures the contrast of a courageous husband, who wishes to grow wheat, and his wife, who longs for the city.

ROLLINS, PHILIP A., 1869-
Jinglebob (Scribner's, 1927). Based on the story of a real cowboy, comparable to Adams' *Log of a Cowboy*.

ROLVAAG, OLE E., 1876-1931
Giants in the Earth (Harper, 1927). Our finest novel of pioneering on the Great Plains. Realistic. Per Hansa, strong and resourceful, Beret, his homesick and neurotic wife, and other Norwegian immigrants open up new lands in Dakota Territory. Emphasizes psychological effects of their struggle.

SANDOZ, MARI, 1907-1966
Slogum House (Little, 1937). A story of rip-roaring days in the sand hills of Nebraska. Slogum House is a country inn (also bawdy house) for teamsters, cowhands, etc. The Slogums, who run the house, are a gang of thieves and lawbreakers. Emphasis on the crude and hard.
Miss Morissa, Doctor of the Gold Trail (McGraw, 1955). Life of a woman doctor in the North Platte area of Nebraska in the 1870's and 1880's. Vivid in its detail about ranchers, cowboys, outlaws, and early businessmen. Sympathetic toward Indians and nesters.
Son of the Gamblin' Man (Potter, 1960). A lively, compelling tale of a gambler who becomes a colonizer in Nebraska. He and his group fight grasshoppers, drought, and cattlemen until he and his family have to leave in disgrace.

SANTEE, ROSS, 1889-
The Bubbling Spring (Scribner's, 1949). A yarn—idiomatic, fresh, comprehensive, flavorsome, richly anecdotal—of the cowboy's West from Montana and Dakota to Texas and New Mexico. Excellent on buffalo, cattle trailing, remudas, bronco busting, on the people of ranches, board towns, and the vast plains.

TAYLOR, ROSS, 1909-
Brazos (Bobbs, 1938). Tells the adventures of a Texas cattleman during the seventies and eighties. Depicts Indian fights, cattle stealing, the drives to Kansas. Realistic.

WELLMAN, PAUL ISELIN, 1898-1966
Jubal Troop (Carrick, 1939). A lively tale of a man who begins as a sheepherder-cowboy, and becomes a cattle baron of Texas and Oklahoma. Vivid.
The Bowl of Brass (Lippincott, 1944). An entrepreneur stakes out a town in western Kansas and deals in land mortgages. "An unlovely world, people. . .primitive. . ., beastly. . .stupid."
The Iron Mistress (Doubleday, 1951). Fictionalized episodes in the life of James Bowie in Louisiana, Mississippi, and especially Texas, including the final fracas at the Alamo. Weak in characterization but good for history of the Old Southwest in the period 1817-1836.

WILDER, LAURA INGALLS, 1867-1957
Little House on the Prairie (Harper, 1935). Intended for young readers, but satisfying to adults. The details of homemaking in a cabin on

the covered-wagon frontier of Indian territory. Part of a series that begins with the family in Wisconsin, *Little House in the Big Woods* (1932), and continues into Minnesota and Dakota Territory in *On the Banks of Plum Creek* (1937), *By the Shores of Silver Lake* (1939), *The Long Winter* (1940), *The Little Town on the Prairie* (1941), and *These Happy Golden Years* (1943). All are soundly historical and autobiographical and in discreet conformity with the Victorian code. Reissued in a uniform edition in 1953.

WILSON, MARGARET, 1882-
The Able McLaughlins (Harper, 1923). The story of the establishment of a home in Iowa by Scotch immigrants. The struggle with nature is dominant.

WINTHER, SOPHUS, 1895-
Take All to Nebraska (Macmillan, 1936). Tells of a Dane who sold all his possessions, came to Massachusetts, then to Nebraska in 1898. Details the family's hardships from 1898 to 1908. Especially good in presenting the psychology of the farm boy.

WISE, EVELYN VOSE
Long Tomorrow (Appleton, 1938). In Minnesota in the 1880's, a Catholic priest becomes the leader of the community, starting co-operative undertakings.

3. THE FAR WEST AND ALASKA

Stories of pioneer days in the eleven western states, Alaska, and western Canada deal with a greater variety of experiences and situations than those of the grasslands. Many of these books deal with the overland trips of the easterners moving westward across the mountains and deserts; the life of the "mountain men," especially in the Rockies; the wild mining towns; the growth of settlements and farming communities; railroad building; the ever-present rancher and cowboy; and the friction between the Yanqui and the earlier Spanish-American settlers.

BEAN, MRS. AMELIA
Fancher Train (Doubleday, 1958). The story of a wagon-train which crossed Mormon territory in 1857. Most of the people in the train are murdered by renegades and Indians. Good characterizations and compelling narrative.
The Feud (Doubleday, 1960). Well-told story of ranchers in the Tonto Basin and a two-family feud of the 1880's. A neat plot.

BINNS, ARCHIE, 1899-
The Land Is Bright (Scribner's, 1939). A wagon party, in the face of many hardships, makes the trip from Independence to The Dalles, over the Oregon Trail. A realistic and dramatic presentation.

You Rolling River (Scribner's, 1947). Astoria in the 1870's and 1880's. Vivid and interesting.

BOYD, JAMES, 1888-1944
Bitter Creek (Scribner's, 1939). A boy runs away to the West and becomes a cowboy. Realistic. Revitalized version of the cowboy story because of a subtle psychological subtheme. The West of the eighties and nineties.

BRINIG, MYRON, 1900-
Wide-Open Town (Farrar, 1931). The love story of a young Irishman and the prostitute, Zola, in a wild Montana copper-mining town before the Civil War.

BRISTOW, GWEN, 1903-
Jubilee Trail (Crowell, 1950). A big, formula-written romance laid along the route of the Spanish Trail between Santa Fe and Los Angeles in the 1840's. Overplotted. Best for social history, as of low life in Los Angeles at the time of the war with Mexico.

CAMPBELL, PATRICIA, 1901-
Royal Anne Tree (Macmillan, 1956). The story of a young girl married to a middle-aged farmer in Washington Territory before the Civil War. The emphasis is on the character of the husband, who is a miser and who is intolerant of Indians and others. His death frees her to marry her lover, who is half Indian.

CANIFIELD, CHAUNCEY L., 1843-1909
The Diary of a Forty-Niner (third edition; Delkin, 1947). A lively description of life in the diggings. Written in 1906. Combines storybook romance and the reminiscences of an old miner named Lewis Hanchett.

CLARK, WATER VAN TILBURG, 1909-
The Ox-Bow Incident (Random, 1940). A searching analysis of members of a lynching party in a western Nevada town in 1885. Shows them getting into the mood to go beyond the law and reacting later to what they have done. Highly competent realism.

COOLIDGE, DANE, 1873-1940
Snake Bit Jones (Dutton, 1936). Of a clever Death Valley prospector who finds much gold and outwits his opponents. A formula "Western."
The Trail of Gold (Dutton, 1937). A wild tale of a gold rush in southern Nevada, resembling the historical excitement at Tonopah and Rhyolite. A representative subliterary "Western."
Gringo Gold (Dutton, 1939). A romance of the Gold Rush to California in 1849 and the adventures of Joaquín Murieta, the Mexican bandit.

CORLE, EDWIN, 1906-
Coarse Gold (Dutton, 1942). Tale of a tungsten strike in a Nevada

ghost town. Contrasts nineteenth-century mining camps with those of the twentieth.

CRONYN, GEORGE W., 1888-
'49, a Novel of Gold (Dorrance, 1925). A novel of the Gold Rush. An interesting tale with good local color.

DAVIS, HAROLD L., 1896-
Honey in the Horn (Harper, 1935). Mr. Davis depicts all the types of old-timers and homesteaders to be found in Oregon in 1906-1908. The hero, mixed up in a "jail delivery," has contacts with Indians, half-breeds, herders, horse traders, and others. Records the manners, dress, speech, and morals of the early settlers. Realistic and racy.
Team Bells Woke Me, and Other Stories (Morrow, 1953). Tales and sketches of early days in eastern Oregon. Vivid, authentic.

DOBIE, J. FRANK, 1888-1964
Coronado's Children (Southwest Press, 1931). A collection and (in part) a retelling of many tales of "lost" mines and treasures in the desert Southwest. Richly detailed and accurate reportage on highly romantic material.
Apache Gold and Yaqui Silver (Little, 1939). Similar to *Coronado's Children.*

EDGERTON, LUCILE SELK
Pillars of Gold (Knopf, 1941). Standard Western characters in a freshly presented background—the gold rushes and hazardous travel in pioneer Arizona in Civil War days.

FELTON, HAROLD W. (ed.), 1902-
Legends of Paul Bunyan (Knopf, 1947). An important collection containing more than one hundred collected tales and a bibliography.

FERBER, EDNA, 1887-
Ice Palace (Doubleday, 1958). A story centering on a young girl in the 1950's in Alaska. The story doubles back to give quite a bit of earlier history of the territory. One of Ferber's best.

FERGUSSON, HARVEY, 1890-
Followers of the Sun: A Trilogy of the Santa Fe Trail (Knopf, 1936). *Wolf Song* (1927) is a heroic Western romance that involves a gringo trapper and a Taos senorita. *In Those Days* (Knopf, 1929) covers a half-century of change from the Civil War to the automobile, including Indian wars and the arrival of railroad tracks. *The Blood of the Conquerors* (1921) is laid in Albuquerque in the early 1900's, and centers on the futile love of a Mexican New Mexican for the sister of an Eastern "lunger." All three novels are vigorous, fresh in detail, and full of feeling for the Southwest, especially the Rio Grande Valley.
The Conquest of Don Pedro (Morrow, 1954). Tells of an immigrant from New York to New Mexico soon after the Civil War; of how he

adapts himself to Mexican customs and builds up a business. Quiet, well-written.

FISHER, VARDIS, 1895-

Toilers of the Hills (Houghton, 1928). A well-rounded picture of dry farmers on the benchland of southeastern Idaho. The husband fights the locusts, the drought, and the heat; his wife is dissatisfied. The fictional counterpart of Annie Pike Greenwood's *We Sagebrush Folks*.

Dark Bridwell (Houghton, 1931). A realistic story of an Idaho frontiersman who is unbelievably brutal to both human beings and beasts. A debunking of the romantic frontier.

In Tragic Life (Caxton, 1932). A sensitive boy grows up amid brutalities in Idaho. A powerful study of a boy's reactions to the unpleasant things in a pioneer community.

City of Illusion (Harper, 1941). A melodramatic, oversexed picture of flush days in Virginia City, Nevada. Built around the rise to wealth of Sandy and Eilley Bowers. Suggests the background of life in a metropolitan mining camp.

The Mothers (Vanguard, 1943). A retelling in fictional form of the adventures and misfortunes of the Donner party. Told from the point of view of the courageous mothers of the party.

FOOTE, MARY HALLOCK, 1847-1938

The Led-Horse Claim (1882). A trite love story with a substantial background of actual life in a mining camp. A story of illegal mining near Leadville, Colorado, in the 1870's.

GABRIEL, GILBERT WOLF, 1890-

I, James Lewis (Doubleday, 1932). Tale of James Lewis, clerk on the ship *Tonquin*, who became a hero by his tragic death. He died in blowing up the ship after a massacre by the Indians. Story of a fur-trading expedition to Oregon sponsored by John Jacob Astor in 1811.

GREY, ZANE, 1875-1940

The U. P. Trail (1918). Melodramatic tale, but a sincere attempt to capture some of the epic importance of the building of the first transcontinental railroad.

GUTHRIE, ALFRED BERTRAM, 1901-

The Big Sky (Sloane, 1947). Story of a boy who fled from the brutality of his home in Kentucky, and then became a "mountain man" of the 1840's, living ruthlessly and violently. The story shows that the violence of the early West brought neither peace nor a solution of personal problems.

The Way West (Sloane, 1949). About an emigrant party crossing from Independence to Fort Hall and on to Fort Vancouver, Oregon, in the 1840's. Excellent for dialog, characterization, the contrast between agricultural pioneers and the earlier mountain men, and for the social history of parties on the Oregon Trail.

HARTE, FRANCIS BRET, 1839-1902
The Luck of Roaring Camp: and Other Sketches (1870). The book which first exploited local color of the early mining camps in California. Skillful in form, sentimental in selection and treatment of material.
Gabriel Conroy (1876). Harte's longest novel. Weak in construction but contains interesting character portrayals and dramatic incidents.

HAYCOX, ERNEST, 1899-1950
Deep West (Little, 1937). Of the jealousies and suspicions of neighboring ranchers in Wyoming. The old theme of cattle rustling and attempts to find the guilty party. Staccato talk and good suspense. Wyoming in 1884.
Sundown Jim (Little, 1938). About fifteen years after the Civil War in a Western territory. Ranchers are both Southerners and Yankees. Tells of their conflicts and how a U.S. deputy, "Sundown Jim," brings order.

HERSCH, VIRGINIA DAVIS, 1896-
The Seven Cities of Gold (Duell, 1946). A story of early Spanish explorers and settlers and of the hero, Carlos, who joins Coronado's expedition in search of the seven cities of Cibola. Good romance about explorations antedating those of the Yankees.

HULBERT, ARCHER, 1873-1933
Forty Niners (Little, 1931). A party crosses from the Missouri to Placerville, California, on the Overland Trail. A clumsy patchwork of quotations and diaries, but realistic and satisfying to read.

IRWIN, WILL, 1873-1948
Youth Rides West; A Story of the Seventies (Knopf, 1925). A tenderfoot meets adventure in a Colorado mining camp.

JANVIER, THOMAS ALLIBONE, 1849-1913
The Aztec Treasure-House (1890). Americans discover an Aztec city. An old-fashioned adventure story.

JONES, IDWAL, 1890-1964
Vermilion (Prentice, 1947). A story of three generations in California from the early 1800's to the twentieth century. Mining, ranching, and finally grape-growing are parts of the story. Old-time romance plus a few modern touches.

JONES, NARD, 1904-
The Petlands (Harcourt, 1931). Story of the Petland family, whose lives through three generations reflect the growth of Seattle and its back country.
Swift Flows the River (Dodd, 1940). Beginning with the Indian massacre at The Cascades, 1856, this novel pictures early steamboating and town-building on the Columbia and Snake rivers and the gold rush to the Clearwater in Idaho.

Scarlet Petticoat (Dodd, 1941). A popular adventure set against the background of the fur trade on the lower Columbia in the early nineteenth century.

KNIBBS, HENRY HERBERT, 1874-
The Tonto Kid (Houghton, 1936). A lively, dry-humored story of the cowboy West. Full of action.

LAUGHLIN, RUTH, 1889-
The Wind Leaves No Shadow (Whittlesey, 1948; "enlarged edition," Caxton, 1952). Laid in Santa Fe and elsewhere in the Rio Grande Valley in 1821-1846, and based on the life of the locally famous gambler, Doña Tules, who was for a time mistress to Armijo. Good for regional flavor, ethnic contrasts, and political and military tensions. The second edition adds thirty pages and six years to the story and supplies a nine-page glossary.

LAURITZEN, JONREED, 1902-
The Rose and the Flame (Doubleday, 1951). A swashbuckling romance about a Spanish journey to New Mexico at the time of the Pueblo Revolt, 1680.

LOTT, MILTON
The Last Hunt (Houghton, 1954). This depicts buffalo hunters in 1882, giving their reactions and those of ranchers and Indians as the buffalo go, forever: "A piece of a continent would be gone, and with it a people and the life they lived."

McKEOWN, MARTHA FERGUSON
Mountains Ahead (Putnam, 1961). Interesting story of one group of immigrants on the Oregon Trail, centering on the adjustment to pioneer life of a young bride from Indiana married to a Kentuckian. The hardships of the trail are vividly portrayed.

McNEILLY, MILDRED M., 1910-
Each Bright River: A Novel of the Oregon Country (Morrow, 1950). A period romance, laid when "54-40" was an issue, based on careful research into Indian relations, the effect of the California gold rush, the growth of settlements, and the political rise of Oregon and Washington territories.

MASON, VAN WYCK, 1897-
End of Track (Reynal, 1943). Wild days in Julesburg, Colorado, when the Union Pacific was being put through.

MEIGS, CORNELIA LYNDE, 1884-
Railroad West (Little, 1937). Deals with the laying of the Northern Pacific railroad from Minnesota to the Yellowstone and the hardships of the undertaking. The love element is between a young engineer and the sister of another engineer.

MILLER, MAY MERRILL
First the Blade (Knopf, 1938). Missouri of Civil War times and California (the San Joaquin Valley) of the sixties and seventies. The struggle with nature and predatory capitalism.

O'CONNOR, JACK, 1902-
Boom Town (Knopf, 1938). Details life in a representative Arizona mining camp of the 1890's. A biography of a boom town from the accidental discovery of the lode through its heyday and the decline into a ghost town. Much action and adventure, also vice and character degeneration. A "hard-boiled" novel that overstresses sex and violence, but is worthwhile nevertheless.

O'DELL, SCOTT, 1903-
Hill of the Hawk (Bobbs, 1947). Historical novel of California in 1846 and 1847, leading up to the march on Los Angeles of the Army of the West.

O'MEARA, WALTER
The Spanish Bride (Putnam, 1954). A Castilian girl becomes mistress of a governor of New Mexico in the early 1700's. A close-up of a Spanish colony and a dramatic romance that includes fighting on the Great Plains against French from La Luisiana.

O'ROURKE, FRANK, 1916-
The Far Mountains (Morrow, 1959). New Mexico from 1801 to 1849. The story of two men who established an important New Mexico family. Much on class distinctions, fights with Indians, trade with North Americans, and the Mexican Revolution.

PETTIBONE, ANITA
Light Down, Stranger (Farrar, 1942). An unretouched picture of a boy growing up in a bustling frontier community in Washington Territory.

RHODES, EUGENE MANLOVE, 1869-1934
Rhodes Reader (University of Oklahoma Press, 1957). A collection made by W. H. Hutchinson of stories by Rhodes that had been out of print for some time and had never appeared in book form. A good selection to give a glimpse of Rhodes' breezy style and of what Westerners of Rhodes' own generation had made of Western tradition in the area of New Mexico and West Texas which remained "The West" after the frontier had disappeared in other regions.

RICHTER, CONRAD, 1890-
Tacey Cromwell (Knopf, 1942). Set in an Arizona mining town about 1890. The title character is a sporting-house madam. Written in a "cold, stereopticon-slide" style.

ROSS, LILLIAN B.
The Stranger. A Novel of the Big Sur (Morrow, 1942). Of a Californian

who married a Kansas spinster in the decade following the Civil War. A story of ranch life.

RUXTON, GEORGE F., 1820-1848
Life in the Far West (1848). (Reprinted in part as *In the Old West. . .*, Macmillan, 1920). An enthusiastic Englishman's description of the delights of wide-open spaces and the mountains. Fictionalized.

SANTEE, ROSS, 1889-
Cowboy (Cosmopolitan Book Co., 1928). Story of a man going out West (Arizona) and becoming a cowboy. Delicate, but realistic.

SEIFERT, SHIRLEY, 1889-
Those Who Go Against the Current (Lippincott, 1943). An adventurous, romantic fiction based on the life and times of Manuel de Lisa, fur trader on the Missouri River frontier.

SNELL, GEORGE D.
And If Man Triumphs (Caxton, 1939). Of adventure going down the Green River, of rescue by Indians, of attempts to cross Death Valley. Based on Lewis Manly's book, *Death Valley in '49*.

STEVENS, JAMES, 1892-
Paul Bunyan (Knopf, 1925). A literary and somewhat sophisticated rendering of the Bunyan legend. Racy enough to be in line with the tradition.
Homer in the Sagebrush (Knopf, 1927). Stories of jerkline teamsters, powder monkeys, and reclamation-project laborers during sprees in town, gamblers, ranch boys. Heroic evocation of the Old West in tales that are somewhat tall.

STEWART, GEORGE R., 1895-
East of the Giants (Holt, 1938). An interesting account of Yankee-Mexican relationship in the area south and east of San Francisco, after the Mexican War. A good realistic tone.

TEILHET, DARWIN LeORA, 1904-
The Road to Glory (Funk, 1956). An appealing treatment of the struggle between Father Serra and the military in California around the year 1800. The hero, a young man from a noble family, is won to Serra's way of thought, as the frontier promotes a more democratic spirit.

TERRELL, JOHN UPTON, 1900-
Plume Rouge (Viking, 1942). A story of the McKenzie expedition to Oregon along the trail of Lewis and Clark. Capable realism.

WHITE, HELEN CONSTANCE, 1896-
Dust on the King's Highway (Macmillan, 1947). The story of the effort to found an inland route from Sonora to the upper California missions.

The central character is a Franciscan priest, Fray Francisco Garces (1738-1781).

WHITE, STEWART EDWARD, 1873-1946
Gold: A Tale of the Forty-niners (1913). The lives of men during the Gold Rush and how many became permanent settlers.
Long Rifle (Doubleday, 1932). Historical novel about the life of a young man who inherited a long rifle from his grandfather's friend, Daniel Boone. He becomes a "mountain man" of the Rockies in the 1820's, where he is captured by the Blackfeet Indians and adopted into their tribe. Full of details about the trappers.

WISTER, OWEN, 1860-1938
The Virginian (1902). A Wyoming cowboy from Virginia wins a prim schoolma'am from Vermont. Romantic treatment of the conflict between Western and Eastern ideas. The "classic" Western story of cowboys and rustlers. Main characters: The Virginian, quick on the draw, and Trampas (from the Spanish word meaning to cheat), the gambler.

ZIEGLER, ISABELLE, 1904-
The Nine Days of Father Serra (Longmans, 1951). An appealing story of Father Serra and his faith during early days in San Diego. He is on the side of the Indians at a time when they are mistreated by some of the Spanish.

4. WARS OF THE WESTWARD MOVEMENT

The pioneers did not travel West in a vacuum. Not only did they meet the hardships described in the three lists of novels preceding this but they fought many wars with the Indians who disputed their progress. Also the "tide of empire" met men of other nationalities who had established claims to various parts of western North America. Aside from Indian wars, the most dramatic struggle was that with the Mexicans (by the Texans in 1836, and by the United States in 1846-1848).

ARNOLD, ELLIOTT, 1912-
Blood Brother (Duell, 1947). A careful historical novel packed with action about conflict between the Army and the Chiricahua Apaches from 1856 to 1872. A clear account of certain historical events, such as the Camp Grant Massacre.
The Time of the Gringo (Knopf, 1953). Of Manuel Armijo, who became Mexican governor of New Mexico after a revolution staged by New Mexicans and Indians. Also of the repercussions set off in New Mexico by events in Texas and by the arrival of General Kearny. Sympathetic to Indians, New Mexicans, and the United States nationals. Excellent.

BARRETT, MONTE
Tempered Blade (Bobbs, 1946). A well-told fictionalized biography of James Bowie, using most that is known about his life in the Southwest from 1815 to 1836.

BARRY, JANE
A Time in the Sun (Doubleday, 1962). A girl on her way to the West to marry an Army officer is kidnapped by Apaches. She marries a man who is half Indian and prefers life with him to that on an Army post. Interesting psychological study.

BINNS, ARCHIE, 1899-
Mighty Mountain (Scribner's, 1940). A picture of the Northwest frontier. A New Englander settles in Washington Territory. The relationship of Indians and whites. Appreciation of both points of view. Indian fighting.

BIRD, ROBERT M., 1803-1854
Nick o' the Woods (1837). A bloodthirsty story of Kentucky as "the dark and bloody ground." Most Indians involved are savage and uncontrollable.

BLAKE, FORRESTER
Johnny Christmas (Morrow, 1948). A serious and adventurous tale of fights against Mexicans and Indians in the Southwest between 1836 and 1846. Based on research and travel, and inspired by the sweep and history and beauty of the land.

BOYD, THOMAS, 1898-
Shadow of the Long Knives (Scribner's, 1928). Pioneers from Kentucky fight British and Indians for the old Northwest Territory.
Simon Girty (Minton, 1928). A fictional reconstruction of the life of the "white renegade" of the Revolution.

BURNETT, WILLIAM RILEY, 1899-
Adobe Walls: A Novel of the Last Apache Uprising (Knopf, 1953). A fictionalized version of Al Sieber's successful pursuit of Chief Victorio, in spite of Army incompetence, amid the savage Southwestern desert country, in 1886. A lively, graphic narrative.

CAMPBELL, WALTER S. (STANLEY VESTAL, pseud.), 1887-1957
Revolt on the Border (Houghton, 1938). A romance laid in and about Santa Fe in 1846. Includes scenes of General Kearny's annexation of the New Mexico territory.

COMFORT, WILL L., 1878-1932
Mangus Colorado (Stein, 1931). A fictional biography of a famous Apache chieftain. Tells of his losing battle to drive the whites from Santa Rita and reunite the Indians. Shows the real Indian—his greatness and his weakness.

Apache (Dutton, 1931). The story of an uprising led by Mangus Colorado. The usual story of white double-crossing and desperate Indian fighting, ending in disaster for the Indian. New Mexico and Arizona.

COOPER, JAMES FENIMORE, 1789-1851
The Last of the Mohicans (1826). Perhaps the most popular of Cooper's works. Uncas, the last of the Mohicans, is a leading character. Of fights against the French and their allies in upper New York.
The Pathfinder (1840). The father of Uncas ("the last of the Mohicans") is a leading character. Uncas and his father are notable examples of Cooper's "good Indians."

DAVIS, JAMES F., 1870-
The Road to San Jacinto (Bobbs, 1936). Romantic story of heroism as far as the main character is concerned, but good feeling for the plight of the Mexicans and a realistic account of the massacre at San Jacinto. Upholds Houston in the Houston *vs.* Austin quarrel.

DERLETH, AUGUST, 1909-
Wind over Wisconsin (Scribner's, 1938). A careful novel centering around Black Hawk and his "war" in Illinois, Wisconsin, and Washington, D.C., for the lands promised the Indian.

DUFFUS, ROBERT L., 1888-
Journada (Covici, 1935). Set in the Mexican War, deals with lovers who have to make La Journada alone after being separated from their wagon train. Describes a Comanche attack. Much background material, Spanish dancing, frontier life, homicide. By the author of the non-fiction *Santa Fe Trail.*

EDMONDS, WALTER DUMAUX, 1903-
Drums Along the Mohawk (Little, 1936). A pro-settler novel of the Revolution, which includes scenes of Indian raids in the Mohawk Valley, especially those led by Walter Butler.
In the Hands of the Senecas (Little, 1947). A brief novel about captivity among eighteenth-century Indians. The characters are believable and the story full of suspense.

FAST, HOWARD MELVIN, 1914-
The Last Frontier (Duell, 1941). A novelized history of the flight of the Northern Cheyennes from Oklahoma to Montana, of the series of whippings they gave the United States Army, of the cold, slow cruelty with which the whites retaliated. A deeply moving picture of a simple people fighting for their homeland.

FLEISHMAN, GLEN
While Rivers Flow (Macmillan, 1963). A satisfactory historical novel dealing with the struggle between the government of Georgia and the Cherokee nation over lands in northern Georgia. The main character is a young Army officer on duty in the area.

FOREMAN, LEONARD LONDON, 1901-
The Road to San Jacinto (Dutton, 1943). A romantic tale of the Texas War of Independence. Contains more down-to-earth detail than does the book of the same title by James F. Davis.

FORREST, WILLIAMS
Trail of Tears (Crown, 1959). A careful attempt to trace the events leading up to and including the removal of the Cherokees from northern Georgia and eastern Tennessee to the Indian Territory, centering around John Ross, the Cherokee leader who was most dominant during the period.

FULLER, IOLA
The Shining Trail (Duell, 1943). Emphasizes the tragedy of the Indians' position in the Black Hawk War.

GORMAN, HERBERT SHERMAN, 1893-
The Wine of San Lorenzo (Farrar, 1945). This romance of the Mexican War presents well-studied social and military history. It contrasts Anglo-Saxon and Latin cultures, and portrays General Santa Anna, old-style hacienda life, and the battles fought by Winfield Scott and Zachary Taylor.

KREY, LAURA (SMITH)
On the Long Tide (Houghton, 1940). Historical novel of the fight for the independence of Texas.

LAIRD, CHARLTON, 1901-
Thunder on the River (Little, 1949). Realistic, strong-flavored, and concerned with the struggles between settlers and Indians at the time of the Black Hawk War and the decline of the Sauk Indians. Interesting for its social history of whites and Sauks.

LeMAY, ALAN
The Unforgiven (Harper, 1957). Story of a family thought to have been friendly with enemy Indians, the Kiowas. They are attacked by the Kiowas, defend themselves bravely, and help to make Texas history. Vivid writing.

O'CONNOR, JACK, 1902-
Conquest: A Novel of the Old Southwest (Harper, 1930). Of Anglo-American domination in Arizona and of a brave villain, killer of many Indians and a conqueror of his environment.

PARKHILL, FORBES, 1892-
Troopers West (Farrar, 1945). Story of violence and of individual character reactions to unusual situations. Critical of the type of person selected for the Indian service. Time, 1879.

PREBBLE, JOHN, 1915-
Buffalo Soldiers (Harcourt, 1959). A white lieutenant in charge of

Negro troops around 1870 in the high plains country comes to understand some of the motivations of his troop and those of the Indians
whom he pursues. A psychologically sound and well-written story.

REMINGTON, FREDERIC, 1861-1909
John Ermine of the Yellowstone (1902). Popular fiction of a young
scout for United States troops sent to subdue the Sioux Indians. Illustrated by the author.

ROBERTS, RICHARD EMERY, 1903-
The Gilded Rooster (Putnam, 1947). Physical and spiritual conflicts
among four captives of the Sioux in Wyoming during the Civil War.
Creates a vigorous mountain man, a cruel captain, and other characters.

SABIN, EDWIN L., 1870-
On the Plains with Custer (Lippincott, 1913). Tells of a youth who is
captured by the Indians and is rescued by Custer. He then serves in
the "fighting Seventh Cavalry" as bugler. Facile romance.

SCHUMANN, MARY
Strife Before Dawn (Dial, 1939). A conscientious, adventurous account
of the struggle for the old Northwest Territory. Pontiac's War, Lord
Dunmore's War, and the Revolution. Introduces several historical
characters, including Simon Girty, Henry Hamilton "the hairbuyer,"
George Rogers Clark, and the famous half-breed, Logan. Imaginative
use of much source material.

SEARS, CLARA ENDICOTT, 1863-
The Great Powwow (Houghton, 1934). King Philip's War in early Massachusetts, 1675-1676. Considered historically accurate.

SHEPARD, ODELL, 1884-   and SHEPARD, WILLARD O.
Holdfast Gaines (Macmillan, 1946). A novel of American expansion
westward, 1780-1815. Holdfast Gaines, a Mohegan adopted by a white
family, is the central character. A twentieth-century "Cooper" story.

SIMMS, WILLIAM GILMORE, 1806-1870
The Yemassee (1835). War between the English and the Yemassee.
Notable Indian characters.

STONE, GRACE Z., 1896-
The Cold Journey (Morrow, 1934). A realistically told history that
deals with the attack on a Massachusetts village by the French and Indians in 1704 and of the journey through the snow to Quebec by the inhabitants and captors of the village. Deals with the fortunes of the
captives when they reach Canada.

STOVER, HERBERT E.
Song of the Susquehanna (Dodd, 1949). Good for a picture of Lancaster,
Pennsylvania, as a trading post and on campaigns and battles during

the French and Indian War. Colonel Bouquet, John Bartram, and other personages appear.

STRAIGHT, MICHAEL, 1916-

Carrington (Knopf, 1960). Story of a disastrous ambush of a small U.S. force by the Sioux. Carrington, with humanitarian ideas, tries to carry out orders from Washington, but is opposed by his fellow officers, who hate all Indians.

A Very Small Remnant (Knopf, 1963). A story of the betrayal of the Cheyenne Indians by Army officers eager for promotion and by corrupt Indian agents. The hero resigns from the Army on the eve of promotion in order to become an Indian agent. He fails to reform the Indian agency system, as he failed previously in his attempts to get the Army to live up to its promises to the Indians.

SWANSON, NEIL H., 1896-

Judas Tree (Putnam, 1933). A historical novel about the siege of Fort Pitt by the Indians and the dauntless Swiss commandant who saved the fort. Details of the Indian tortures of the time.

TURNBULL, AGNES SLIGH, 1888-

The Day Must Dawn (Macmillan, 1942). Western Pennsylvania during the Revolution. Good detail on pioneer life and Indian fighting.

WARREN, CHARLES MARQUIS, 1912-

Only the Valiant (Macmillan, 1943). A psychological dramatic story of a small Army detail fighting hopelessly against the Apaches.

WILDER, ROBERT, 1901-

Bright Feather (Putnam, 1948). A story of the bloody fights between settlers and Seminoles on the Florida frontier. Authentic military and social history compounded with gusty romance.

FARM AND VILLAGE LIFE

In each section of the country after the early stages of exploration and settlement, the pioneer way of life was succeeded by "farm and village life." This stage, which still exists everywhere except in cities and their immediate environs, came to each section at a different time. Our division, then, is not chronological exactly but rather in accordance with how people lived. If a novel represents a settled way of life on the farm or in the village, rather than early hardships, it belongs in this section rather than under pioneering. Such a settled way of life was established in the Northeast throughout most of the nineteenth century, in the Middle West approximately from the Civil War onward. Since in the regions farther west the pioneering stage was passed at divers times, some pioneering books may have their settings in the twentieth century; other books may represent a settled stage which certain sections reached much earlier. The South, of course, reached one "settled" way of life before the Civil War and an entirely different one after Reconstruction.

The story of American life in the village or small town or on the farm became a major theme in letters when a country-raised generation found itself in crowded cities after the Civil War. From the beginning the treatment varied from the starkly realistic to the romantically optimistic. The later farm books have been heavily sociological, taking up tenant farming, disease, decay, and the farm laborer, who isn't a farmer in the older sense at all. The books about the village or town have followed much the same development, with much satire and debunking during the 1920's and since then a good deal of fresh psychological reevaluation.

The regional novel was at its height in the period from 1920 to 1950. Since then the peculiarities of regions has been a declining topic.

1. THE NORTHEAST

The "recorders of the New England decline" (Pattee: *History of American Literature Since 1870)* first made daily life in New England a popular subject for fiction in the 1870's and 1880's. There has been a great variety of treatments, with a general trend of development from the sentimental toward the more matter-of-fact picture. This area of the country is characterized by small, diversified farms and old-fashioned villages. Stories of New York, New Jersey, Pennsylvania, and New England are included in this section of the book.

ALCOTT, LOUISA MAY, 1832-1888
Little Women (1868). A story of childhood and home life in a New

England village. Immensely popular. Shows the integrity and virtues of the American villager.

ALDRICH, THOMAS BAILEY, 1836-1907
The Story of a Bad Boy (1869). Tells a boy's experiences in a New England seaport town. A wholesome account of a normal life.

ALLIS, MARGUERITE, 1886-
Charity Strong (Putnam, 1945). Against the opposition of her Puritan father a Connecticut girl of the 1820's struggles to become an opera singer.
Water over the Dam (Putnam, 1947). Fair-to-middling story of the building of a dam across the Connecticut River in the early 1800's. Triangle story of two sisters and the man who married one of them.

ASCH, NATHAN, 1902-
The Valley (Macmillan, 1935). A group of sketches and short stories of life in a small decadent place in the Berkshires as told by a native of Warsaw, Poland. Shows the essentials of Yankee rural life with all its simple delights.

BEALS, HELEN RAYMOND, 1888-
The River Rises (Macmillan, 1941). Through the eyes of a minister and his wife and a construction engineer the reader sees a cross section of life in a Massachusetts village which is to be flooded for a reservoir.

BEER, THOMAS, 1889-1940
Collected Stories of Thomas Beer: Mrs. Egg and Other Americans (Knopf, 1947). Adroit and entertaining stories of rural, village, and small-city people in New England, New York, and Ohio. Discerning presentations of American behavior and mentality, in several series that were popular in the *Saturday Evening Post*.

BRACE, GERALD WARNER, 1901-
Bell's Landing (Norton, 1955). An account of two generations of New Englanders—and especially of a young man who inherits Bell's Landing, but who is of the generation involved in World War II and is on the way toward developing new attitudes.
The Wind's Will (Norton, 1964). A story centering on a seventeen-year-old and his summer between high school and college, as he escapes from his father's moralistic teachings and begins to understand the customs of his time. An excellent portrayal of New England village life.

BROWN, ALICE, 1857-1948
Tiverton Tales (1899). Full details of New England village life and the peculiarities of its folk. Discusses an old maid and an annual village fair.
The Country Road (1906). Thirteen stories of New England folk, their

love affairs and domestic difficulties. Little of the shadows of life;
plenty of its comedy.
Country Neighbors (1910). Short stories emphasizing the romance of
humble lives.

BUCK, PEARL SYDENSTRICKER, 1892-
Portrait of a Marriage (Day, 1945). An interesting study of the effect
of the land and farm life on a sensitive artist who marries a Pennsylvania farm woman and spends his life in the country. Interesting
speculations, a rather unbelievable plot, and live characters.

BUCKLER, ERNEST
The Mountain and the Valley (Holt, 1952). A detailed picture of daily
and seasonal work and social life on a Nova Scotia farm. "In the
country the day is the determinant. The work, the thoughts, the feelings, to match it, follow." Much attention to the emotional needs and
outlets of adolescents and young men and women.

CANNON, LeGRAND, 1899-
A Mighty Fortress (Farrar, 1937). Story of a boy farmer who grew up
to become a minister at the time of the abolition movement during the
middle of the nineteenth century. New Hampshire setting.

CARROLL, GLADYS H., 1904-
As the Earth Turns (Macmillan, 1933). A story of the events of one
year in the life of a Maine farmer in the early twentieth century.
Neighbor to the Sky (Macmillan, 1937). Of a girl who escaped the
farm, fell in love with a Maine farmer, and tried to remake him but
decided in the end not to do so.

CHASE, MARY ELLEN, 1887-
Mary Peters (Macmillan, 1934). Mary Peters spends her childhood on
her father's sailing ship, and in her teens goes to live with her family
in a Maine village. Her anxiety, sorrow, loneliness, and final serenity.
An amiable recollection.
Silas Crockett (Macmillan, 1935). Chronicle of four generations of a
New England family. Depicts seafaring people of Maine from Silas,
captain of a clipper, to his great-grandson Silas, who cannot follow the
ways of his seafaring family but is forced to leave college to work in a
herring factory.

COATSWORTH, ELIZABETH, 1893-
Here I Stay (Farrar, 1940). Story of a woman who lived alone and
liked it on a New England farm. She is contrasted with other New
Englanders who wish to escape their environment.

COFFIN, ROBERT PETER TRISTRAM, 1892-1955
Lost Paradise; a Boyhood on a Maine Coast Farm (Macmillan, 1934).
Childhood on a Maine coast farm of the late 1890's, with its pleasura-
ble toil and sheer delights.

COOKE, ROSE TERRY, 1827-1892
Rootbound and Other Sketches (1885). Perhaps the best collection of short stories by this author. Gives the authentic flavor of New England.
Huckleberries Gathered from New England Hills (1891). Vernacular tales of plain, hardy characters.

COZZENS, JAMES GOULD, 1903-
The Last Adam (Harcourt, 1933). Presents the seamy side of a New England village.
The Just and the Unjust (Harcourt, 1942). "A presentation and an analysis of the American way of discipline" in a small village.

CRANE, STEPHEN, 1871-1900
Twenty Stories (Knopf, 1940). Contains five stories of a New England town, including "The Monster," one of Crane's finest tales.

CUDDEBAK, JANE, 1891-
Unquiet Seed (Pellegrini, 1947). Good detail about life on a tobacco farm in New York, mostly from the viewpoint of a child.

D'AGOSTINO, GUIDO, 1910-
The Barking of a Lonely Fox (McGraw, 1952). A rounded picture of the struggle for existence and love on a dairy farm in Pennsylvania. Although the book admits flaws in the environment, especially in the towns, it is essentially optimistic; it is *pro* country living.

DOAN, DANIEL, 1914-
Amos Jackson (Beacon, 1957). A romance about the marriage of a poor New England farm boy to the daughter of a wealthy family. New England common sense and the unbelievable goodwill of both family groups make the marriage a success. The forsaking of the land by the old New England families is a sub-theme.

DUFFUS, ROBERT L., 1888-
West Hill (Macmillan, 1942). Excellent character studies centering about a ninety-five-year-old man and his doctor. Vermont from the Revolution to mid-twentieth century.

FERBER, EDNA, 1887-
American Beauty (Doubleday, 1931). Tells the story of a family mansion in Connecticut from 1700 to 1900. Shows Polish peasants replacing the "old-stock" Yankees.

FISHER, DOROTHY CANFIELD, 1879-1958
Hillsboro People (Holt, 1915). Centered around the lives of simple village folk in Vermont. Their lives may not be eventful, but the people are real and smart in the ways of life itself.
The Brimming Cup (Holt, 1916). Family life in a little Vermont community.

Rough Hewn (Harcourt, 1922). A picture of family life in the ideal American home. Deals with a couple who return from Paris to live a contented life in a small Vermont village.

FLINT, MARGARET, 1891-
Enduring Riches (Dodd, 1942). Appealing story of Maine country people. The building of a happy family life by two people who marry in their thirties.

FORBES, ESTHER, 1894?-
The Running of the Tide (Houghton, 1948). A long novel, better realized as history than as literature, that gives a period picture of people in Salem, Massachusetts, in its great days as a seaport for the China trade.
Rainbow on the Road (Houghton, 1954). About an itinerant peddler and portrait painter. An episodic re-creation of New England life, speech, and scenery in the 1830's. Entertaining as social history and interesting as a parallel to Hawthorne's *American Notebooks.*

FREDERIC, HAROLD, 1856-1898
Seth's Brother's Wife (1887). A drab, bitter tale of farm life in upper New York State. Pictures country journalism and politics and rural frustration. A good companion for *Main-Travelled Roads* by Garland, published in 1891.

FREEMAN, MARY E. WILKINS, 1862-1930
A Humble Romance (1887). Twenty-eight realistic stories and sketches of a Massachusetts village. All deal with unhappiness.
A New England Nun; and Other Stories (1891). The title story is the author's most famous, and a true portrayal of New England character.

GREBENC, LUCILE, 1893-
The Time of Change (Doubleday, 1938). A story of a Connecticut woman in the early nineteenth century, centering on details of farm life.

HALL, LELAND, 1883-1957
They Seldom Speak (Harcourt, 1936). Full of detailed daily events of average American farm life. Deals with a family from the eighties until the close of the war of 1914-1918, showing the changing ideas during this time.

HOUGH, HENRY BEETLE, 1896-
New England Story (Random, 1958). An appealing story in which a young writer of the 1950's attempts to get the true story of an old New England sea captain who died in 1889. He learns much of New England character and family tradition and marries the old captain's grand-daughter.

HOWARD, ELIZABETH METZGER
Before the Sun Goes Down (Doubleday, 1946). The year 1880-1881 in

the town of Willowspring, Pennsylvania. Fine treatment of social classes and problems of the time.

HUMMEL, GEORGE F., 1882-1952
Subsoil (Liveright, 1924). One of the better early forerunners of the down-to-earth stories published in the 1930's. Separate stories of various people, all connected with each other by residence in or near Norwold, Long Island.
Heritage (Stokes, 1935). Set in Norwold, Long Island, this is a chronicle of village life from the time the railroad came in 1846, bringing with it a sturdy German immigrant family. Concerned with domestic problems.

IRVING, WASHINGTON, 1783-1859
Knickerbocker's History of New York (1809). A humorous, kindly re-creation of events in early New York. Irving pretends to be presenting a firsthand account written by one Diedrich Knickerbocker, who lived in the Dutch period.
The Sketch Book (1819). The best-known volume by Irving. Contains such famous stories of early New York as "The Legend of Sleepy Hollow," "Rip Van Winkle," and "The Devil and Tom Walker."

JEWETT, SARAH ORNE, 1849-1909
A Country Doctor (1884). Based on the life of Miss Jewett's father. Realistic. Intimate.
A White Heron (1886). Stories of rural New England. Humble people and Puritan character.
A Native of Winby and Other Tales (1893). Of deserted farms, occasional returns of those who went west, and of summer boarders.
The Country of the Pointed Firs (1896). Portraits and scenes of a seaside village in Maine. Homely and old-fashioned characters.

LAING, DILYS B.
The Great Year (Duell, 1948). This tells of three generations of Vermont farming folk. Catches the flavor of rural New England, in appealing poetical fashion.

McINTIRE, MARGUERITE
Free and Clear (Farrar, 1939). A novel of Maine farm life. Good in details of country life.
Heaven's Dooryard (Farrar, 1940). The story of the building of a farm and the establishment of a family in New England. Setting: New Hampshire, Maine, and Vermont.

MacLENNAN, HUGH, 1907-
The Precipice (Duell, 1948). The marital story of a girl from a sleepy, narrow-minded Ontario town and a New Yorker in the advertising business. A thoughtful novel that studies the differences between Canadians and Americans and between their civilizations.

MARQUAND, JOHN PHILLIPS, 1893-1960
Point of No Return (Little, 1949). There is much here on a small town in Massachusetts up to 1930, when the central character moves away to become a suburbanite working in a Manhattan bank. Most of the book is his recollections—in flashback—of the environment that molded him.

MAYO, ELEANOR R., 1920-
Turn Home (Morrow, 1945). The town bad boy returns after five years' absence to make good in his home town. Emphasis on small-town narrowness.
Loom of the Land (Morrow, 1946). The portrait of a self-made man in Maine—a dictator, Yankee model—who caused unhappiness to his children but kept the respect of the townspeople.

MERRICK, ELLIOT TUCKER, 1905-
From This Hill Look Down (Daye, 1934). A series of sketches interpreting life in Vermont in the 1930's.
Ever the Winds Blow (Scribner's, 1936). Story of a sensitive lad on a Vermont farm during the pre-Depression years.

METALIOUS, GRACE, 1924(?)-1964
Peyton Place (Messner, 1956). A routine but commercially successful novel laid in a small town in the period 1935-1944. A naturalistic and sensational regional slice-of-life full of typical people, clichés of phrase, and fresh journalistic detail.

MOORE, RUTH
The Walk Down Main Street (Morrow, 1960). A story which plays up the shortcomings and distorted values of a small northeastern town, willing to maim the youth morally and physically in order to produce a championship high-school team.

MUIR, EMILY
Small Potatoes (Scribner's, 1940). An authentic portrait of country life in the Penobscot Bay region of Maine.

NABOKOV, VLADIMIR V., 1899-
Lolita (Doubleday, 1958). A story told by a middle-aged man who lives for several years in an intimate relationship with the adolescent daughter of his former wife. A good psychological study of this man, but also pictures to some extent the more normal attitudes of youth in the mid-twenties, as contrasted to those of various middle-aged folk.

NATHAN, ROBERT, 1894-
Barly Fields (Knopf, 1938). A collection of five short novels. Of these, *Fiddler in Barly* is an excellent fantasy of life in a small village, with neighborly gossip carried on by the poultry, the birds, etc.

OGILVIE, ELISABETH, 1917-
Storm Tide (Crowell, 1945). An appealing story of a lack of understanding between husband and wife in a carefully drawn portrait of a
small island community off the coast of Maine.
The Ebbing Tide (Crowell, 1947). A well-told psychological novel of a
woman whose husband is away from home in World War II. Bennett's
Island, the locale, and the people represent an authentic northeastern
community. Continues *Storm Tide*.
Rowan Head (People's Book Club, 1949). A struggle between two ship-
building families in a small New England town. The hero and heroine
maintain personal integrity in face of great odds. A story with real
emotional appeal.
No Evil Angel (McGraw, 1956). A young man who has grown up in a
small coastal town dominated by his father, whom he hates, succeeds
to the family business upon the death of his father. He perceives that
he is unalterably a part of the community.
Call Home the Heart (McGraw, 1962). The jealousies and gossip of
women left behind in a small fishing village as the men go out to sea.
The heroine befriends the friendless and outwits those who wish to
punish the underprivileged.
There May be Heaven (McGraw, 1964). A story centering on the relationships between four brothers in a small Maine fishing village, and
on the courtship of a young widow by the youngest. The widow, who
comes to the village to escape her grief over her dead husband, becomes an integral part of the community.

PARMENTER, CHRISTINE (WHITING), 1877-
Swift Waters (Crowell, 1937). A love story in which a few descendants
of the foreign-born begin to mingle with older members of New England society.

PARTRIDGE, BELLAMY, 1878-1960
January Thaw (McGraw, 1945). A city couple buy a Connecticut farm
which has a flaw in the title. A country couple with a claim on the
place move in with them. The struggle between the two couples serves
to bring out various New England attitudes and customs.

ROBINSON, ROWLAND EVANS, 1833-1900
Uncle Lisha's Shop (1887). One of the more satisfactory "local color"
stories; township life centering about a shoemaker's shop.
Sam Lovell's Camps (1889). Stories of the fishing and hunting expedi-
tions of Samuel Lovell, a neighbor of Uncle Lisha. Sequel to *Uncle
Lisha's Shop*. A French-Canadian is an important character.
Danvis Folks (1894). Satisfactory presentation of details of country
happenings and folkways of Danvis township, Charlotte County, Vermont.

SCHRAG, OTTO, 1907-
Sons of the Morning (Doubleday, 1945). Two veterans returned to a New England village find themselves alien to the townspeople (although their friendship with the town's conscientious objector remains unbroken).

SETTLE, MARY LEE
The Love Eaters (Harper, 1955). An acidulous report on the upper class in a coal town in the Alleghenies.

STOWE, HARRIET BEECHER, 1812-1896
The Minister's Wooing (1859). A valuable picture of villagers in the undiluted Puritan tradition. Full of authentic detail.
The Pearl of Orr's Island (1861). Faithful portraits of New England village life. A pioneer book in portraying this section.
Old Town Folks (1869). A Massachusetts village, similar to *The Pearl of Orr's Island*.
Sam Lawson's Oldtown Fireside Stories (1872). A Massachusetts village about 1800. Indians, Hibernians, English, Puritans, ghosts. Good old-style humor.

WALKER, MILDRED, 1905-
The Quarry (Harcourt, 1947). Life in a Vermont village from 1857 to 1914, emphasizing the New Englander's sense of duty.
The South-West Corner (Harcourt, 1951). A simply told story of an eighty-four-year-old woman determined to end her days on the old farm on top of a hill in Vermont. Rich in presenting folkways and folk habits of thought and speech.

WESTCOTT, EDWARD N., 1847-1898
David Harum (1898). A rural "Yankee" of New York. Considered an excellent portrayal of a shrewd country banker who is also a good horse trader and a rustic humorist. A very popular novel about 1900.

WHARTON, EDITH NEWBOLD (JONES), 1862-1937
Ethan Frome (1911). A realistic story of the restricted moral atmosphere of a bleak New England farm. The hero is compelled by circumstances to stay on his farm—to deny himself the chance to practice his chosen profession or to enjoy a normal life. One of the best books for this section.

WILDER, ISABEL
Let Winter Go (Coward, 1937). A story of life in a New England university town. Shows the havoc one selfish woman is able to create and its effect on the four intelligent people around whom the story is centered.

WILDER, LAURA INGALLS, 1867-1957
Farmer Boy (Harper, 1933). Intended for young readers but satisfying

for adults. A detailed account of family life and the annual cycle of tasks on an upstate New York farm in the 1880's.

WINSTON, CLARA, 1921-
The Closest Kin There Is (Harcourt, 1952). A vigorous story of the bitter lives of an emotionally trapped family on a New England farm in the 1940's. Catches many aspects of isolated farm life.

2. THE MIDDLE WEST

In the Middle Western states and Ontario with their vistas of productive land, the farms are somewhat larger than those of New England. The principal products of these farms are corn, wheat, soybeans, and livestock—hogs, cattle, mules, horses, and poultry. The writers have concentrated to a great extent on the frankly realistic, sometimes naturalistic, presentation of farm life. Many of the later books emphasize ethical problems.

ADE, GEORGE, 1866-1944
Fables in Slang (1900). Short, humorous, and satirical sketches of small-town life at the end of the nineteenth century. Sharp portraits of social climbers, drummers, bashful boys, mandolin players, merchants, Spanish-American War heroes. A convenient collection of Ade stories is *Thirty Fables in Slang* (Arrow Editions, 1933).

ANDERSON, SHERWOOD, 1876-1941
Winesburg, Ohio (1919). A famous book of short stories dealing with the frustrations and inhibitions of many sorts of people in a small Ohio village. Sentimental, bitter. Attacks the hypocrisies and the pharisaic code of villagers.
Triumph of the Egg (Viking, 1921). A collection of short stories, told very simply in the style of *Spoon River Anthology*, about the ugliness, emptiness, and misery of the lives of people with repressed emotions, petty desires, and thwarted instincts.

AYDELOTTE, DORA, 1878-
Long Furrows (Appleton, 1935). Midwestern farm life, centering on homely activities, such as threshing, quilting, skating, and picnicking.
Full Harvest (Appleton, 1939). Shows the disasters that follow after an ambitious farmer's wife has succeeded in moving the family to town for the sake of the children.

BELLAMANN, HENRY, 1882-1945
Kings Row (Simon, 1940). A sardonic picture of village life in the tradition of *Winesburg, Ohio*. The rottenness and corruption that follow in the wake of economic stagnation.

BELLAMANN, HENRY, 1882-1945, and BELLAMANN, KATHERINE J.
Parris Mitchell of Kings Row (Simon, 1948). Story of a well-educated

doctor fighting the cause of simple people against political bigotry, especially during the war of 1914-1918. Sheds light on a town in the St. Louis area.

BLAKE, ELEANOR, 1899-
Seedtime and Harvest (Putnam, 1935). Pictures a young, eager Norwegian immigrant girl forced by marriage into a lifetime of drudgery and work on a Michigan farm in the early twentieth century.

BLUMENTHAL, ALBERT, 1902-
Small Town Stuff (University of Chicago, 1932). A sociological study of a small town of about 1,400 inhabitants, showing the activity of the town, its agencies of social control, its social life, and changes which take place.

BOYD, THOMAS, 1898-
Samuel Drummond (Scribner's, 1925). Story of a family's struggle to make their farm in Ohio prosper. The advent of the Civil War destroys all their work and they are forced in middle age to start anew in town.

BROMFIELD, LOUIS, 1896-1956
The Farm (Harper, 1933). Contrasts the purposes of the two types of early Ohio settler—the one rich and well educated, the other the "no-account." Details of the settling of the Ohio Valley, the religion of these people, their work on the farm, etc. Really the biography of the farm told in terms of the people who worked it.

CARLETON, JETTA
The Moonflower Vine (Simon, 1962). The story of a farmer-schoolmaster, his wife, and four daughters, in Missouri. Good presentation of customs and attitudes, and a modest amount of sexual entanglement.

CLEMENS, SAMUEL LANGHORNE (MARK TWAIN, pseud.), 1835-1910
The Adventures of Tom Sawyer (1876). Missouri village life. A famous story giving much detail of life around 1850.
The Adventures of Huckleberry Finn (1885). Some presentation of village life and much of the customs and ideas of the mid-century in Missouri. The American classic of boy life on the river.
Pudd'nhead Wilson (1894). A small Missouri town looks with disfavor upon the intellectual lawyer, Wilson, who later proves his superiority. Clever, cynical, but thin.

COREY, PAUL, 1903-
Three Miles Square (Bobbs, 1939). Struggle of a widow to keep her farm and educate her four children in Iowa. Develops the life of a family against this rural community background. Realistic.
The Road Returns (Bobbs, 1940). Continues story begun in *Three Miles Square*. Covers the period immediately after the war of 1914-1918.

County Seat (Bobbs, 1941). A many-threaded story of life in an Iowa county in the late 1920's. Third of the trilogy.

Acres of Antaeus (Holt, 1946). A story of the Depression years in Iowa and of the development of a corporation farm by those who were foreclosing mortgages on the land of small farmers. A realistic story, ending with an argument for farm co-operatives.

CROY, HOMER, 1883-
West of the Water Tower (Harper, 1923). Excellent picture of a Missouri village.

DELL, FLOYD, 1887-
Moon Calf (Doran, 1920). Of a dreamy youth fighting against poverty and the conventions of a small factory town on the Mississippi. The two bondages of American youth of 1920: "his environment and his sentimental heritage."

DERLETH, AUGUST, 1909-
Still is the Summer Night (Scribner's, 1937). A love story set in a small town in Wisconsin in the 1880's. Good pictures of the everyday life of town and prairie.

Village Year (Coward, 1941). An unforced chronicle of life for three years in Sac Prairie, Wisconsin. Sensitive and mellow.

Sweet Genevieve (Scribner's, 1942). Of a girl who hated her life in the small town of Sac Prairie and finally had a chance to go on a showboat.

DOWNING, J. HYATT, 1888-
Sioux City (Putnam, 1940). Life in Sioux City in the gaudy boom period of the middle eighties.

DUNCAN, THOMAS WILLIAM, 1905-
Gus, the Great (Lippincott, 1947). Of a circus man in the Midwest. Long and rambling. Varies from burlesque to straight realism in style and characterization—but seems to recapture some of the spirit of 1890 nevertheless.

ELLISON, JAMES WHITFIELD
I'm Owen Harrison Harding (Doubleday, 1955). The social, academic, and "romantic" problems of a sixteen-year-old high-school boy in a Michigan town. A conversational report on adolescence.

ENGSTRAND, SOPHIA, 1908-
Miss Munday (Dial Press, 1940). This shows the limited but secure life of a schoolma'am in a Wisconsin village. Miss Munday chooses easy security rather than romance with a poor fisherman.

ERDMAN, LOULA GRACE
Years of the Locust (Dodd, 1947). Story of a successful Missouri farmer and his community, emphasizing neighborliness and common-sense customs.

FREEMAN, MARTIN JOSEPH, 1899-
Bitter Honey (Macmillan, 1942). An amusing sketch of a small Ohio town in 1908. Filled with a myriad of details of ordinary people and their lives.

GALE, ZONA, 1874-1938
Friendship Village (Macmillan, 1908). An old-fashioned story of "neighborly friendships and quiet lives."
Birth (Macmillan, 1918). A faithfully realistic picture of life in a Wisconsin small town.
Miss Lulu Bett (Appleton, 1920). A story of the restrictions of small village life. Miss Lulu Bett revolts.

GARLAND, HAMLIN, 1861-1940
Main-Travelled Roads (Harper, 1891). Renowned as the first truly realistic picture of the Middle Western farm. A collection of short stories of the drab, debt-ridden lives of farmers in Wisconsin and neighboring states. An epoch-making book.
Prairie Folks (Harper, 1892). Continues the style of *Main-Travelled Roads*, with stories nearer to the daily lives of average people.

GLASPELL, SUSAN, 1882-
Judd Rankin's Daughter (Lippincott, 1945). Story of Midwestern mores in 1944. Shows that not all Midwesterners are isolationist and provincial.

HARNACK, CURTIS, 1927-
The Work of an Ancient Hand (Harcourt, 1957). Varied characters in a Midwestern community. The story centers on the pastor of a fundamentalist church and his guilt complex.
Love and Be Silent (Harcourt, 1962). A family of four farm children whose father dies, leaving them to inherit his four farms and to pursue four separate ways of life. Iowa farm life and folk attitudes well presented.

HOWELLS, WILLIAM DEAN, 1837-1920
The Leatherwood God (1916). Story of a man who claimed to be God, causing excitement in a small community.

JOHNSON, JOSEPHINE, 1910-
Now in November (Simon, 1934). Beautifully written, tragic story of life on a run-down farm in Missouri during a terrible drought.
Jordanstown (Simon, 1937). One year in the life of a little city on a Midwest river.

KITCH, KENNETH HAUN (VICTOR HOLMES, pseud.), 1907-
Salt of the Earth (Macmillan, 1941). An understanding and sympathetic account of ordinary people in an ordinary town. Good-natured realism.

KRAUSE, HERBERT ARTHUR, 1905-
The Thresher (Bobbs, 1946). A realistic picture of rural life in Minnesota. The hardening effect of toil and brutal competition is a major theme.

LANE, ROSE WILDER, 1887-
Old Home Town (Longmans, 1935). Short stories of small-town life during the first decade of the century, with its neighborly intimacy, conventional morality, gossip, and isolation from the world.

LARDNER, RING, 1885-1933
Round Up (Scribner's, 1924). A collection of thirty-five of Lardner's stories. He excels in portraying the life of the Midwest village. Exact dialect.
How to Write Short Stories (Scribner's, 1924). Contains some of Lardner's best stories, with a few interspersed remarks.

LEWIS, SINCLAIR, 1885-1951
Main Street (Harcourt, 1920). A book centering on life in a small Midwestern town, "Gopher Prairie." The heroine tries to make the town over, but in the end becomes one of the people (almost). Emphasis on the pettiness and deadly dullness of the townfolk. An important satire.

LOCKRIDGE, ROSS FRANKLIN, 1914-1948
Raintree County (Houghton, 1948). A long novel of Indiana life from 1844 to 1892, with particular emphasis on the life of an introspective, idealistic character who becomes the village schoolmaster, a man who never seems quite to belong among his daily associates. Many glimpses of village mores and ways of thinking prevalent in the period. A book which debunks some of the myth about the good old days, and succeeds in presenting some phases of the horse-and-buggy days quite realistically.

LUTES, DELLA THOMPSON, 1872?-1942
Millbrook (Little, 1938). A charming reminiscence of farm life early in the century.

MacLEOD, LEROY, 1893-
Three Steeples (Covici, 1931). A farm community of Indiana. The life of the town is revealed through a story telling of the building of the community church.
Years of Peace (Century, 1932). The everyday life of farming folk in the Wabash Valley after the Civil War.
Crowded Hill (Reynal, 1934). A sequel to *Years of Peace,* covering the years 1876 to 1878. The conflicts between two families under one roof.

MANFRED, FREDERICK FEIKEMA (originally FEIKE FEIKEMA), 1912-
This Is the Year (Doubleday, 1947). Excellent account of a farmer's

life in northwestern Iowa. In the tradition of showing the hardening effect of harsh conditions on character. The major characters are Frisian, and there is considerable about their European customs and folkways.

MARQUIS, DON, 1878-1937
Sons of the Puritans (Doubleday, 1939). Illinois in the latter nineteenth century, emphasizing changing conventions and the results of suppression and frustration.

MARQUISS, WALTER
Brutus Was an Honorable Man(Scribner's, 1946). The development of a community from 1899 to 1941, showing that the business leaders do things for a community through coercion or to salve conscience.

MASTERS, EDGAR LEE, 1869-1950
The Tide of Time (Farrar, 1937). Follows the development of Ferrisburg, Illinois, from the time of its first land grants in 1812 to the end of the century. The conventions of the village defeat a natural Jeffersonian aristocrat.

MAXWELL, WILLIAM, 1908-
Time Will Darken It (Harper, 1948). An entertaining and sympathetic chronicle of events in an Illinois town in 1912. Probes into the psychological elements in human relationships but presents sweeter matters than those in the Henry Bellamann novels. Written in a poetic, thought-bearing style.

MOODIE, SUSANNA, 1803-1885
Life in the Clearings (1853, reprinted by Macmillan, 1959). An autobiographical account of settled, post-frontier town and country life in "Canada West"—in Ontario—told from the point of view of a genteel, English-born lady.

MORRIS, WRIGHT, 1910-
The Home Place (Scribner's, 1948). An off-beat documentary novel, illustrated with fine photographs of a Nebraska farm and town that typify "folk depletion." Strong in dialog and in details of farm life.

POUND, ARTHUR, 1884-
Once a Wilderness (Reynal, 1934). A family chronicle having for its background a large Michigan farm. Many of the farming activities, especially cattle breeding, described in detail.

PRICE, EMERSON
Inn of that Journey (Caxton, 1939). A dreary, small Ohio town. A realistic portrayal of boyhood therein.

RICHTER, CONRAD, 1890-
The Town (Knopf, 1950). Follows the rise of a town on the site of the

cabin of *The Trees*. A recognizable, credible story of physical and social changes, including the coming of the first railroad locomotive and
individual reactions to altering circumstances. The author has fully
digested his research, he writes in an easy style, and he imaginatively
communicates a feeling for past times.

ROBERTS, DOROTHY JAMES, 1903-
A Man of Malice Landing (Macmillan, 1943). Of a small town in Ohio,
with emphasis on the theme of narrow-mindedness.

SANDOZ, MARI, 1907-1966
The Tom-Walker (Dial, 1947). A study of three postwar periods in the
Middle West (after the Civil War, World War I, and World War II), and
leading up to the period when a dictator takes over in Washington. The
"tom-walker" or man on stilts is a symbol of giantism and irresponsibility.

SEAGER, ALLAN, 1906-
Inheritance (Simon, 1948). An attack, using graphic characterizations
and incidents, on the stultifying effect of life in a small Michigan town
upon its inhabitants. Exposes the double standard, the snobbery, the
unvarying cultural patterns that pass from father to son.

SHEEAN, VINCENT, 1899-
Bird of the Wilderness (Random, 1941). Curious tangle of psychological elements in an Illinois town in the spring of 1917. Midwestern
village "Morbidia" in Sheean's seemingly light vein. Shows attitudes
toward the coming war.

SHROYER, FREDERICK, 1916-
Wall Against the Night (Appleton, 1957). A good glimpse at changing
family mores around the time of World War II. The central character
gains understanding of the psychological factors underlying the life of
his wife, who committed suicide, of her lover, and of himself.

SINCLAIR, HAROLD, 1907-1966
American Years (Doubleday, 1938). Story of the development of an
Illinois small town for thirty years, following the stories of its first
settlers until Lincoln's election and the fall of Fort Sumter.
The Years of Growth (Doubleday, 1940). Continues *American Years*.
Everton, Illinois, from 1861 to 1893. Careful re-creation of nine-
teenth-century life.
Years of Illusion (Doubleday, 1941). Third of the trilogy. Period,
1900-1914.

SMITH, LABAN C., 1911-
No Better Land (Macmillan, 1946). Vigorous novel about a Wisconsin
farmer, with authentic detail about the life of one family.

STEGNER, WALLACE, 1909-
Remembering Laughter (Little, 1937). A novelette of farm life in Iowa, reminiscent of Mrs. Wharton's *Ethan Frome*.

SUCKOW, RUTH, 1892-1960
Country People (Knopf, 1924). Chronicle of three generations of German-American Iowa farmers. Tells of the early hardships of pioneers and their way of living until they became prosperous farmers.
Iowa Interiors (Knopf, 1926). A group of sixteen sketches of the drabness of existence on farms and in small Midwestern towns of the corn country.
The Bonney Family (Knopf, 1928). Twenty years of life in a minister's family in a small Iowa town.
The Folks (Farrar, 1934). Lengthy, detailed novel of the folks in a small Iowa town during the 1920's. Two parents find security and happiness but cannot transfer their sense of well-being to their children.
The John Wood Case (Viking, 1959). Well-told story of a small Iowa village and the ethical problems growing out of one man's misuse of funds. The story centers on his son, a high school boy.

TARKINGTON, BOOTH, 1869-1946
The Gentleman from Indiana (1899). A popular novel of the romantic type. Pictures the Midwest village as the home of democracy. Things turn out right for the hero and his sweetheart.
Penrod (1914). A popular story of a boy. Good details of life in a small Indiana town, the folk habits, moral codes, etc., of fifty years ago.

THOMAS, DOROTHY, 1899-
The Home Place (Knopf, 1936). A Nebraska farm after the Depression. The sons and their families all return to the old farm. A year of turmoil ensues. Realistic.

TROYER, HOWARD W., 1901-
The Salt and the Savor (Wyn, 1950). A folksy, leisurely, aphoristic, scrapbook-like picture of pioneer and rural Indiana from 1840 to 1865. "Every incident. . .has historical authenticity. . . ."

WALKER, MILDRED, 1905-
Fireweed (Harcourt, 1934). A quiet, natural story of a young couple in a Michigan lumber-mill town.

WELLMAN, MANLY WADE, 1898-
Not at These Hands (Putnam, 1962). Interesting, quite complete analysis of a community in Iowa. Centers on the minister and his wife, and his guilt complex over the death of his adopted son, who hanged himself.

WESCOTT, GLENWAY, 1901-
  The Apple of the Eye (Dial, 1924). Interesting story of Wisconsin country life, showing accurate knowledge of the people and their mores.
  Good-Bye Wisconsin (Harper, 1928). A group of short stories emphasizing the landscape of Wisconsin. Unemotional. By an expatriate who spent many years in Paris.

WEST, JESSAMYN
  The Friendly Persuasion (Harcourt, 1945). Contains fourteen tales about a Quaker farm family in southern Indiana in the Civil War period. Quiet characterizations and antiquarian charm.
  The Witch Diggers (Harcourt, 1951). Indiana in 1899-1900. Rural life and life on a country "poor farm" with its "sheltered" existence.

WHITLOCK, BRAND, 1869-1934
  J. Hardin and Son (Appleton, 1923). Small-town life in Ohio. The story centers around Hardin, Junior, who doesn't share his father's religious and moral enthusiasms but leads a colorless, unexciting life of duty.

3. THE NORTHWEST

The Northwest includes the United States from the great bend of the Missouri northwestward and the provinces of Saskatchewan, Alberta, and British Columbia in Canada. It is a land characterized by large farms and ranches, where wheat, cattle, and sheep are raised. A major variation in the setting is the fruit-growing areas of Oregon, Washington, and British Columbia. The general themes used by writers are much the same as those for the Middle West, with an added tendency toward grimness. The difficulties of dry-land farming and battles with winter storms are major themes.

BOLSTER, EVELYN, 1909-
  Come Gently Spring (Vanguard, 1942). Story of an Idaho farming community. A pastoral view of people who blend naturally into the landscape.

CANNON, CORNELIA JAMES, 1876-
  Red Rust (Little, 1928). Story of Swedish immigrants in the farm lands of Minnesota. Discusses their hardships, mostly economic; the search for a rust-resisting wheat is a central theme.

CASTLE, MARIAN (JOHNSON), 1898-
  Deborah (Morrow, 1946). A story of three generations, beginning on a Dakota farm in the early nineties and ending in the same place during the Depression. Indicates the changes that took place in the attitudes and cultural ambitions of America during that period.

CATHER, WILLA SIBERT, 1876-1947
Youth and the Bright Medusa (Knopf, 1920). Various stories showing
the restrictions on expressive living in towns and on ranches.

COMSTOCK, SARAH
Speak to the Earth (Doubleday, 1927). Shows an ex-service man trying to make a living from an arid sheep ranch in the Dakota Badlands.

CURRY, PEGGY (SIMSON)
So Far From Spring (Viking, 1956). A novel of ranch life in northern
Colorado in the early 1900's. Believable characters and a vivid pic-
turing of conditions in a cattle-raising area. Winter storms and the
Western code of violence lend a grim tone to the narrative.

DAVIS, HAROLD L., 1896-1960
Honey in the Horn (Harper, 1935). A novel collecting much of the folklore about early settlers in Oregon. Realistic detail about ranches,
hop-pickers, dry-land farmers, etc., shortly after 1900. In the main,
realistic. Written in a brisk style.
Winds of Morning (Morrow, 1952). Laid in rural Oregon in the 1920's.
A strong story, free of clichés and notable for its contrast of petty
people and noble natural settings. Good characterizations, exciting
incidents, and a direct style that is rich in idiom.

DOWNING, J. HYATT, 1888-
A Prayer for Tomorrow (Putnam, 1928). A story of the coming of
wheat farmers, the ruin of grazing land, a boom during war years, and
the letdown afterward. Comprehensive treatment of an era in South
Dakota (approximately 1890-1930). Good details concerning small-
town life.
Hope of Living (Putnam, 1939). Of a woman farmer and her ambition-
less husband on a South Dakota farm.

EUNSON, DALE
Homestead (Farrar, 1935). Homesteading in Montana. Written in the
matter-of-fact style popular in Western action stories. Cattleman
versus farmer theme.

FISHER, VARDIS, 1895-
Orphans in Gethsemane (Swallow, 1960). The first half of this immense volume (987 pages) about the life of Vridar Hunter is a rehash
and condensation of a tetralogy published in the 1930's. The whole
volume comes out as an ironic presentation of a twentieth-century
character, a sensitive boy who grew up in revolt against the sadism
and misery of his early life, and in turn caused great misery to those
who loved him, without, seemingly, realizing his own shortcomings.

HART, ALAN, 1892-
Doctor Mallory (Norton, 1935). A general practitioner in a bleak little

Oregon town battles against dishonest competition, ignorance, poverty, and disease.

HUDSON, LOIS PHILLIPS
The Bones of Plenty (Little, 1962). A detailed story of a renting farm family in North Dakota in the Depression years of 1933-1934. Forced from their farm, in May, 1934, they start west to join other migrants.

JOHNSON, ALVIN SAUNDERS, 1874-
Spring Storm (Knopf, 1936). The record of a few years of a boy's life on a Nebraska farm in the early 1900's.

JONES, NARD, 1904-
Oregon Detour (Harcourt, 1930). A good picture of a small town in eastern Oregon, also of farm life in the same community.
Wheat Women (Duffield, 1933). Set in wheat lands of Washington, a story of three generations of wheat growers and their families.
Still to the West (Dodd, 1946). Live, real account of people living in the area to be affected by the building of the Grand Coulee.

KRAMER, HORACE
Marginal Land (Lippincott, 1939). About farmers and ranchers on the high plains, where farming is not very successful. A textbook on soil conservation in the form of a novel.

KRAUSE, HERBERT, 1905-
Wind Without Rain (Bobbs, 1939). An intense picture of emotionally hardened farmers in Minnesota.

McKAY, ALLIS
They Came to a River (Macmillan, 1941). Farm life in the apple-growing region of Washington from 1900 to 1920. A richly colored study of a countryside and its people.

MACLEOD, NORMAN, 1906-
The Bitter Roots (Smith and Durrell, 1941). Thirty-eight episodes from a Montana boyhood during the war of 1914-1918.

NELSON, IRA S., 1912-
On Sarpy Creek (Little, 1938). A good realistic novel of Montana in the 1920's and 1930's, with emphasis upon the homely goodness and reliability of the folk when faced by adversity.

O'ROURKE, FRANK, 1916-
Window in the Dark (Morrow, 1960). A simply written, but clever whodunit about a bank robbery in a small Nebraska town and a twenty-year-old suspect. Nice portraiture of a small town in the 1930's.

OSTENSO, MARTHA, 1900-
Wild Geese (Dodd, 1925). Shows a greedy and heartless farmer

dominating his household so that his children get no chance for self-realization. Scandinavians on a Minnesota farm.

The Dark Dawn (Dodd, 1926). A drama of grim psychological conflict, resulting from an ill-advised and disastrous marriage. Laid against a background of farm life.

There's Always Another Year (Dodd, 1933). Story of early twentieth-century life on a Dakota farm. Concerned mostly with a farm-loving young man, his selfish wife, and the young girl on whose farm he worked.

SNELL, GEORGE D.
The Great Adam (Caxton, 1934). An uncensored presentation of the slow disintegration of the influential banker in a small Idaho town.

STEGNER, WALLACE, 1909-
The Big Rock Candy Mountain (Duell, 1943). A long biography of a trapshooter, gambler, bootlegger, and real-estate man in the post-pioneer West. The book reveals life in the early twentieth century; its theme is the frontiersman's dreams and frustrations.

STEWART, GEORGE, 1892-
Reluctant Soil (Caxton, 1936). Story of a widow and her two small children who struggle to make a living on the desert soil of the south-western part of Idaho between 1900 and 1920.

THORPE, BERENICE, 1900-
Reunion on Strawberry Hill (Knopf, 1944). A warm, understanding novel of life and love on a small berry ranch in Washington.

WALKER, MILDRED, 1905-
Winter Wheat (Harcourt, 1944). A strong, simple story of the wheat country of Montana, with emphasis on place and character rather than plot. Shows the inexorability of nature, its influence on human lives.

The Curlew's Cry (Harcourt, 1955). Pictures a Montana town in a cattle region during a period of change, 1905-1941, as a woman lives through the main events of her life.

WINTHER, SOPHUS K., 1895-
Mortgage Your Heart (Macmillan, 1937). Continuation of *Take All to Nebraska*. About this family's experiences on the Nebraska farm as rent farmers. Showing the differences between the father and his Americanized sons. Time of the story about 1906-1917.

This Passion Never Dies (Macmillan, 1938). Continuation of *Mortgage Your Heart*. Speaks of the family's struggle after their father's death, and of the personal conflicts of these Americanized Danish immigrants.

Beyond the Garden Gate (Macmillan, 1946). Story of an Oregon college boy who partially solves some difficult personal problems by taking the advice of a doctor friend. Throws some light on changing mores in regard to sex and family life.

ZIETLOW, E. R.
These Same Hills (Knopf, 1960). Excellent local-color story of a boy in the Badlands of South Dakota as he gives up his romantic dreams of being a trapper and plans to go to college.

4. THE SOUTH

(a) The Old South

Novels in this section of the book represent the South before the Civil War and during the war and Reconstruction. Ever since the 1830's, fiction has treated plantation life from varied viewpoints. Novels have been pro-South, anti-South, pro-Negro, anti-Negro, pro-abolition, anti-North—but whatever their point of view, they have generally attributed glamour to the vanished plantation civilization, and they have taken up, at least by implication, the problem of human freedom.

Writing about the plantation has been divided into two major streams, the sentimentalists of the 1880's and 1890's—Allen, Page, and Harris—and the realists of the twentieth century—Gaither, Stribling, Bontemps, and others. Aside from this, of course, there have been lesser streams: Harriet Beecher Stowe and her followers; a comparable group of propagandists for the South; flamboyantly romantic writers like John Esten Cooke and Stark Young; and historical romanticists, such as Mary Johnston and Margaret Mitchell.

ALLEN, JAMES LANE, 1849-1925
A Kentucky Cardinal (1895). Lyrical and sentimental, but famous for its descriptions of the Kentucky of about 1850.

BARKER, ROLAND, 1905-   , and DOERFLINGER, WILLIAM
The Middle Passage (Macmillan, 1939). Pedestrian fiction based on much research. An informative picture of the slave trade from the purchase of slave captives in the island cities of the Gold Coast to delivery to smugglers off South Carolina.

BEAUMONT DE LA BONNINIERE, GUSTAVE AUGUSTE DE, 1802-1866
Marie; or Slavery in the United States: a Novel of Jacksonian America (1835; Stanford University Press, 1958). A study of the racial attitudes of Negroes and non-Negroes (and also Indians and non-Indians) in both the South and the North. A sentimental and melodramatic tale in the tradition of *Atala* and *Pierre et Virginie,* and much interesting non-fictional comment on American civilization.

BONTEMPS, ARNA, 1902-
Black Thunder (Macmillan, 1936). About an attempted slave insurrection in the early nineteenth century. Good on realistic detail.

BRADFORD, ROARK, 1896-1948
Kingdom Coming (Harper, 1933). Plantation life. Some pictures of voodoo and of the Underground Railroad and of unhappy "free" Negroes.

CARUTHERS, WILLIAM ALEXANDER, 1800-1846
Kentuckian in New York, or the Adventures of Three Southerns (1834). "A contribution to the cause of intersectional good-will." In a series of letters, several Southerners make charming, intelligent comment on Yankees, slavery, poverty in Virginia, and so on.

CATHER, WILLA SIBERT, 1876-1947
Sapphira and the Slave Girl (Knopf, 1940). Beginning in the South in 1856, the story deals with Sapphira Dodderedge Colbert, a Virginia lady, whose husband ran a mill on the frontier. There is great conflict between the Colberts over the beautiful slave girl, Nancy, and the plot centers around Sapphira's unfounded jealousy. Artistic but lifeless writing.

CLEMENS, SAMUEL LANGHORNE (MARK TWAIN, pseud.), 1835-1910
Life on the Mississippi (1883). An autobiographical narrative, mostly about Twain's experiences as a river pilot. Perceptibly but entertainingly fictionalized. The classic account of steamboating on Old Man River.

COOKE, JOHN ESTEN, 1830-1886
The Virginia Comedians (1854). A romantic and fairly expert picture of the social life of colonial Virginia, with its charm, irresponsibility, and aristocratic code of love. One of the early fixers of the romantic interpretation of old plantation days.

CRABB, ALFRED LELAND, 1884-
Dinner at Belmont (Bobbs, 1942). An effective, romantic picture of the Old South and its fine first families.
Home to the Hermitage: A Novel of Andrew and Rachel Jackson (Bobbs, 1948). Laid in the Nashville area. A story of Jackson's marriage and his fights against slanderers who accused his wife of bigamy.

DOWDEY, CLIFFORD, 1904-
Gamble's Hundred (Little, 1939). Historical novel of Gamble's Hundred, a plantation in tidewater Virginia in the early eighteenth century. The hero is the surveyor employed by the owner of the plantation. Gives good historical information about the South of this period.

ENDORE, GUY, 1901-
Babouk (Vanguard, 1934). A revolutionary Marxist novel, opposed to slavery and imperialism, which presents in ghastly detail the horrors of the African slave trade.

FAULKNER, WILLIAM, 1897-1962
Absalom, Absalom! (Random, 1936). An involved and complicated novel of the Old South and of an ambitious planter who settled near Jefferson, Mississippi, in 1833.

GAITHER, FRANCES O., 1889-1955
Follow the Drinking Gourd (Macmillan, 1940). A beautifully written novel of pre-Civil War days in Georgia and Alabama. Presents the economic wastefulness of slavery and the social effect of such an institution on all concerned.
The Red Cock Crows (Macmillan, 1944). Shows how even the best plantation life was a failure because of its unreconcilable combination of human values. Of a slave revolt on a model plantation in Mississippi.
Double Muscadine (Macmillan, 1949). A story of love and slavery on a Mississippi plantation. The plot centers in a dramatic murder trial, which crosscuts existence in a Southern community.

GORDON, CAROLINE, 1895-
The Forest of the South (Scribner's, 1945). Sixteen well-told stories of the South, ranging in time from pioneer days to the present.

HARRIS, JOEL CHANDLER, 1848-1908
Nights with Uncle Remus (1883). Humorous and charming folklore created by the slave. Pictures a pleasant relationship between white and black.

HEARN, LAFCADIO, 1850-1904
Chita: A Memory of Last Island (1889). A terrific storm destroys L'Ile Derniere off the Louisiana coast. One of the few survivors is a small child rescued by a Spanish-American family who bring her up as their own child. The story is rich in descriptions of the storm, of the coastal islands near Barataria, and of the fisher folk of the region.

HERGESHEIMER, JOSEPH, 1880-1954
The Limestone Tree (Knopf, 1931). A Kentucky family chronicle covering part of the eighteenth and most of the nineteenth century.

JOHNSTON, MARY, 1870-1936
Lewis Rand (1908). Lively portrait of interaction between the various classes of people in Virginia in Jefferson's time.
The Slave Ship (Little, 1924). A well-told novel about the slave trade in the eighteenth century, giving one man's reaction to the buying and selling of human flesh.
Miss Delicia Allen (Little, 1933). The cultured and gracious life on Indian Leap plantation in Virginia before and during the Civil War.

JOHNSTON, RICHARD M., 1822-1898
Dukesborough Tales (1871). Stories of yeomen and nobodies during

plantation days in Georgia. Some sharp characterizations in the "local-color" manner.

KANE, HARNETT T., 1910-
Bride of Fortune (Doubleday, 1948). A true account, adorned by fictional scenes and conversations, of Mrs. Jefferson Davis. Rich details of wealthy Mississippi planting society, Washington City in the 1850's, and also the Confederate period. A clear portrait of a remarkable woman.

KENNEDY, JOHN P., 1795-1870
Swallow Barn (1832). This is a mellow, well-rounded, Southern account of a plantation in the Old Dominion. Slow but satisfying reading.

KING, GRACE, 1852-1932
The Pleasant Ways of St. Médard (Holt, 1916). Reminiscent, nostalgic sketches of the old regime in New Orleans during and right after the Civil War. Much on the folkways of French, "Americans," and Negroes and on the role of the father in a patriarchal society.

LEWIS, BESSIE
To Save Their Souls (Christopher, 1939). Running from 1810 to about 1870, this story shows that the Negroes gained a great deal in being brought to America. Satirizes Northerners who tried to "save their souls," and implies that Southerners know best.

MARGULIES, LEO, 1900-   , and MERWIN, SAMUEL
The Flags Were Three (Curl, 1945). Novel of New Orleans and its development from a wilderness outpost in 1732 to the sophisticated city of the early nineteenth century. The romance of the old city is preserved. Three generations of believable characters.

MARQUAND, JOHN PHILLIPS, 1893-1960
The Black Cargo (Scribner's, 1925). An adventure story of illicit slave trade in the New England clipper-ship era, with the interest centered on the black deeds and tormented conscience of an elderly slaver and "pirate" who has come home from the sea.

MITCHELL, MARGARET, 1900-1949
Gone with the Wind (Macmillan, 1936). Full-length portrait of a Georgia plantation before and after the Civil War. A conventional plot combined with lively social history and interesting human psychology. Shows how war wiped out an integrated way of life.

ODUM, HOWARD WASHINGTON, 1884-1954
Cold Blue Moon (Bobbs, 1931). An old Negro tells things he remembers of plantation days.

PAGE, THOMAS NELSON, 1853-1922
In Ole Virginia (1887). Stories of plantations, slaves, and masters,

containing much Negro dialect. A sentimental, nostalgic treatment of the Old South which did much to "set up" the plantation tradition.

PARRISH, ANNE (MRS. CHARLES A. CORLISS), 1888-
A Clouded Star (Harper, 1948). Of Harriet Tubman, the notable Negro who helped lead the Underground Railroad. A fictional account of one of her trips north from Maryland toward Canada, in 1860.

PIERCE, OVID WILLIAMS, 1910-
On a Lonesome Porch (Doubleday, 1960). A simply told and appealing story of a Southern lady returning to her plantation in North Carolina after the Civil War. Her widowed daughter-in-law and her grandson adapt to the terms of their new life after the war, but she prepares to return to her friends in Raleigh.

SASS, HERBERT RAVENAL, 1884-
Look Back to Glory (Bobbs, 1933). The story is weak, but the background of South Carolina aristocracy is fully depicted, especially the Secessionists' rationalizations.

SCOTT, EVELYN, 1893-
Migrations (Boni, 1927). A record of unpleasant and tragic aspects of slavery.

SETTLE, MARY LEE (MRS. DOUGLAS NEWTON)
Know Nothing (Viking, 1960). A slight variation on the old plantation theme. Events from 1837 to 1861 leading up to the Civil War in a West Virginia setting, with the families of the story being divided by the war.

STEWARD, DAVENPORT, 1913-
Rainbow Road (Tupper and Love, 1953). A romantic tale with an authentic background of the gold rush in the Georgia hills in the 1820's. This rush had, the author says, "its tide of blatant greed, its seething undercurrent of animal ferocity."

STOWE, HARRIET BEECHER, 1812-1896
Uncle Tom's Cabin (1852). One of the greatest of our propaganda novels. A sentimentalized and also sensationalized version of antebellum plantation life. Kentucky and Louisiana.
Dred, A Tale of the Dismal Swamp (1856). Rich in background material of the ordinary life on the plantation. A study of the economic problems of Negro emancipation.

STRIBLING, THOMAS SIGISMUND, 1881-
The Forge (Doubleday, 1931). Good realistic treatment of a middle-class family at the time of the Civil War, a family ranking between the plantation owner and the poor white or hillbilly. All the traditional classes are represented but with a better feeling of actuality than is usual.

The Store (Doubleday, 1932). Gives the atmosphere of a small town in Alabama—the folkways, the class distinctions, the religions, the business practices. The ruthless, unethical main character becomes an important man in the town.

TATE, ALLEN, 1899-
The Fathers (Putnam, 1938). A dramatization of the plantation code in Virginia in the decade before the Civil War, when social forces were rapidly hatching a national crisis.

TOURGEE, ALBION W., 1838-1905
A Royal Gentleman (1874). A melodramatic story of a Southern gentleman who made a mistress of his slave girl. Presents forcibly the effect of the slave system on the white owner as well as the effect on the slave.

WARREN, LELLA, 1899-
Foundation Stone (Knopf, 1940). Novel of Alabama in the last century. A chronicle of a family of planters who came to Alabama from South Carolina. Follows their lives from the 1820's to the end of the Civil War. Shows their economic struggles and their relations with Negroes.

WELD, JOHN, 1905-
Sabbath Has No End (Scribner's, 1942). A South Carolina cotton plantation in 1815. Good portrayal of Negro character.

YOUNG, STARK, 1881-1963
Heaven Trees (Scribner's, 1926). A picture of a Mississippi plantation before the Civil War. Contrasts the spacious, lazy, easy life with that which the young kinswoman from Vermont knew.

(b) The South After 1880

Since about 1880 the South has become the land of the sharecropper and its economy is dominated, as it was before the Civil War, by the raising of cotton, tobacco, and cane. The people engaged in farming have been divided into a new set of classes: owners, tenants, sharecroppers, and hired hands. There has been much realistic and naturalistic writing, particularly since 1920, but also a persistent, perennial reappearance of the old-fashioned romantic story.

The 1920's and 1930's were marked by the emergence of an unusual number of realistic writers picturing many facets of life in the South. Among the most notable were: Erskine Caldwell, William Faulkner (a Nobel Prize winner), Ellen Glasgow, Edith Summers Kelley, George Milburn, and Thomas S. Stribling. Writers of the 1940's and 1950's tended to present more clearly the psychological patterns emerging from the peculiar stresses of changing ways of life. Prominent among writers of those decades were William E. March Campbell, Mrs. Worth

Tuttle Hedden, Carson McCullers, Lillian Smith, William Styron, and Robert Penn Warren. Since 1954, many new writers dealing with the civil rights struggle have emerged.

ARMFIELD, EUGENE MOREHEAD
Where the Weak Grow Strong (Covici, 1936). A picture of Tuttle, North Carolina, in the autumn of 1912. A cross-section view of all the types of people in the town.

BASSO, HAMILTON, 1904-1964
Cinnamon Seed (Scribner's, 1934). Life on a twentieth-century plantation near New Orleans, given perspective by the memories of a veteran of the Civil War.
The View from Pompey's Head (Doubleday, 1954). A discursive study of the hold his Southern background has on a man who has achieved a career in Manhattan. Deals with the psychological complications and the sociological castes in a Southern town and throws an angular light on New York literary life.

BEAUMONT, CHARLES, 1929 or 1930-
The Intruder (Putnam, 1959). A story of a small Southern town in the late 1950's during the school desegregation crisis. The events taking place in Clinton, Tennessee, are followed in close detail, but the town is given the name Caxton and the characters all have fictitious names. The character Cramer (Kasper?) is thoroughly analyzed.

BETHEA, JACK, 1892-1928
Cotton (Houghton, 1928). Larry Maynard returns to Alabama to try to raise cotton by the scientific methods he has learned in school. After many failures, he succeeds in convincing his fellow planters.

BOLES, PAUL DARCY, 1919-
Deadline (Macmillan, 1957). A moving story of a Southern editor, who after great travail comes out in a public speech and in his column for integration. Shows good understanding of Southerners and their folkways.

BRADDON, RUSSELL, 1921-
The Proud American Boy (St. Martin's, 1961). A British writer tells the story of an eight-year-old boy in the American South, accused of rape and sent to a juvenile home. The story gives many glimpses of Southern customs and attitudes, as well as the political connections between such customs and the world today.

BURMAN, BEN LUCIEN, 1895-
Steamboat Round the Bend (Farrar, 1933). A gently humorous story of an old shanty-boat dweller who always longed to own a steamboat.
Blow for a Landing (Day, 1938). Self-respecting shanty-boat people strive to establish a little farm on the land. Realistic yet charming.

CALDWELL, ERSKINE C., 1903-

Tobacco Road (Duell, 1932). The story of a sharecropper shelved by the plantation owner, allowed to live in a tumble-down shack but not allowed to raise a crop. Pictures a family unbelievably degraded and destitute—the end result of a bad system. Contains grim farcical humor.

God's Little Acre (Viking, 1933). Story of a dirt farmer who for fifteen years dug holes in his Georgia soil, hoping to find gold. The only other occupation indulged in by him and his two sons was sex. Outrageous details given in a casually humorous manner. A social and economic study of the poor white.

We Are the Living (Duell, 1933). A collection of twenty stories ranging in setting from North to South, mostly concerned with the sex impulses of the characters.

Kneel to the Rising Sun (Viking, 1935). A book of short stories of which the title story is an unusual presentation of the relationships between a poor white, a Negro, and the plantation owner. A classic story of "the system" and its effect on the people.

CAMPBELL, WILLIAM E. MARCH, 1894-1954

Come in at the Door (Smith, 1934). Story of the childhood of a white boy in Alabama and the lasting impression that the hanging of his Negro comrade, following his childish betrayal, has upon his later life.

The Looking Glass (Little, 1943). A psychoanalytic picture of Reedyville, Alabama, about 1917. Sardonic writing in the tradition of *Spoon River Anthology*.

CARTER, HODDING, 1907-

The Winds of Fear (Farrar, 1944). A study of a small Southern town during World War II. Built around the civil struggle over Negro rights.

Floodcrest (Rinehart, 1947). Of a great flood and how a corrupt Southern senator tried to make the people believe he was doing all he could for them.

CHAMBERLAIN, WILLIAM WOODROW, 1914-

Leaf Gold (Bobbs, 1941). Of tobacco-growing in Kentucky. Realistic detail.

CHASTAIN, THOMAS

Judgment Day (Doubleday, 1962). A simply told story of a Negro minister who does much to keep a small town from the violence which threatens after a white man kills a Negro after an illicit affair with the Negro's wife.

CHAZE, ELLIOT

Tiger in the Honeysuckle (Scribner's, 1965). A small Mississippi town in 1964. A middle-aged reporter on the town paper finds himself on the side of the civil rights workers. He defends a Negro accused of assault, falls in love with a Negro girl, and dies a hero saving the people in a rights rally from being blown up by a bomb.

CHEVALIER, ELIZABETH PICKETT, 1896-
Drivin' Woman (Macmillan, 1942). From the time of the Civil War to 1911. A mingling of sentimentality with a good story of the tobacco war between Kentucky planters and New York financiers.

CLAYTON, JOHN BELL, 1906-1955
Six Angels at My Back (Macmillan, 1952). An intimate view of have-nots in Florida—their essential decency, their uneducated groping for a home and a good life, and their attitudes toward tourists and flashy resorts. Told in the words of a nineteen-year-old boy who becomes involved in crime. Dramatic, suspenseful, excellent style.

COCHRAN, LOUIS
Son of Haman (Caxton, 1937). Of the delta land of Mississippi in the late eighties and early nineties. Effective local color written in the style of the "stark realism" school.
Boss Man (Caxton, 1939). Continues the story of *Son of Haman*. A fair, sympathetic analysis of miserable sharecroppers and the Southern economic system that causes their troubles.

COFFIN, TRISTRAM, 1912-
Mine Eyes Have Seen the Glory (Macmillan, 1964). Of a Congressman from Arkansas, a typical demagogue, and his son who becomes a "Mississippi Freedom" worker. Practically burlesque in its treatment of the Congressman, but quite sympathetic in handling the story of the son.

COMMAGER, EVAN CARROLL (MRS. HENRY STEELE COMMAGER)
Valentine (Harper, 1961). A simple story of a New England girl transplanted to the South. In a sentimental story of the remnants of an old Southern family for whom the New England girl becomes a baby-sitter, Mrs. Commager succeeds in giving quite a bit of Southern customs and attitudes.

COOPER, MADISON ALEXANDER, 1894?-
Sironia, Texas (Houghton, 1952). This two-volume, 1,731-page novel tells a great deal about a town during the period 1900-1925, as mores disintegrate. Good reportage.

DEAL, BABS H. (MRS. BORDEN DEAL)
It's Always Three O'Clock (McKay, 1961). Setting in the South from 1923 to 1946. The leading characters are high school age at the beginning. Good treatment of Southern ways.

DOUGHTY, LEGARDE S.
Music Is Gone (Duell, 1945). Story of a country doctor and his struggle

to bring health and some happiness to his patients, in a Southern village. Good, simple, realistic picture.

DOUGLAS, MARJORY STONEMAN, 1890-
Road to the Sun (Rinehart, 1952). The locale is the Miami district in the 1910's and 1920's. A picture of rapid development of farm and city areas and a drama of conflicts between the old established inhabitants—crackers—and the new exploiters and boomers—rice farmers, canal builders, and real estate men included.

FAULKNER, JOHN, 1901-1963
Men Working (Harcourt, 1941). A comic folk epic in the manner of *Tobacco Road*. Matter-of-fact presentation of a Mississippi tenant-farmer family that moves to town and makes a meager living on checks from "the WP and A."
Dollar Cotton (Harcourt, 1942). A vigorous tale of a Mississippian who leaves the hills and founds a cotton plantation in the rich delta country. A case-study of the poor white.

FAULKNER, WILLIAM, 1897-1962
The Sound and the Fury (Cape, 1929). Of the decay of a Southern family of gentle blood and of its members who become drunkards, suicides, idiots, pathological perverts, etc. Comparable to works of Dostoevsky and James Joyce in its picture of insanity and futility. Notable for Faulkner's use of four points of view and of stream-of-consciousness technique.
Sartoris (Harcourt, 1929). Story of life in the hills of northern Mississippi. About Bayard Sartoris, whose brother's death during the war of 1914-1918 makes him on his return from war more reckless than even the traditional Sartorises.
As I Lay Dying (Smith, 1930). About a moronic but heroic Mississippi family and their trek across the state with the corpse of their dead mother on a wagon. A morbid social and psychological study of family solidarity, told by use of a multiple, first-person point of view.
Sanctuary (Smith, 1931). A violent, disjointed narrative of the downfall of a flighty, college-age, Mississippi girl (Temple Drake) and of the sadistic pervert who has her in his control as she becomes a prostitute in Memphis. The author makes complicated use of the stream of consciousness.
Light in August (Smith, 1932). At base, this is a simple, small-town idyll, but in execution it becomes a complex novel packed with comedy, violent misfortune, and implicit moral and social commentary. Four major characters lead frustrated lives: a part-Negro who passes for white and finally ends the victim of a mob; a preacher whose religion doesn't meet reality; a lonely woman; a migratory worker. Clearer, better writing than some of Faulkner.
The Wild Palms (Random, 1939). Contains two long separate stories.

"The Wild Palms" is a study of integrity in love. "Old Man" is an astonishing account of the Mississippi River flood of 1927 and of an "escaped" convict's adventures in trying to get back to prison; the tale is a tribute to the essential courage, dignity, and reliability of the Mississippi hillfolk.

The Hamlet (Random, 1940). Details the arrival of Flem Snopes and other Snopeses in Frenchman's Bend, Mississippi. Shows a grasping poor-white family using any means to get ahead. Full of comedy, anecdote, symbolism, and evocative description. Studies aspects of love and possession. First in a trilogy in which *The Town* is second.

Collected Stories of William Faulkner (Random, 1950). A carefully selected list of 42 short stories from Faulkner's works. Arranged in groups: country, village, wilderness, wasteland (on war), middle ground, and beyond. A fine collection.

Requiem for a Nun (Random, 1951). Partly a dramatic dialogue that involves the former Temple Drake (of *Sanctuary*) in a murder case and that calls forth philosophical talk about guilt and faith; partly a clear, poetical evocation of the history of Faulkner's city of Jefferson and his county of Yoknapatawpha, especially as symbolized by the courthouse and the jail.

Big Woods (Random, 1955). Contains four hunting stories, including a new version of the splendid and important "The Bear" with its evocation of Mississippi forests, an almost mythical bear, and a boy's growing up.

The Town (Random, 1957). Centers on the economic rise of Flem Snopes in the city of Jefferson, as he becomes president of the old Colonel Sartoris bank and discovers civic virtue and the need for a good name and a house that looks successful. A complicated yarn with some tall-story anecdotes about various Snopeses.

The Mansion (Random, 1959). Concludes the life story of Flem Snopes, and follows through with his stepdaughter and other Jefferson people.

FERBER, EDNA, 1887-

Show Boat (Doubleday, 1926). Ultraromantic and rather popular, but nevertheless a robust treatment of a colorful aspect of river life.

FLEMING, BERRY, 1899-

Colonel Effingham's Raid (Duell, 1943). Good-natured satire on Dixie politics in 1940. Probes the dry rot of local corruption.

Lightwood Tree (Lippincott, 1947). Of a Georgia community in 1943, and the fight of an academy history teacher to get the people to uphold civil rights.

The Fortune Tellers (Lippincott, 1951). Centers on an attempt of the leading citizen of a Southern town to keep hidden a family secret: a murder for which a Negro was unjustly condemned. Catches aspects of present-day mores.

GIBBONS, ROBERT, 1915-
Bright Is the Morning (Knopf, 1943). A first novel, full of warmth and
humor, which portrays the life and emotions of ordinary Alabamans
"who live neither behind the great white columns nor beneath the leak-
ing roof."

GLASGOW, ELLEN, 1874-1945
Barren Ground (Doubleday, 1925). An American *Far from the Madding
Crowd.* A story of the worn-out land of Virginia and its rehabilitation
by the use of scientific methods.
They Stooped to Folly: A Comedy of Morals (Doubleday, 1929). De-
lightfully ironic treatment of changing attitudes toward feminine conduct.
The Sheltered Life (Doubleday, 1932). Of a young girl "sheltered"
from a knowledge of life in true Southern fashion.
Vein of Iron (Harcourt, 1935). The fifth generation of a Virginia fam-
ily of Scotch Presbyterians.
In This Our Life (Harcourt, 1941). A story of family relationships in
Queensborough, Virginia. Shows philosophic understanding of Southern
ways.

GORDON, CAROLINE, 1895-
Aleck Maury (Scribner's, 1931). Biographical novel about Aleck
Maury, whose predominant interest is his love for hunting and fishing.
He finally satisfies his desire at the age of seventy in a Virginia val-
ley, after all his family cares are in order.
The Garden of Adonis (Scribner's, 1937). Shows the Southern share-
cropper, the plantation owner, and the industrialist in conflict.

GRAU, SHIRLEY ANN, 1929-
The Hard Blue Sky (Knopf, 1958). Kaleidoscopic picture of fisher folk
on a small island off the coast of Louisiana. Details of speech and
custom seem accurate.
The Keepers of the House (Knopf, 1964). Of a wealthy landowning family
in an unnamed state (Mississippi perhaps). The white branch of the
family keep the estate. The colored descendants move north. Psychologically interesting.

GREEN, PAUL, 1894-
This Body the Earth (Harper, 1935). A study of the Southern share-
cropper who is condemned forever to the system no matter how industrious he may be.
Salvation on a String, and Other Tales of the South (Harper, 1946).
Short stories about the Raleigh, North Carolina, back-country area,
several of them about revivalism. Traditional treatment of hillbillies
and Negroes, in the main.

HAAS, BEN
Look Away, Look Away (Simon, 1964). A picture of one Southern
community from 1946 to 1963, a composite of various real places in

THE SOUTH   61

which dramatic events occurred at the time. The central character is
a Negro teacher who becomes a civil-rights leader. A story display-
ing real understanding of the Southern scene.

HAMILL, KATHARINE
Swamp Shadow (Knopf, 1936). Of a strong, responsible woman who
contrasts with the shiftless, fever-ridden poor whites in the swamp
region of the Mississippi coast. A picture of these backwoods people—
their language, habits, and customs.

HARRIS, BERNICE K.
Purslane (University of North Carolina, 1939). An excellent presentation of the comfortable life of an independent Southern farmer about
1900. Slim in plot but abundant in sensuous descriptions of country
food.
Sweet Beulah Land (Doubleday, 1943). An honest picture of life among
landlords and tenants, good and bad alike—simple ordinary Americans
who live on a neck of the Carolina coast. Rich in the everyday business of planting, harvesting, worshipping.

HEDDEN, MRS. WORTH TUTTLE
The Other Room (Crown, 1947). Tells of the daughter of an old
Virginia family who becomes a teacher in a Negro college in New
Orleans. Throws into relief the difficulties of young people, both black
and white, south of Mason and Dixon's line.

HOFFMAN, WILLIAM, 1914-
A Place for My Head (Doubleday, 1960). The life of the last McCloud
of McCloud, Virginia. He tries to become a successful lawyer and to
rehabilitate the old estate, but he fails.

HUMPHREY, WILLIAM, 1924-
Home from the Hill (Knopf, 1957). A well-done whodunit. The psychological factors are well worked out. The Southern setting is inci-
dental. The story centers on a Puritanic woman and what her attitudes
did to her husband and her son.

HURSTON, ZORA NEALE, 1901-1960
Jonah's Gourd Vine (Lippincott, 1934). Story of Negro life in the Southern cotton lands told in authentic Negro dialect. Story is concerned
with a Negro preacher and his irresistible attractiveness to women.
Seraph on the Suwanee (Scribner's, 1948). A tender, simple story of
life and love among Florida crackers in swamp and turpentine camps.
Catches the literary flavor of "illiterate" Southern speech.

KELLEY, EDITH SUMMERS
Weeds (Harcourt, 1923). Good presentation of life of renters on a
tobacco farm. The heroine, Judy Pippinger, is said to be the first
"poor-white" woman to become a leading character in a novel.

KELLEY, WILLIAM MELVIN, 1937-
A Different Drummer (Doubleday, 1962). The story of a Negro who causes a migration of all the Negroes out of one Southern state. An interesting speculation. Excellent writing.

KEYES, FRANCES PARKINSON (WHEELER), 1885-1957
River Road (Messner, 1945). A long, romantically told story of a family living along the river road between Baton Rouge and New Orleans, descendants of the earlier great plantation owners trying to live up to the great traditions of the past.

LANHAM, EDWIN M., 1904-
The Stricklands (Little, 1939). Of a family of Oklahoma tenant farmers. One son organizes unions; another is an outlaw. Good arguments against "Jim Crow" and for unions.

LEE, CLARENCE P., 1913-
The Unwilling Journey (Macmillan, 1940). The story of a small boy in an Arkansas village. The story traces his life from the village to Pine Bluff and through one year of high school.

LEE, HARPER
To Kill a Mockingbird (Lippincott, 1960). A small Alabama town in 1935, through the eyes and ears of an eight-year-old girl. A lovely picture of family relationships, in a town committed to discrimination and class lines. Well-written.

LLOYD, NORRIS
A Dream of Mansions (Random, 1961). From the standpoint of a thirteen-year-old girl, the author gives us a perceptive picture of the elements making up a small Georgia town of the 1950's. The smug churchgoers, the sincere Christians, the Negroes, and the non-conformists are all present.

LUMPKIN, GRACE, 1898-
A Sign for Cain (Furman, 1935). Story of the organization of Negro and white workers of the South by a Negro Communist who has returned from the North, showing the deterioration of the former ruling families and the power of organized protest. A Marxist novel.
The Wedding (Furman, 1939). Story set in a small Georgia town in 1909. The lovers have a quarrel on the eve of their wedding, and the novel traces subsequent happenings. Shows the folkways of the Southern middle class.

MALLY, EMMA LOUISE, 1908-
The Mocking Bird Is Singing (Holt, 1944). A story of the changing South. Shows nineteenth-century businessmen engaged in blockade-running, railroad-building, and cotton- and cattle-dealing.

McCULLERS, CARSON (SMITH) 1917-

The Heart is a Lonely Hunter (Houghton, 1940). A psychological study of the relationships of five lonesome people in a small city. Attests the seriousness of many Southern problems, such as the suppression of the intelligent Negro and the brutal slum environment of mill workers.

Clock Without Hands (Houghton, 1961). Glimpses into the lives of a few village characters around the 1950's. The change being made by the young from the older patterns is evident.

MEDEARIS, MARY, 1916-

Big Doc's Girl (Lippincott, 1942). Presents the dignified, virtuous, heroic side of village life. Set in the back country of Arkansas.

MILBURN, GEORGE, 1906-

Oklahoma Town (Harcourt, 1931). Short stories of country and village life in Oklahoma. In part reminiscent of older Southern themes (Southern colonels, Southern attitudes toward Negroes, etc.)

No More Trumpets (Harcourt, 1933). A better collection than *Oklahoma Town*. Contains representative Southern humor, similar to that of Erskine Caldwell but mellower. More realistic than Caldwell, if not so pointedly satiric as Caldwell at his best.

The Catalogue (Harcourt, 1936). Shows the place of mail-order catalogues in the lives of farmers and small-town folk. Satisfying humor.

MILLEN, GILMORE, 1897-

Sweet Man (Viking, 1930). Story of John Henry, son of a mulatto and a white man, set on a Southern cotton plantation. His interest in women leads him into many adventures, climaxing in his job as chauffer to a white woman in Los Angeles. A good description of Negro life on the plantation.

MILLS, CHARLES, 1914-

The Choice (Macmillan, 1943). Of a Southern boy who considered himself an aristocrat and his conflicts with the materialistic world of the small town.

MOLLOY, ROBERT, 1906-

An Afternoon in March (Doubleday, 1958). Story of a murder trial in a South Carolina town in 1889. Class relationships clearly shown.

MUNZ, CHARLES CURTIS, 1905-

Land Without Moses (Urquhart, 1938). A strong picture of sharecroppers and their absolute dependence on the boss. Implies their need for leadership.

OWEN, GUY, 1925-

Season of Fear (Random, 1960). A compassionate portrayal of a man's struggle with his own passions and beliefs. A middle-aged Southern farmer, ridden by his religious beliefs and Victorian prejudices, commits a murder and upsets his small community.

PALMER, FLORENCE G., 1895-
Spring Will Come Again (Bobbs, 1940). The story of a cotton planter and his family in Alabama from 1880 on, and his struggles to succeed.

PERRY, GEORGE SESSIONS, 1910-1957
Hold Autumn in Your Hand (Viking, 1941). A wholesome, well-rounded account of a good-natured, independent Texas tenant-farmer in a river bottom. A miniature *Grapes of Wrath* seen through rose-colored glasses.
Hackberry Cavalier (Viking, 1944). Short stories of backwoods Texas. Happy and romantic regionalism.

PRATT, THEODORE, 1901-
Florida Roundabout (Duell, 1959). A group of short stories with settings in southern Florida. The places vary from the sophisticated homes of newcomers to real backwoods; the times from 1840 to the 1950's.

ROBERTS, DOROTHY JAMES, 1903-
With Night We Banish Sorrow (Little, 1960). Concerns a Virginia family of six girls in the period 1930-1950. A sort of Southern *Little Women.* Twentieth-century attitudes and ideas well presented.

ROBERTS, ELIZABETH MADOX, 1885-1941
The Time of Man (Viking, 1926). Excellent portrayal of poor whites in Kentucky, their ambitions and daydreams, and the inescapability of their lot, generation to generation.
My Heart and My Flesh (Viking, 1927). Of half-sisters, one with a white mother, the other with a Negro mother.
He Sent Forth a Raven (Viking, 1935). With the death of his second wife a wealthy Kentucky farmer vows he will never again leave the house. He directs his workers on the farm from the balcony. His news from the outside is related to him by his great-granddaughter.

ROGERS, LETTIE HAMLETT, 1917-
Birthright (Simon, 1957). A well-told story of the impact of the desegregation struggle on one community. The major character, a minister, makes a turn in his road and begins working on the side of civil rights for all.

SALAMANCA, J. R., 1924-
The Lost Country (Simon, 1958). Of a Virginia boy, growing up in the area near Charlottesville in mid-twentieth century. His innocence, and consequent feeling of guilt as he is seduced by one of his former teachers, is rather unbelievable. Good detail on country sights, sounds, and customs.

SAXON, LYLE, 1891-1946
Children of Strangers (Houghton, 1937). An excellent story of the colored Creoles of Louisiana, a group entirely different in folkways from other Negroes of the United States.

SCARBOROUGH, DOROTHY, 1858?-1935
In the Land of Cotton (Macmillan, 1923). Presents the contrast of the rich, full life on the Texas cotton plantation and the meager, hard life of the poor tenant farmer.
Can't Get a Red Bird (Harper, 1929). Much on country customs, etc. Sentimental. Comes up to present day with its talk of farmer co-operatives.

SIMON, CHARLIE MAY, 1897-
The Share-Cropper (Dutton, 1937). Story of sharecroppers in Arkansas. A novel of social injustice. The main character takes part in union activities.

SIMS, MARIAN, 1899-1961
The City on the Hill (Lippincott, 1940). A realistic and dramatic account of a young lawyer's rebellion against the evil and corruption of a small North Carolina city.

SMITH, LILLIAN EUGENIA, 1897-1966
Strange Fruit (Reynal, 1944). The story of a love affair between a white man and a Negro girl, a murder, and a lynching in a representative Georgia town. An informed and sensitive exploration of the effect of Southern ideas and customs on family and race relations.

SPENCER, ELIZABETH, 1921-
This Crooked Way (Dodd, 1952). Of a religious man, both mean and tender, who gets what he wants. A Faulknerian version of psychic decay and physical violence, in the Mississippi hills and delta. Several styles and points of view.
The Voice at the Back Door (McGraw, 1956). Well-worked-out story of a small Southern town during the Truman administration. Shows the methods used to keep a believer in civil rights for Negroes from being elected sheriff.

STRIBLING, THOMAS SIGISMUND, 1881-
Bright Metal (Doubleday, 1928). The crudity of Tennessee farm life and the community class distinctions as seen by a girl of "tarnished metal" who marries a Tennessee farmer.
Backwater (Doubleday, 1930). The love affair of the son of the local bootlegger of a small town in Arkansas and the daughter of an aristocratic family is halted because of their different social status. The breaking of the levee changes the situation.
Unfinished Cathedral (Doubleday, 1934). Continues the story of

The Store. In his nineties Colonel Miltiades Vaiden is the village patriarch, the chief donor toward a cathedral.

STYRON, WILLIAM, 1925-
Lie Down in Darkness (Bobbs, 1951). Skillful, immediate writing in the tradition of Joyce and Faulkner, about the minds and memories, the loneliness and love-seeking of soul-sick members of an old Virginia family. Strong probing of alcoholism, Puritanism, and lostness. Notable for a 52-page paragraph that plumbs a girl's stream of consciousness.

SYLVESTER, HARRY, 1908-
Dearly Beloved (Duell, 1942). Of the attempts of a young Catholic layman to start a co-operative including Negroes in a Maryland community. Satirizes the church and Southern mores.

TAYLOR, PETER H., 1917-
A Long Fourth and Other Stories (Harcourt, 1948). Stories of middle-class life in Southern towns—the night's leave of a soldier, changes in a growing suburb, and so on. Concerned with growing boys, evolving social attitudes, and crises in moral understanding.

TILLERY, CARLYLE, 1904-
Red Bone Woman (Day, 1950). A touching story of the marriage of a poor Red Bone girl (a "Spanish white") and an elderly white man on a declining farm in southeastern Louisiana. Excellent for dialect, folkways, and social tensions.

VINES, HOWELL H., 1899-
This Green Thicket World (Little, 1934). Story of a large landowner of "the thicket" in Alabama. Some good details about daily life—socials, food, fishing, and hunting.

WARREN, ROBERT PENN, 1905-
Night Rider (Houghton, 1939). Deals with a Kentucky tobacco war in the early 1900's and with the men who resort to terrorism in this fight between the manufacturers and growers.
Circus in the Attic, and Other Stories (Harcourt, 1948). In many of these stories of Tennessee, the author explores "the integral relation between a rural folk and the land." The title story diagrams the social relationships in a Tennessee town.
Flood (Random, 1963). The story of a Southern man who comes back to his home town after a twenty-year absence to help make a movie about the town, which is to be flooded. It is in the main a psychological probing into the past, as he comes to see more clearly the strands that have made up his quite unsatisfactory "successful" career. The reader is led into seeing some of the strands in modern life that lead to disaster, strands which the leading character does not see.

WELTY, EUDORA, 1909-

Delta Wedding (Harcourt, 1946). A week in the life of the Fairchilds of Shellmound Plantation, in the Mississippi Delta. A subtle and slow-moving story.

Golden Apples (Harcourt, 1949). A series of short stories that chronicle the passing of some forty years of a group of persons in a small Mississippi town. Artistic, perhaps even overwrought, with undertones and adroit immediacy. One remarkable tale deals with a Mississippian in San Francisco.

The Ponder Heart (Harcourt, 1954). An amusing brief comedy, appropriately written, of characters in a Mississippi village. A genre yarn with a tall-tale quality, told in the first person by a participant in a funny trial at the courthouse.

WERTENBAKER, GREEN PEYTON, 1907-

Rain on the Mountain (Little, 1934). A study of living in modern Virginia and of a romantic's search for "reality" in and around Charlottesville.

WILLIAMS, JOAN (MRS. EZRA BOWEN), 1928-

The Morning and the Evening (Atheneum, 1961). A book throwing light on the people and mores of a small Mississippi town as it is faced with the problem of what to do with and about a forty-year-old imbecile left all alone when his mother dies. Excellent writing. Sympathetic understanding of people and their problems.

WILSON, JOHN W., 1920-

High John, the Conqueror (Macmillan, 1948). A touching short regional novel of cotton farmers in the Brazos River bottoms. Presents the feel of the land, the life and problems of Negro tenant farmers, and the economic conflict of small landholders with aggressive monopolists.

WOLFE, THOMAS, 1900-1938

Look Homeward, Angel (Scribner's, 1929). The story of Eugene Gant, a Southern boy. Much material on Southern mores and many unforgettable pictures. The boy breaks away from his pathetic family but is nevertheless caught in a web of futility and despair.

Of Time and the River (Scribner's, 1935). Continues Eugene Gant's story.

YOUNG, STARK, 1881-1963

River House (Scribner's, 1929). Set in a little Mississippi town, *River House* tells of the conflict between the South of old and the modern South. Most of the characters are types rather than individuals, but the picture of the South is real.

YOUNGS, DELIGHT

The Gladesman (Dodd, 1955). Of the marginal farmers who live in a frontier fashion in the sawgrass Everglades region. A story of inner and outer struggles brought on by human nature and social "progress."

4. (c) The Southern Mountain Regions

Unlike the planters and farm workers in the cotton-raising low-lands, the mountaineers were little affected by the Civil War, though they have been gradually influenced by industrialism and modernization in the South. Their way of life, unbroken for two centuries (until the coming of the automobile), has been characterized by eighteenth-century customs and attitudes. Independent in spirit, picturesque in speech, increasingly antiquated in culture, the mountain folk have interested writers ever since the local-colorists appeared in the 1870's.

No tradition has been more colorful and pleasing to the American public than the picture of the Southern hillbilly with a still in every other "holler" and with a disposition to carry on unending feuds with his neighbors. The traditional story is best represented by the works of Mary Murfree, Charles Neville Buck, and John Fox. While "proletarian" writers of the 1930's like Grace Lumpkin and Olive Dargan lean heavily on the old tradition for their portraits of the hill folk, others (seemingly more in touch with their materials), for example, T. S. Stribling, Rose Wilder Lane, Borden Deal, and Harriette Arnow, have created entire novels picturing what seem to be flesh-and-blood people living in the Southern highlands in the twentieth century. Stories of these mountain people are segregated in this section as the most extreme and picturesque examples of the local-color school. Few new writers have emerged in recent years.

ARNOW, HARRIETTE LOUISA, 1908-
Hunter's Horn (Macmillan, 1949). Excellent for many sides of life in the Kentucky hills during the 1930's—housework, fox hunting, molasses making, selling sheep and heifers at the yards, Federal farm relief, and so on. Excellences in style, including rendition of dialect.

BOONE, JACK, 1908-
Dossie Bell Is Dead (Stokes, 1939). A story of the hill people of West Tennessee in much the same style as *Tobacco Road*. Deals with the death of Dossie Bell, Luster Holder's woman, and of the confession of the minister at the funeral when he tells the part he played in the drama.

BUCK, CHARLES N., 1879-
The Call of the Cumberlands (1913). A story of the typical Kentucky mountain feud with all the expected local color and atmosphere.
Mountain Justice (Houghton, 1935). Story of a district attorney of the Kentucky of the Cumberlands and how he served mountain justice on three men convicted of murder.

CHAPMAN, MARISTAN, 1895-
Happy Mountain (Viking, 1928). A simple and pungent story of Cumberland Mountain folk.

The Weather Tree (Viking, 1932). Story of the conflict between a small conservative settlement in the Tennessee mountains and a man who tried to rebuild the town, only to meet with hate and resentment.

COAN, OTIS WELTON, 1895-
Rocktown, Arkansas: An Ozark Novel (Exposition, 1953). A series of brief episodes that dramatize simply and directly most facets of life in a small community. Sympathetic and tender.

DARGAN, OLIVE T. (FIELDING BURKE, pseud.)
Highland Annals (Scribner's, 1925). Chronicles of neighborly kindness on an upland farm, revealing the Southern mountaineer folk in all their contradictions of character. Sketchy short stories leaning heavily on the traditional treatment of mountain folk.

DEAL, BORDEN, 1922-
Dunbar's Cove (Scribner's, 1957). Relates a struggle between an old settler in the Tennessee Valley and the new ideas brought by the T.V.A. He finally makes peace with his daughter and her lover, a worker for T.V.A. Satisfactory romance.
The Insolent Breed (Scribner's, 1959). A somewhat picaresque story of a "pagan" Southern family in conflict with old-fashioned religionists. Symbolic treatment of a conflict involving two attitudes toward life—with the artistic, paganistic gaining the edge.

FOX, JOHN W., 1862-1919
The Trail of the Lonesome Pine (1908). A very popular mountain story, with all the traditional trappings.

FURMAN, LUCY, 1869-
The Quare Women (Little, 1923). Of the Kentucky hills, with feuds, moonshine whisky, dialect, and quaint ways. Tells of the coming of a settlement school and of its work among the mountaineers as these "furrin" women try to teach the women to cook, sew, play, and sing.

GILES, JANICE (HOLT), 1905-
The Enduring Hills (Westminster, 1950). A hill boy from south central Kentucky gets away from home, makes good in business, hates the lack of ethics in the business world, and goes back to "the enduring hills."

GIVENS, CHARLES G.
The Devil Takes a Hill Town (Bobbs, 1939). An easygoing tale of Tennessee hillbillies. The Devil and God, in the persons of mountain men, are the chief characters. They speak in their native, colorful dialect and discuss the problems of capitalism and the class struggle together.

GOWEN, EMMETT, 1902-
Mountain Born (Bobbs, 1932). A tale of members of two rival families who fall in love. Gives insight into the lives of the mountain folk, their language, loves, and hates.

HANNUM, ALBERTA PIERSON, 1906-
Thursday April (Harper, 1931). A story of West Virginia mountaineer
life.
The Hills Step Lightly (Morrow, 1934). Of a hill woman and her life
from childhood to old age. Good detail of daily life in the late nine-
teenth century, but a romantic plot.
The Gods and One (Duell, 1941). A simple, pleasant story of a North
Carolina mountain girl.
Roseanna McCoy (Holt, 1947). A satisfactory romance of the love of
Roseanna McCoy for one of the Hatfields during the famous Hatfield-
McCoy feud.

HARRIS, BERNICE (KELLY)
Janey Jeems (Doubleday, 1946). A Blue Ridge Mountains story told
in the vernacular. Seemingly true to the life of the people.

HARRIS, GEORGE WASHINGTON, 1814-1869
Sut Lovingood (1867; new edition, Grove, 1954). Twenty-two yarns
that deal hilariously with many sides of life in the Great Smokies.
Notable for vivid, often Rabelaisian details and for rich imagery. A
masterpiece of American dialect humor.

HAUN, MILDRED, 1912-
The Hawk's Done Gone (Bobbs, 1940). About the people of eastern
Tennessee. Shows changes the motor roads, schools, and traveling
libraries have made in their lives.

KANTOR, MacKINLAY, 1904-
The Voice of Bugle Ann (Coward, 1935). A long short story of a man
and his fox hound, Bugle Ann, in the hills of Missouri. A glimpse
into a long-settled community.

KROLL, HARRY HARRISON, 1888-
Their Ancient Grudge (Bobbs, 1946). The story of the Hatfield-McCoy
feud, which flared in the southern Appalachians during the nineteenth
century, told from the standpoint of the six women most closely involved.
Darker Grows the Valley (Bobbs, 1947). A story of the Clinch Valley
in East Tennessee, covering five generations from 1778 to the coming
of T.V.A. A satisfactory record of common experience.

LANE, ROSE WILDER, 1887-
Hill-Billy (Harper, 1926). Laid in the Ozarks of Missouri. A lively,
authentic presentation of folkways and ideas, accompanied by the usual
romantic plot.

LUMPKIN, GRACE, 1898-
To Make My Bread (Macaulay, 1932). An important proletarian novel
showing the old ways of the North Carolina mountaineers completely
disintegrating under the impact of modern industry.

MacKAYE, PERCY, 1875-
Tall Tales of the Kentucky Mountains (Doran, 1926). A group of twelve tall tales supposedly by one Solomon Shell as he went from one cabin to another spinning them. Fantastic and with quaint description, each yarn gives a picture of the Kentucky mountain area.

MARSHALL, ROBERT K., 1901-
Little Squire Jim (Duell, 1949). A story of mountain folk in North Carolina, especially of a boy. Acceptable for style and for accounts of lore and ways of living.

MURFREE, MARY N., 1850-1922
In the Tennessee Mountains (1884). The book that "made" the tradition. Emphasizes the peculiarities of mountain folk.
The Prophet of the Great Smoky Mountains (1885). A local-color story of religion and superstition in the Tennessee hills.

RANDOLPH, VANCE, 1892-
From an Ozark Holler; Stories of Ozark Mountain Folk (Vanguard, 1933). A collection of anecdotes about the Ozarks. Deals with homely melodramas and local superstitions, stories more imaginative than realistic.

SIMON, CHARLIE MAY (HOGUE), 1897-
Straw in the Sun (Dutton, 1945). A simple story, rich in detail, of kindly folk in the Ozark Mountains. Told as an autobiography of the author's experiences living in the Ozarks during the Depression years.

SIMPSON, HARRIETTE, 1908-
Mountain Path (Covici, 1936). The experience of a young girl teacher in a rural school in the Kentucky hills who witnesses a mountaineer feud and its effect on the women and children.

SKIDMORE, HUBERT, 1911-1946
I Will Lift Up Mine Eyes (Doubleday, 1936). Pictures farmers of the Blue Ridge in a year of drought.
Heaven Came So Near (Doubleday, 1938). Continues the story of *I Will Lift Up Mine Eyes*.

STILL, JAMES, 1906-
River of Earth (Viking, 1940). A simple episodic novel of life in the hills and coal camps of Kentucky. Gives a vivid picture of the hard life of the hill people. Develops universal themes: man's search for security, man's bewilderment at the ways of destiny.

STRIBLING, THOMAS SIGISMUND, 1881-
Teeftallow (Doubleday, 1926). Of mountain whites in the early twentieth century in a Southern village. Realistic.

STUART, JESSE, 1907-
Head of W-Hollow (Dutton, 1936). A collection of poetically written

short stories containing some beautiful descriptions of the Kentucky
mountains and of the Kentucky people. Written by a native who loves
his land, its trees, crops, streams, and storms.
Trees of Heaven (Dutton, 1940). An amusing, robust story of the Kentucky hills. Depicts the farmer's love of land, his agricultural activities the year around, his attitude toward squatters.
Taps for Private Tussie (Dutton, 1943). A warm-hearted story of a
generous, ever-squabbling clan of mountaineers. More than a stereotyped hillbilly tale, more than a sociological case study; humorous,
poetic, sympathetic.
The Good Spirit of Laurel Ridge (McGraw, 1953). An episodic folk
tale that catches the natural setting, the lore, and the people of the
Kentucky hills.

TENNESSEE WRITERS' PROJECT
God Bless the Devil (University of North Carolina, 1940). Twenty-five
anecdotes of life from the Great Smokies to the Mississippi levees.
Such themes as milk snakes, lady-killing, horse races, hunting dogs.

WARREN, ROBERT PENN, 1905-
The Cave (Random, 1959). Story growing out of an incident in which a
young man is trapped in a cave. The author uses the incident to present a very complete analysis of the family and of others in the small
Tennessee mountain town.

WILLIAMSON, THAMES ROSS, 1894-
Woods Colt (Harcourt, 1933). Arkansas and Missouri. Of an illegitimate boy and his young manhood in the Ozarks.

5. THE SOUTHWEST

In this list "Southwest" means the agricultural valleys and the dry-
land farming areas of Kansas, Texas, Oklahoma, New Mexico, Arizona,
Nevada, Colorado, Utah, and California. Economically and culturally
the region displays a great variety of patterns. East of the Rockies are
wide plains, wheat farms, and sheep and cattle ranches. Farther west
are the irrigated valleys growing great varieties of fruits and vegeta-
bles and cotton. And oil as well as other minerals is produced in many
areas. The cultural subdivisions take in the Mormons as a distinct
group, and various ethnic groups including Indians, Mexicans, Negroes,
and Orientals. The migratory worker figures in more stories of the
Southwest than he does in stories of regions farther east. Subject matter of the stories ranges from early attempts to establish the small
farm, such as Norris's *The Octopus*, to stories of "factories in the
field," such as Steinbeck's masterpiece, *The Grapes of Wrath*.

ABBEY, EDWARD, 1927-
Fire on the Mountain (Dial, 1962). A story centering on an "old

timer's" attempt to hold on to his land in New Mexico after it has been condemned as part of the White Sands Proving Ground. The independent attitudes of the early settlers are a major point.

BEZZERIDES, A. I., 1908-
There Is a Happy Land (Holt, 1942). Of a family who come from the Great Plains to California and—in contrast to Steinbeck's Joad family—get along very well.

CHIDESTER, ANN, 1919-
The Lost and the Found (Doubleday, 1963). An appealing story, set around the kidnapping of the eight-year-old daughter of a migratory worker in California's Central Valley. The events set in motion are used by the author to give a quite extensive portrait of the people of one community.

CLARK, WALTER VAN TILBURG, 1909-
City of Trembling Leaves (Random, 1945). Of a sensitive boy, a composer in the making, growing up in Reno, and after experiences in California identifying himself again with Nevada. Much on sex and love, and much literary allusion and symbolism.
The Track of the Cat (Random, 1949). Written in a good style and with much dialog, this takes place on a remote Nevada ranch and concerns itself symbolically with the struggle of good and evil.

DEWLEN, AL, 1921-
Twilight of Honor (McGraw, 1961). The story of a public defender in an important murder trial in a West Texas town. He succeeds in showing that the guilty man was actually fighting for his life against a man found in bed with the killer's wife. The attitudes and customs of the Texas Panhandle town are a part of the story.

FERBER, EDNA, 1887-
Giant (Doubleday, 1952). A plump job of journalistic research on present-day Texas. Casual in construction and repeatedly critical of Texans for "a mania for bigness" and the "littleness" of mind and culture that they hide. Points out maladjustments of Texans, their bigotry and hypocrisy and un-American treatment of Mexican-Americans. Centers on a vast cattle ranch.

FERGUSSON, HARVEY, 1890-
Grant of Kingdom (Morrow, 1950). A strong, skillful treatment of a private empire in New Mexico from the mid-nineteenth century to the 1940's. Notable for characterizations of Indians, Spaniards, Mexicans, and American frontiersmen.

GILLMOR, FRANCES, 1903-
Fruit Out of Rock (Duell, 1940). A story of fruit-growing country in Arizona. Good local color.

HALDEMAN-JULIUS, EMANUEL, 1889-1951, and HALDEMAN-JULIUS,
    A. M., 1888-
Dust (Brentano's, 1921).   Pictures the drudgery of farm life on the
Kansas plains. Story of the unsuccessful marriage of a coarse farmer
and a sacrificing wife.

HAYES, CHARLES EDWARD, 1912-
The Four Winds (Macmillan, 1942). A swift and merciless account of
a tenant-farm family in Kansas that is wrecked and scattered by economic misfortunes in the mid-1930's. A pessimistic picture of rural
life, told with some humor and tenderness.

HILL, WELDON (pseud.)
The Long Summer of George Adams (McKay, 1961). Of a small Oklahoma town. As the railway begins to go out of business, George
Adams, night watchman, makes a shift over to farming. Good picturing of the customs of the small town.

HOBART, ALICE TISDALE (NOURSE), 1882-
The Cup and the Sword (Bobbs, 1942). A family chronicle of French-
men who establish vineyards and wineries in California. Their enterprise is almost ruined by the Eighteenth Amendment but rises slowly
again after 1934. A dramatic story told in terms of clearly realized
characters.
The Cleft Rock (Bobbs, 1948). A thesis novel dealing with ownership
and control of both land and irrigation water in the San Joaquin Valley.
The problems set forth are made more important than the characters.

HORGAN, PAUL, 1903-
The Return of the Weed (Harper, 1936). Six short stories showing
man's inability to adjust himself to his environment. New Mexico.
Each story deals with some ruin or destroyed mission or abandoned
habitation.
Lamp on the Plains (Harper, 1937). Sequel to Main Line West. Story
of a boy's life in a town on the plains of New Mexico. Good in detailed
description of a small town and of the ranches. Typical plains people.
Mountain Standard Time (Farrar, 1962). Contains three novels form-
erly published: Main Line West (1936), story of a Kansas girl who
married a salesman, went to California, was deserted by her husband,
and then supported herself and child, finally, by becoming a traveling
evangelist; Far From Cibola (1938), a novelette of Depression days in
New Mexico; The Common Heart (1942), story of a medical doctor in
Albuquerque in the 1920's, a triangle story in which the "other woman"
loses as the wife attempts suicide, then learns to be a better wife.

HOWE, EDGAR W., 1854-1937
The Story of a Country Town (1883). One of the better early village
stories. Realistic. Pictures farm life, especially the life of appren-
ticed farmhands. The piety of the community is a point for satire.

JOHNSON, RICHARD (SIKES JOHNSON, pseud.)
Hope of Refuge (Little, 1956). Story of an American man married to a Russian immigrant. Asked to leave a small Texas town during the Korean War, he refuses and is killed by his enemies. Simple and appealing. Well written.

KING, MARY PAULA, 1909-
Quincie Bolliver (Houghton, 1941). Of a Texas town in oil-boom times and a girl from the age of twelve to eighteen. A picture of social customs and of labor in the oil fields.

LAMAN, RUSSELL, 1907-
Manifest Destiny (Regnery, 1963). Of one family in Kansas from the 1880's until after World War I. Comprehensive picture including the Populist movement, attitudes toward two wars, drought, and other farm problems.

MARION, FRANCES, 1890-
Valley People (Reynal, 1935). Short stories of a small valley in northern California. Some are reminiscent of Sherwood Anderson in their emphasis on frustration. Others are light and happy in tone.

MARTIN, CURTIS, 1913-
The Hills of Home (Houghton, 1944). Seventeen stories of a New Mexico town called Sangre de Cristo. Sincere, youthful, and simple in style.

NORRIS, FRANK, 1870-1902
The Octopus (1901). A California classic. The story of the struggle of the early wheat farmers of the San Joaquin Valley to be independent, to establish the sort of neighborhoods of farmers that had long been the pattern in the Middle West. Shows what the monopolistic railroad, the "Octopus," did to their hope.

OSKISON, JOHN M., 1874-
Brothers Three (Macmillan, 1935). Story of three brothers who owned an Oklahoma farm from 1873 to the 1930's. The three are a town merchant, a cattleman, and a writer.

PERRY, GEORGE SESSIONS (editor), 1910-1957
Roundup Time: A Collection of Southwestern Writing (McGraw, 1943). Stories, biographies, and essays. Stories by Atlee, Horgan, Thomason, Lanham, Richter, Porter, La Farge, Dobie, Steinbeck, and others. An introduction to the best of Southwestern literature.

RICHTER, CONRAD, 1890-
The Lady (Knopf, 1957). The story of an Anglo-Mexican family in New Mexico in the 1880's and 1890's. The leading character, from an old Mexican family, lives up to the traditions of her clan. Good writing.

ROE, WELLINGTON
The Tree Falls South (Putnam, 1937). A tragic story of dust storms
and drought in Kansas, and of grim farmers who stage a riot.

SINCLAIR, JOHN L., 1902-
In Time of Harvest (Macmillan, 1943). Of nesters from Oklahoma who
settle in New Mexico. An earthy regional novel of the strengths and
weaknesses of a bean rancher.

SORENSEN, VIRGINIA (EGGERTSEN), 1912-
The Neighbors (Reynal, 1947). *Beloved Enemy* plot laid in sheep
country of Colorado highlands. Combines the open-air romance of a
good Western with the realism of social and economic actualities such
as water rights, stockmen's associations, and pressures of mores.
The Evening and the Morning (Harcourt, 1949). Among Danish Mormons. Contrasts life in a Utah town as lived by children in the 1920's
and decades before by their grandmother, but shows the essential con-
tinuity of pattern.
Many Heavens (Harcourt, 1954). A love story containing much of life
in a mountain-enclosed valley town in Utah in 1890, just after poly-
gamy came to an end.

STEINBECK, JOHN, 1902-
Pastures of Heaven (Viking, 1932). Describes farm life in California's
Central Valley. Theme of the book is the people's failure to find happiness in these perfect surroundings. Supposes this failure to be
caused by people's inability to look at neighbors with tolerance. Effective characterizations.
To a God Unknown (Viking, 1933). Story of a man who plants a tree on
his California ranch to symbolize his father's spirit. The ranch prospers until his brother, not understanding his sacrifices to the tree,
cuts it down. Years of famine and drought follow. An almost mystical
treatment of farming.
In Dubious Battle (Viking, 1936). A story of attempts to organize migratory fruit pickers in California. In the fights between pickers, vigi-
lantes, owners, etc., not only is the outcome "dubious" but even the
motives and desires of the various elements are not clear to themselves or others. Incompletely convincing.
Of Mice and Men (Viking, 1937). Discusses the problems of the migratory ranch workers who cherish the unrealized dream of some day
owning their own land. Shows the physical and spiritual conditions of
these laborers, who work for not much more than their food. A pathetic story of frustration.
The Grapes of Wrath (Viking, 1939). An outstanding book describing
the plight of the migratory farm worker in the 1930's. The Joad family travel from Oklahoma to California looking for work. In California
they live in poverty and degradation. Shows the "factory in the field"
system of farming. Realistic, and beautifully written.

The Long Valley (Viking, 1938). Realistic short stories of people in the Salinas Valley. Shows how people live there, and their relationship to the migrants who are a constant part of the scene.

East of Eden (Viking, 1952). Contrasts two families over a fifty-year period on ranches and in towns of the Salinas Valley, California. A self-conscious reworking of the story of Cain and Abel. Effective in certain scenes but weak in key characterizations and naïve in philosophy.

STEWART, GEORGE R., 1895-

Storm (Random, 1941). About a low-pressure storm center that crosses the Pacific and brings disaster in California and the Sierra Nevada Range. The storm's "birth, growth, adventures, and final death," says Stewart, are the "main vortex of the story," with "the various little human beings. . .isolated here and there around the edges." No characterizations.

Fire (Random, 1948). A taut story of the birth, work, and death of a forest fire in a California national forest. Dramatizes mankind versus an element on the rampage. The nonfiction far surpasses the fiction.

SYKES, HOPE WILLIAMS, 1901-

Second Hoeing (Putnam, 1935). The beet fields of Colorado. A picture of unending toil.

TOTHEROH, DAN, 1898-

Wild Orchard (Doran, 1927). An outstanding novel of the California fruit country and of the daughter of an Italian prune picker. Tells of her coming maturity through a series of tragic love episodes and of the nomadic life of prune pickers.

VAN DER VEER, JUDY, 1912-

November Grass (Longmans, 1940). Of a girl who belonged to the intellectual world of Eastern friends and also to the everyday world of her father's ranch in California.

WEST, JESSAMYN

Cress Delahanty (Harcourt, 1954). Amusing episodes in the life of a bright girl growing up from her twelfth to sixteenth year on a southern California orange ranch and attending her first year in "Woolman" College.

South of the Angels (Harcourt, 1960). A story set in a project development southeast of Los Angeles during the years 1916-1917. Mostly about inter-family relationships, centering on the love affairs of the women in the small community. Rather weak in plot; but characters are messy and real.

WHITE, WILLIAM ALLEN, 1868-1944

In Our Town (Century, 1904). A chatty story of a small town in Kansas. Emphasizes the neighborliness and moral uprightness of the people.

In the Heart of a Fool (Macmillan, 1918). Of three generations from the Civil War to 1914. Plays up the idealism of the pioneer, decries the attitudes of later generations. Looks forward to the war of 1914-1918 reawakening our idealism.

A Certain Rich Man (Macmillan, 1926). Pictures the growth of a Kansas town from the Civil War to the war of 1914-1918.

WHITE, W. L., 1900-

What People Said (Viking, 1938). About life in a small plains city, telling of people's manners, clothes, food, and ideas. The chief interest is in the struggle between "liberals" and "conservatives." Neither group is pictured as being very intelligent.

INDUSTRIAL AMERICA

Just as pioneering was superseded in the United States during the nineteenth century by a more stable way of living, so the farm-and-village pattern has been superseded in many sections by urban-industrial life in the late nineteenth and twentieth centuries. As this change took place, it was reflected immediately in the work of American writers, who led the world in the production of fiction regarding the industrial-business complex of modern times. The most noticeable effect of the industrial age on literature has been the development of realism, with its twin facets of reform and naturalism, and the fostering of analytical, critical attitudes. Of course the romantic element is still in evidence, too, and amid all the realistic and critical treatments of labor, business, the city, modern society, and modern war there are hundreds of books creating a romantic picture of the same elements.

1. LABOR AND THE INDUSTRIAL MACHINE

The earliest and most persistent subject matter in the fiction of the industrial age has been, quite naturally, the laborer and his relation to the industrial machine. In general, writers have sympathized with the worker's plight. The Depression years produced a flood of the so-called proletarian novels. Mostly they were propagandistic, but there was much solid writing too. Many interesting books have pictured the work in certain industries and the "leisure-time" activities of the workers. Settings range from the industrial cities of the Northeast and Midwest to the oil fields of the Southwest and the lumber mills of the Northwest.

ADAMS, SAMUEL HOPKINS, 1871-1958
Sunrise to Sunset (Random, 1950). A dramatic novel of work, love, and mystery laid in the collar and cotton mills of Troy, New York, in the 1930's, at the time when labor was winning the 12-hour day. Interesting as an enlivened piece of history and as a contrast and parallel to Dreiser's *An American Tragedy*.

ALDRICH, THOMAS BAILEY, 1836-1907
The Stillwater Tragedy (1880). Various aspects of life in a manufacturing village, including a love story, the detection of a murder, and the passions and calamities of a strike.

ALGREN, NELSON, 1909-
Somebody in Boots (Vanguard, 1935). A story of jobless youth and their disillusionment. Bitter indictment of a social system that condemns its younger generation to soup lines and a hobo existence.

ANDERSON, SHERWOOD, 1876-1941
Poor White (Huebsch, 1920). Of a poor country man who became an
inventor. The story of how out-of-place he felt among industrialists.

ARNOW, HARRIETTE LOUISA, 1908-
The Dollmaker (Macmillan, 1954). A strong sociological presentation
of Cumberland Mountain people who migrate to Detroit to work during
World War II and there endure shack housing in an impoverished environment. Centers on the wife and children and the impact on them of
conditions in the industrial city.

ATTAWAY, WILLIAM, 1911-
Let Me Breathe Thunder (Doubleday, 1939). Strong novel of two migratory laborers and a small Mexican boy they pick up on the road.
Their life as migrants forces them to be hard, but their feelings
underneath show through the staccato language and harsh deeds.

BELL, THOMAS, 1903-
Out of This Furnace (Little, 1941). A gripping story of Slovak immigrants in the steel mills of Pennsylvania.
There Comes a Time (Little, 1946). An urbane, realistic, sociological
novel dealing with a middle-aged bank teller's work for his union, and
incidentally with politics of the 1930's.

BELLAMY, EDWARD, 1850-1898
Looking Backward (1888). The most popular Utopian novel. Pictures
a perfect Socialist state in the year 2000. Some comment on political
life of 1887.
Equality (1894). A sequel to *Looking Backward*. Gives more details
and shows how the revolution came about.

BINNS, ARCHIE, 1899-
The Timber Beast (Scribner's, 1944). Story of an elderly man, an old
"timber beast," and his sons. A quiet, intimate tale of family life, with
interesting glimpses of the logging business.

BISSELL, RICHARD, 1913?-
A Stretch on the River (Little, 1950). A rollicking report of towboat
workers on the upper Mississippi in the early 1940's. Gives glimpses
of interesting characters afloat and ashore.
7 1/2 Cents (Little, 1953). Light, comic treatment of labor-manage-
ment relations and a strike at the Sleep Tite Pajama Company, in an
Iowa river town.
High Water (Little, 1954). Another high-spirited towboat story, from
St. Louis north, in flood time. Like Clemens, Bissell is entranced by
local color and riverbank vernacular.

BOYD, THOMAS, 1898-1935
In Time of Peace (Minton, 1935). The story of one man's struggles

from 1919 to 1929. He meets unemployment, boom times, labor violence. The title is ironic. The hero is becoming a radical at the end of the story.

BRINIG, MYRON, 1900-
The Sun Sets in the West (Farrar, 1935). The setting is Copper City, a large mining town, in which the characters, who spend their lives underground, spend much of their time talking and thinking of their unrealized dreams.

BRODY, CATHARINE
Nobody Starves (Longmans, 1932). A story of workers in an industrial city. Realistic portrayal of a man and his wife, their work, their tragedy growing out of the Depression. A better feeling of actuality than in most such novels.

CANTWELL, ROBERT, 1908-
Land of Plenty (Farrar, 1934). Realistic story of a lumber mill. Good portraits of brutalized workers, owners, and their families.

CHURCHILL, WINSTON, 1871-1947
The Dwelling Place of Light (Macmillan, 1917). Of American industrialism, the harsh lot of women caught in its toils, and the alleged misdoings of the Industrial Workers of the World.

CLEMENS, SAMUEL LANGHORNE (MARK TWAIN, pseud.), 1835-1910
A Connecticut Yankee in King Arthur's Court (1889). A comic fantasy that is a confused but thought-provoking study of the social role of the inventor and capitalist in a world dominated by church and state. The inventor who sets about to bring progress is from a gun factory.

COLMAN, LOUIS, 1904-
Lumber (Little, 1931). Laid in a lumber-mill town in the Northwest. A drifting and uneducated jobber marries and starts a home. Strikes lead to economic difficulties. He is unable to adjust himself to the demands of modern industry.

DAHLBERG, EDWARD, 1900-
Bottom Dogs (Simon, 1930). A realistic indictment of American institutions and the futility of life for the lower classes. The story of one who spent his early life in an orphans' home and his later life as a salesman and hobo.

DARGAN, OLIVE TILFORD (FIELDING BURKE, pseud.)
Call Home the Heart (Longmans, 1932). Leans on old-style romance for hill traditions. A proletarian novel of a hill woman from the Blue Ridge who goes down into the factory town to work.
A Stone Came Rolling (Longmans, 1935). Sequel to *Call Home the Heart*. Tract-like in argument. Both contain Communist propaganda.

DOS PASSOS, JOHN, 1896--
U.S.A. (Harcourt, 1938). Contains *The 42nd Parallel* (1930), *1919* (1932), and *The Big Money* (1936). A trilogy which captures much of American life during the first thirty years of the century. Life stories of six men and six women from various social and occupational groups. Contains brief, vivid biographies of national leaders of the time and fragments of the news and songs of the time.
Mid Century (Houghton, 1960). A long novel in the same style as *U.S.A.*, with documentary pages, biographic sketches of prominent figures, and fictional episodes. The main emphasis is on labor racketeering and labor's failure to protect the common man, during the period 1935-1960. A remarkable and lively summary of the period.

DREISER, THEODORE, 1871-1945
An American Tragedy (Boni, 1925). An outstanding American novel with a naturalistic philosophy. The ironic title refers to the sordid life and pathetic death of the main character, a weakling—the only sort of life and death a common man could have when controlled absolutely by his environment and his biochemic machine—the sort of "tragedy" modern America produces, according to the Naturalists.

DUNCAN, DAVID, 1913-
The Serpent's Egg (Macmillan, 1950). Focuses on a labor-dispute panel that is arbitrating a controversy about overtime pay for bus drivers. Crosscuts into several lives. A clear, firm story with a residuum of theatricality.

FAST, HOWARD MELVIN, 1914-
Power (Doubleday, 1962). The story of a man who becomes powerful in a mine workers union and in the auto industry. He comes to value power more than human understanding.

FREEMAN, MARY E. WILKINS, 1862-1930
The Portion of Labor (1901). One of the earlier labor novels. The struggle between capital and labor in a New England town.

GARSIDE, EDWARD B.
Cranberry Red (Little, 1938). A proletarian novel which shows poor Irish workers, among others, oppressed by a Yankee landlord in the Cape Cod cranberry region.

GELLHORN, MARTHA E., 1908-
The Trouble I've Seen (Morrow, 1936). Of four sets of people from divergent backgrounds who are driven on to the relief rolls.

GILKYSON, THOMAS WALTER, 1880-
Oil (Scribner's, 1924). Vivid details of the actual scouting and drilling for oil and of the ruthless business methods of some oil men.

GREENE, JOSIAH E., 1911-1955
Not in Our Stars (Macmillan, 1945). Relationships between individuals and between families working for a dairy farm in the East.

HALPER, ALBERT, 1904-
The Foundry (Cassell, 1936). Seemingly realistic picture of all classes and individuals working in a foundry.
The Chute (Viking, 1937). Human character study of ordinary people, young Jews, swallowed up in continually feeding the package chute in a Chicago mail-order house. A gifted high-school student sees his dream of an architect's drawing board disappear as he is forced to become an order picker. Good material, but pedestrian writing.
The Little People (Harper, 1942). Depicts the lives of the employees of a huge department store. Shows half-inarticulate people on the job and at home. Sympathetic literary treatment of the repressed and exploited.

HARRIS, FRANK, 1855-1931
The Bomb (1909; republished by University of Chicago Press, 1963). An imaginative story about a young German immigrant who arrives in Chicago and throws the bomb precipitating the Haymarket Riot. Much on the oppression of labor and the corruption of the police.

HAY, JOHN, 1838-1905
The Bread-Winners (1884). Pictures a provincial town realistically. Conservative in ideas.

HEMINGWAY, ERNEST, 1898-1961
To Have and Have Not (Scribner's, 1937). Both a satire on the idle rich and a brutally realistic depiction of the desperate plight of the unemployed. Contrasts the underdogs of Key West with decadent socialites down for the winter season.

HERBST, JOSEPHINE, 1897-
The Rope of Gold (Harcourt, 1939). Deals with the economic conditions in America from 1933 to 1937. Story centers around a farm organizer, his wife, and an automobile manufacturer.

HULL, MORRIS
Cannery Anne (Houghton, 1936). Cannery workers in central California. Of the hope of the workers some day to own homes of their own, a seemingly hopeless dream.

HUXLEY, ALDOUS, 1894-1963
Brave New World (Harper, 1932). A sharp and pointed satire on human beings in America, in the Machine Age.

IDELL, ALBERT EDWARD, 1901-
Stephen Hayne (Sloane, 1951). Pennsylvania anthracite miners after the Civil War when there was bitter economic conflict, stirred up by overlords, between Pennsylvania Germans and Irish immigrants.

Goes into a strike and the charges made in court against "Molly Maguires." Shows how scapegoats were made of the Irish.

KING, EDWARD, 1848-1896
Joseph Zalmonah (1893). An informed, realistic account of the living and working conditions of Russian-Jewish clothing makers in Manhattan's East Side. Shows sweatshop horrors, a strike, a lockout, the "framing" of the leader of the Cloakmakers' Union, and attitudes of police and Socialists.

LANHAM, EDWIN, 1904-
Thunder in the Earth (Harcourt, 1941). Of Texas oil fields in the 1930's, the oil business and industrial relations. Graphic accounts of wildcat oil promotion and production.

LEE, EDNA L., 1890-
The Southerners (Appleton-Century-Crofts, 1953). The heart of the book is a series of labor and promotion problems faced by the owner of a cotton mill. Scenes portray the liberalization of labor policies, the facing of financial and marketing issues, and the good fortune of hitting the trend toward "good-looking cottons." Deals with *some* Southerners, in Atlanta and nearby, 1900-1917.

LEVIN, MEYER, 1905-
Citizens (Viking, 1940). Little Steel and the Memorial Day massacre in South Chicago in 1937.

LUMPKIN, GRACE, 1898-
To Make My Bread (Macaulay, 1932). Of mountaineers who became part of the factory system when it reached the South. An account of the Gastonia strike.

McCAGUE, JAMES P., 1909-
Fiddle Hill (Crown, 1960). A dramatic story of a fight to save a branch railway in a western state after a merger with a larger company. Vivid picturing of Westerners and railroaders and their families.

McCORMICK, JAY, 1919-
November Storm (Doubleday, 1943). Describes life on a Great Lakes freighter, in the bunkrooms, the messrooms, the pilothouse, and the stokehold. Clear portraits of picturesque freshwater sailors and of a boy who is seeking self-confidence.

McINTYRE, JOHN T., 1871-1951
Ferment (Farrar, 1937). A Philadelphia story of strikebreakers, racketeers, and labor spies. Expresses the hopelessness of the struggle of insignificant little people against Fascism.

McKENNEY, RUTH, 1911-
Industrial Valley (Harcourt, 1939). A vivid pro-labor account of

rubber workers in Akron, Ohio. Shows the birth of the sit-down strike and the turbulent growth of the C.I.O.

MALTZ, ALBERT, 1908-
The Way Things Are (International, 1938). Eight short stories of underdogs, underprivileged or abused persons, who the Marxist author implies are victims of the capitalist system. Contains the moving and much-reprinted story of the ravages of silicosis at Gauley Bridge, West Virginia, "Man on a Road."
The Underground Stream (Little, 1940). The struggle for union recognition in Detroit in 1936 before the C.I.O. and before the validation of the Labor Relations Act. A book centering on the lives of real people rather than the propagation of "proletarian" theory.

MARQUAND, JOHN PHILLIPS, 1893-1960
B.F.'s Daughter (Little, 1946). Of an industrialist and his daughter, who tries to dominate her husband's life as her father dominated hers.

MELLINGER, MAY
Splint Road (Putnam, 1952). Laid in a shingle mill camp in the Louisiana cypress swamps, before and after 1900, among very simple people. Emphasis on the problems of the children and wives of sawyers and shingle weavers.

MEYERSBURG, DOROTHY, 1902-
Seventh Avenue (Dutton, 1941). Of a New York garment manufacturer who fights the unions and finally becomes a "runaway manufacturer."

MORGAN, MURRAY C., 1916-
Viewless Winds (Dutton, 1949). Of the murder of the wife of a labor leader in an Oregon lumber town and the violent tensions that build up between the workers and the mill owners as the crime comes under investigation.

MORLEY, CHRISTOPHER, 1890-1957
Kitty Foyle (Lippincott, 1939). Of the life and loves of an office girl in Philadelphia. Centers upon her mental conflicts.

NICHOLS, EDWARD J., 1900-
Danger! Keep Out (Houghton, 1943). Laid in a Midwest oil refinery; a clear, human story of industrialists and the industrial system. Tellingly dramatizes personnel problems, labor problems, the psychology of industrialists, and especially technological unemployment.

NORRIS, CHARLES G., 1881-1945
Flint (Doubleday, 1943). A melodramatic but illuminating account of strife between capital and labor on the San Francisco waterfront in the 1930's. Sets forth impartially the claims of employers and strike leaders but predicts ultimate, bloody victory for labor.

OWENS, WILLIAM A., 1905-
Fever in the Earth (Putnam, 1958). A story centering on one worker in the oilfields near Beaumont, Texas. The "fever in the earth" dominates his life and leads to his death. Good in picturing Southern speech and mores.

POOLE, ERNEST, 1880-1950
The Harbour (1915). The story of New York harbor through three stages: individual ownership, monopolistic ownership, and finally worker control (not yet realized).

ROLLINS, WILLIAM, 1897-
The Shadow Before (McBride, 1934). An excellent account of the effects of a strike in a large American textile mill. The major characters are a wealthy neurotic, a winding-room girl, a Puritanical reformer, a "playboy" proletarian sympathizer, and an ambitious young immigrant.

SANDOZ, MARI, 1907-1966
Capital City (Little, 1939). Politics, labor, and strife in the capital of a high-plains state, Kanewa, a city with its Hooverville, its upper set, and all classes in between. The "radicals" (laborites) are punished by the forces of "law and order" (a horse doctor is elected governor). Excellent.

SAXTON, ALEXANDER
Bright Web in the Darkness (St. Martin's, 1958). Story of shipyard workers in the San Francisco area during World War II. The major conflict involved is the struggle of Negroes to get full recognition within the unions to which they belong.

SCHULBERG, BUDD, 1914-
Waterfront (Random, 1955). A realistic narrative about New York harbor—about the exploited lives of longshoremen in "a jungle" of quiet murders, the iniquities of the "shape-up" method of hiring for the day, and the tie-in of rackets to the city administrations and the ecclesiastical hierarchy. Shows the problems faced by decent workers, sincere priests, and official investigators. A mixture of artistic creation and reporting on the way things are.

SINCLAIR, UPTON B., 1878-
The Jungle (1906). Of packing houses in Chicago early in the century. Exposes filthy conditions and the mistreatment of workers. The hero becomes a Socialist.
King Coal (Regan, 1917). Of greedy capitalists and their exploitation and maltreatment of workers. The coal fields of Colorado.
Little Steel (Farrar, 1938). A dramatic story of attempts to organize unions and of the steel barons' fight to protect "the old ways."

SKIDMORE, HUBERT, 1911-1946
Hawk's Nest (Doubleday, 1941). An indignant recounting of the famous

tunnel-drilling episode at Gauley Bridge, West Virginia, that gave silicosis its first wide publicity.

SLADE, CAROLINE, 1886-
The Triumph of Willie Pond (Vanguard, 1940). An indignant and convincing presentation of the plight of the unemployed with families.
Job's House (Vanguard, 1941). An honest and starkly realistic picture of one man's solution of the problem of poverty in old age.
Lilly Crackell (Vanguard, 1943). Novelized social history. An understanding case study of a generous and beautiful woman born to a life of horrible poverty. Detailed and convincing, this story plumbs a weakness in the American economic system.

SMITTER, WESSEL, 1894-
F.O.B., Detroit (Harper, 1938). Of an automobile factory. Shows what the "machine" does to man.

SPADONI, ANDRIANA
Not All Rivers (Doubleday, 1937). Story of a woman's decision to fight for social justice, after realizing that being an "indignant intellectual" is not enough. Good descriptions of strikes and the methods used by the employer to combat them.

STEGNER, WALLACE, 1909-
The Preacher and the Slave (Houghton, 1950). Fictionalizes and expands the biography of Joe Hill, the Wobbly poet and musician, for his final years, 1910-1916. Illuminates a violent phase of the labor movement in the Western states.

TIPPETT, THOMAS, 1894-
Horse Shoe Bottoms (Harper, 1935). An English miner comes to the Illinois coal fields and becomes a leader in the early unionization movement. Presents the problems of a man who sees a relation between his work and human happiness. Competent presentation.

TRAVEN, BRUNO
The Death Ship (Knopf, 1934). The adventure of an American who is stranded in Europe without identification, is shunted from place to place, and finally gets on a ship which is being sunk for its insurance. A strong picture of the toughened worker ripe for such doctrines as anarchism.

VAN LOAN, CHARLES E., 1876-1919
Buck Parvin and the Movies: Stories of the Motion Picture Game (1917). Comic tales that catch the spirit of movie-making in the years around 1915, as seen by a hard-working "extra."

WALKER, CHARLES RUMFORD, 1893-
Bread and Fire (Houghton, 1927). Excellent sociological material, telling of actualities in steel mills and labor conditions in mill towns. Radical and intellectual groups.

WARD, ELIZABETH S. PHELPS, 1844-1911
The Silent Partner (1871). The wrongs of labor in New England. Our oldest American labor novel of any significance.

WHITCOMB, ROBERT
Talk United States! (Smith, 1935). Story of a skilled American workman, covering the early twentieth century. Told in the semiliterate language of the worker.

WHITE, LIONEL
Rafferty (Dutton, 1959). The story of Rafferty, a labor leader, on the stand before the "Rackets Committee." His ruthlessness and drive for power become so obvious that he loses his former friends and also his family. Surely not a "pro-labor" book.

WHITE, STEWART EDWARD, 1873-1946
The Blazed Trail (1902). Of an unscrupulous lumber corporation in Michigan. A realistic picture of logging and timber-getting.

WILLIAMS, BEN AMES, 1889-1953
Owen Glen (Houghton, 1950). The story takes place in the Ohio mining region in a small town that could be "any one of ten thousand other little towns." The book is careful social history, 1890 to 1898, picturing the problems of coal miners and the rise of the United Mine Workers.

WOLFF, MARITTA, 1918-
Night Shift (Random, 1942). A ruthless, dramatic, fatalistic picture of cruelty and fear in a small factory town in wartime. Naturalistic treatment of boardinghouse, restaurant, hospital, factory, night club. A studied representation of how the other half lives.

ZUGSMITH, LEANE, 1903-
A Time to Remember (Random, 1936). A novel of the strike of white-collar workers in a large New York department store. Many detailed descriptions of the life of the employees and the execution of a strike.

2. BUSINESS AND FINANCE

An attempt has been made here to list books that deal directly with the handling of business and financial matters. The subject matter to a great extent overlaps that on labor, city life, and the leisure class. The first books of this type were written by William Dean Howells and H. E. Hamblen in the eighties and nineties; but a real deluge of such books appeared after the "muckrakers" of the Progressive Era had shown the corrupting influence and undemocratic methods of American business. In the 1920's the attitude toward business was often satirical, as in the work of Sinclair Lewis, and in the 1930's it was generally antagonistic, but numerous books in the 1950's and 1960's have been neutrally realistic or even compassionate portrayals of businessmen—who are shown as realizing too late that man does not live by commercial values alone. Most novels about businessmen are antidotes for the Horatio Alger tradition and the success-story myth.

ANDERSON, SHERWOOD, 1876-1941
Windy McPherson's Son (Cape, 1916). The tale of an Iowa village boy who goes to Chicago and becomes a millionaire, only to rebel against a life of greed for money. Theme: the utter futility of modern America's ideals.

ASCH, NATHAN, 1902-
The Office (Harcourt, 1925). The story of a broker's office that failed and of the subsequent actions of twenty separate members of the office force.

ASINOF, ELIOT, 1919-
Man on Spikes (McGraw, 1955). About professional baseball as seen by a minor-league player who ends up in the sporting-goods department of a hardware store. Fresh insight into the sports business.

BEZZERIDES, A. I., 1908-
Long Haul (Carrick, 1938). An account of the economic and social plight of the wildcat produce trucker in California. Gives a sense of the exhausting, sleepless life of men who haul oranges and asparagus between Los Angeles and Oakland. Simple and somewhat melodramatic.
Thieves' Market (Scribner's, 1949). A melodramatic version of the hard life of an independent fruit and vegetable trucker and his troubles at the San Francisco wholesale market. A novel in the hard-boiled genre.

BRINIG, MYRON, 1900-
The Sisters (Farrar, 1937). A story of the lives and loves of the three daughters of the local druggist of Silver Bow, Montana. Plenty of local color.

BROMFIELD, LOUIS, 1896-1956
Escape (Stokes, 1927). A series of four novels dealing with the founders of a factory town and their descendants. Shows the decay of the Puritan tradition and the rise of Western industrialism. The individual titles are: *The Green Bay Tree, Possession, Early Autumn,* and *A Good Woman.*

BROOKS, JOHN, 1920-
The Big Wheel (Harper, 1949). On the editorial offices of a big and successful news magazine called *Present Day.* Concerned with the ethics and integrity of the journalistic magazine business.

BROOKS, RICHARD, 1912-
The Producer (Simon, 1951). A brisk, topical, nonsatirical novelizing of all major phases of the making and distribution of an independent motion picture.

BURLINGAME, ROGER, 1889-
The Heir (Scribner's, 1930). Shows the development of a great chemical business through the war of 1914-1918 and also the thwarting of a son's artistic inclinations by a father's enforcement of a business career.

CAHAN, ABRAHAM, 1860-1951
The Rise of David Levinsky (Harper, 1917). An excellent portrait of an immigrant adjusting himself to the American business world. He is quite successful in business but spiritually unsatisfied.

CALDWELL, JANET TAYLOR, 1900-
Dynasty of Death (Scribner's, 1938). Follows the lives of two families —the Barbours and the Bouchards—armament makers, from 1837 until 1914. A detailed and forceful account of death merchants.
The Eagles Gather (Scribner's, 1940). Sequel to *Dynasty of Death;* continues the story of the Bouchard family from 1918 to President Hoover's election.
The Final Hour (Scribner's, 1944). The story of a family of rapacious opportunists who hate democracy and love Fascism. A lone humanitarian stands against the forces of evil.

CARSE, ROBERT, 1903-
The Beckoning Waters (Scribner's, 1953). Built around "empire builders" in lumbering, shipping, and iron in Great Lakes states in the period 1865-1930. A realistic, sympathetic portrait of an Ulsterman become millionaire.

CARSON, ROBERT, 1909-
The Magic Lantern (Holt, 1952). A novelized history that should have been nonfiction; of all aspects of the movie industry before and after 1920, including the making and financing of pictures, distribution problems, the star system, and scandals. Developed around a producer and his "boy wonder" of a son, who succeeds him.
Love Affair (Holt, 1958). A detailed, credible account of an actor's rise and fall in Hollywood. Sheds much realistic light on the film industry and the beginnings of television. Free from the thin satire and fantastic card-stacking of many novels about Hollywood.

CHAMALES, TOM T., 1924-
Go Naked in the World (Scribner's, 1959). Life of a five-hundred-dollar prostitute (call girl) from the height of her career to her death under slum conditions, and of the wealthy Greek-American boy who pursues her instead of joining his father's business.

CHIDESTER, ANN, 1919-
The Long Year (Scribner's, 1946). Story of the turmoil caused in a small Minnesota town by a ruthless woman who is part owner of its factory, and who comes to live for one year in the town. The ethics of modern business is a major theme.
Mama Maria's (Scribner's, 1947). A tense, brief story about a tourist camp on Route No. 61, between Duluth and New Orleans, the proprietress, her employees, and guests. Real people.

CHURCHILL, WINSTON, 1871-1947
A Far Country (1915). Of a corporation lawyer, a man who "sells his intellect" to get on in the world.

COLWELL, MIRIAM, 1917-
Day of the Trumpet (Random, 1947). Story of the development of a ruthless businessman, 1873-1888, who sacrifices friendship and other values for success.

DAVENPORT, MARCIA (GLUCK), 1903-
The Valley of Decision (Scribner's, 1942). A long chronicle of four generations in an intelligent, honest industrial family who mill steel in Pittsburgh. Dramatizes the struggles between titans, ownership, and labor, and shows the growing place of science and enlightened labor policy in American heavy industry since the Civil War. Shows the role played by Slovaks and "Hunkies."

DEISS, JOSEPH JAY
Blue Chips (Schuster, 1957). A scientist is torn between the ethics of the scientist and those of big business as represented by a pharmaceutical company. Business wins, and the man loses his dearest friends and the woman he loves. But he is not particularly conscious of the loss, as he has become a modern, successful businessman. Excellent job in what the author attempts.

DELAND, MARGARET, 1857-1945
The Iron Woman (1911). Story of an American business woman who holds her own in the driving world of industrial competition, but even more the story of another character who holds everybody in line with Puritan tradition in regard to marriage.

DeMARE, GEORGE
The Empire (Putnam, 1956). A composite story of five men working for a big corporation. At middle age each is worn out and convinced that the flame was not worth the candle. A neatly handled plot.

DIBNER, MARTIN, 1911-
Showcase (Doubleday, 1958). A hard and brittle treatment of life in a big department store. Rather good in detail and character presentation.

DOS PASSOS, JOHN, 1896-
The 42nd Parallel (Harper, 1930).   Presents the financial-economic setup around 1900.   Uses the author's new techniques—the "camera eye," the "news reel," etc.
The Big Money (Harcourt, 1936).   The business world, as well as the laboring classes and the leisure class, is a part of this excellent kaleidoscopic picture of the "roaring twenties."

DOWNING, J. HYATT, 1888-
Anthony Trant (Putnam, 1941).   A story of business in the corn belt. Set in Sioux City, 1890-1920.

DREISER, THEODORE, 1871-1945
The Financier (1912).   Shows the methods of big business and the ruthlessness demanded of the man who succeeds.   Story of a broker in Philadelphia about 1870.   Rich detail.
The Titan (1914).   Sequel to *The Financier*.   Another detailed account of a grasping capitalist.   Laid in Chicago and dealing with the fight for control of street railways.
The Stoic (Doubleday, 1947).   Continues *The Financier* and *The Titan*. In this the central character, Cowperwood, attempts to gain control of London's transportation system.   He dies as his fortune begins to dissolve, but much of his money goes into a great hospital that he has dreamed of.   The three novels make a complete unit showing Dreiser's conception of modern American business.

EDDY, ROGER WHITTLESEY, 1920-
Family Affair (Crowell, 1957).   The business of an old Connecticut family is taken over by a poor boy who grew up in the town.   He marries one of the daughters, puts new life into the dying business, and is finally accepted by the family.

FARRELL, JAMES T., 1904-
Gas House McGinty (Vanguard, 1933). Of routine in a large distributing company.   The lives of employees and their boss, McGinty.

FERBER, EDNA, 1887-
Emma McChesney & Co. (1915).   Experiences of a shrewd traveling saleslady, who meets men on their own ground.
Come and Get It (Doubleday, 1935).   In terms of a chore boy who becomes a paper-mill baron, tells of the rise and fall of the lumber industry in Wisconsin and Michigan from 1850 to 1930.

FITZGERALD, F. SCOTT, 1896-1940
The Last Tycoon (Scribner's, 1941).   An uncompleted novel that gives insight into the Hollywood movie industry.   Shrewdly analyzes a picture producer.   Especially interesting for notes and fragments illustrating the author's concern for point of view, tone, characterization, and structure.

FLAVIN, MARTIN, 1883-
Journey in the Dark (Harper, 1943). A careful, artistic tale of an
Iowa boy in his rise to success in business (wallpaper) and his failure
in spiritual adjustment. Neither dishonest nor greedy, the hero is in
essence a lonely man in the dark.

FOWLER, GENE, 1891-1960
Timber Line (Covici, 1933). Sensational fictionalized biography of the
builders of the *Denver Post*, Bonfils and Tammen. Gives an impres-
sive insight into "yellow journalism."

GILBERT, EDWIN
The New Ambassadors (Lippincott, 1961). A perceptive novel compar-
ing the way of life of an American high-pressure businessman with
the life of an old French family. The girl of the family, who loves him,
finally decides not to marry him and disrupt her way of life.

GRAHAM, DOROTHY, 1893-
The China Venture (Stokes, 1929). Tale of three generations of a New
England family engaged with China in a trading business unbroken
from 1835 to the 1920's.

GREEN, GERALD, 1922-
The Heartless Light (Scribner's, 1961). A satiric account of the per-
formance of the mass media (newspapers, broadcasting companies,
etc.) and of the police of the Los Angeles area after a kidnapping of a
child in one of the suburbs.

HARRIMAN, JOHN, 1904-
The Career of Philip Hazen (Howell, Soskin, 1941). A story of high
finance and ruthless competition in Wall Street. A picture of the rich
struggling for survival.

HAWLEY, CAMERON, 1905-
Executive Suite (Houghton, 1952). Of the struggle among vice presi-
dents to succeed to the top position in a furniture company. A clever,
knowing, closely timed story that is quasi-satirical toward top execu-
tives.
Cash McCall (Houghton, 1955). A plot-filled, slickish story of suspense.
About businessmen—their private lives, ethical codes, and methods of
work—and especially about a man who buys and sells whole enterprises.
The Lincoln Lords (Little, 1960). A long, melodramatic account of a
"job jumper," a tycoon who is an itinerant, professional corporation
president. His drive is for power, the feeling of personal success.
Much about financing and promotion in the cannery business and the
supermarket chains.

HERBST, JOSEPHINE, 1897-
The Executioner Waits (Harcourt, 1934). Deals with a large scattered

American family of the middle class, after the Armistice of 1918. Condemns the economic condition after the war—days which saw strikes, unrest, and the I.W.W.

HERGESHEIMER, JOSEPH, 1880-1954
The Three Black Pennys (Knopf, 1917). Of three generations of Pennsylvania iron founders. Over-ornate in style.
The Foolscap Rose (Knopf, 1934). Of the development of a Pennsylvania paper mill from the time when handmade papers were produced by its owners until a hundred years later when the mill had become a slave of Wall Street and the one-time owning family was destroyed.

HERRICK, ROBERT, 1868-1938
The Memoirs of an American Citizen (1905). On the ethics of modern business. The story of a man's rise in the Chicago meat-packing business, told by the character himself.

HERRMANN, JOHN, 1900-
The Salesman (Simon, 1939). Story of the average traveling salesman —the hard-working one who worries about balancing his family budget on his meager salary.

HOBART, ALICE TISDALE (NOURSE), 1882-
Pidgin Cargo (Century, 1929). About a Yankee trader on the upper Yangtze during the war of 1914-1918.
Oil for the Lamps of China (Bobbs, 1933). American business in China. Centers on the struggle of a young man to better his position in Shanghai.
Their Own Country (Bobbs, 1940). Continues *Oil for the Lamps of China*. The main character manages an industrial alcohol plant in Kansas. A study of man's search for security.

HORWITZ, JULIUS, 1920-
The Inhabitants (World, 1960). Gives documented, shocking details of the lives of Negroes, Puerto Ricans, and others on relief in New York City today, as seen by a sympathetic welfare worker carrying a load of eighty-five families. A picture of unemployed people, of Central Park winos, of persons who dream of the good life but are caught in the wretched poverty of a world without birth certificates in apartment houses "where the pushers peddled narcotics like popcorn."

HOWELLS, WILLIAM DEAN, 1837-1920
The Rise of Silas Lapham (1885). One of our earliest books about American business. A careful portrait of a paint merchant in Boston who aspires to crash Beacon Hill society.
A Traveller from Altruria (1894). An adroit satire on American business ideals and the rationalizations used by the well-to-do to justify their wealth and power. Howells uses the device of having a man from a utopia visit a fashionable resort town in Maine and converse with representatives of the "upper" and "lower" classes.

JONAS, CARL
Jefferson Selleck (Little, 1952). A sympathetic novel about a "successful" but not happy real estate man, community leader (in Gateway), and manufacturer (the Yaw-Et-Ag Company). Loaded with social history for the period 1915-1950 and discerning about the discrepancies in American civilization. Told by means of a new fictional device: an autobiographical tape recording.

KAUP, ELIZABETH (DEWING), 1885-
Not for the Meek (Macmillan, 1941). A portrait of a rugged individualist, a Danish immigrant, rising in capitalistic society. Comparable to *The Financier* and *The Titan* of Theodore Dreiser.

KELLAND, CLARENCE BUDINGTON, 1881-1964
Hard Money (Harper, 1930). Tells of the career of a financier in New York in the days of Jefferson, Jackson, and the first Vanderbilt.

KERN, ALFRED, 1919-
Width of Waters (Houghton, 1958). Story of a befuddled young man doing publicity work in a small factory town. He rebels, but succumbs, as do most such young men, according to the author, to the mores of the town.

KOBER, ARTHUR, 1900-
That Man Is Here Again (Random, 1946). Sketches from the *New Yorker* that create Benny Greenspan, a Hollywood artists' agent, who is colorful and ungrammatical in his speech.

LAING, ALEXANDER, 1903-
The Sea Witch (Farrar, 1933). Competition in shipping in old New York. The "Sea Witch," built in 1846, was destroyed at sea in 1856.

LAING, FREDERICK
The Giant's House (Dial, 1955). Of a tough man who builds up a chain of grocery stores by dominating his employees and independent grocers.

LAWRENCE, JOSEPHINE
The Sound of Running Feet (Stokes, 1937). Of clerks and bosses in a small real estate office where no one is actually secure. The worries and burdens of middle-class America.
If I Have Four Apples (Grosset, 1938). Discusses the economic difficulties of a family who cannot budget their income. A worker in the financial department of a newspaper and her suggestions in solving the problems of this family.
No Stone Unturned (Little, 1940). The story of a realtor who was prosperous in the 1920's but whose business was gone in the 1930's. He continues, Micawber-like, to believe he is important.

LEE, HARRY, 1914-
No Measure Danced (Macmillan, 1941). A grim story of a woman

business executive who gains success but loses happiness. A detailed picture of high-pressure business and ruthless opportunism.

LEWIS, SINCLAIR, 1885-1951

Babbitt (Harcourt, 1922). Real estate business. A famous book about the "average business man." Babbitt is an individual, however; it is the town that is portrayed as a "type." Babbitt attempts to revolt but rejoins the herd. A deservedly popular work.

The Man Who Knew Coolidge (Harcourt, 1928). A series of monologues, spoken by Lowell Schmaltz, a deadly dull devotee of "democracy, manly sports, family life, efficiency, culture, and religious uplift." Written in the actual language of the little businessman.

Dodsworth (Harcourt, 1929). Of an automobile magnate who escapes from American business to Europe in order to preserve his individuality and find freedom for his personality. *Half a Loaf* by Grace Livingstone (Hegger) Lewis (Liveright, 1931) gives the ex-Mrs. Sinclair Lewis's version of the marriage Sinclair Lewis put in *Dodsworth*. It tells of the life of the wife of a successful author—her romantic marriage, travels with her husband, disillusionment, and divorce in Reno. Portrays the artist as a man.

Work of Art (Doubleday, 1934). A hotelkeeper's life. Gets in a number of satirical jabs at business in general and conveys practical information about what goes on behind the scenes in hotels.

Gideon Planish (Random, 1943). Of an organizer of charities, uplift societies, etc. Rich satire on organizations of the 1930's.

LONDON, JACK, 1876-1916

The Iron Heel (1908). A story of the remaking of America into a collective society, called a "plutocracy" by London. A forerunner of books on the coming of Fascism, like Sinclair Lewis's *It Can't Happen Here*.

LORIMER, GEORGE HORACE, 1869-1937

Letters from a Self-made Merchant to His Son (1902). An old-style philosophy of life and business not unlike that of David Harum.

LYNDE, FRANCIS, 1865-1930

The Helpers (1899) and *The Grafters* (1904). Business and politics in Denver and the Colorado mining regions.

The Quickening (1906). The Tennessee coal and iron fields. The conflicts of commercialism.

Empire Builders (1907). Railway building in the West, plotting contractors in Denver, and the New York Stock Exchange.

MARQUAND, JOHN PHILLIPS, 1893-1960

Sincerely, Willis Wayde (Little, 1955). Exhibits a man's rise from mill hand to industrialist—his habits of behavior and the crises he meets. Told with many flashbacks and sure craft.

MERWIN, SAMUEL, 1874-   , and WEBSTER, HENRY K., 1875-
Calumet "K" (1901). Of the building of a two-million-dollar grain elevator by the main character, who is hampered by his opponents and by "walking delegates."
The Short-Line War (1901). A fight for the possession of a line connecting two great railways.

NORRIS, FRANK, 1870-1902
The Pit (1903). Of wheat speculation in the stock market of Chicago.

O'BRIEN, BARBARA
Operators and Things (Arlington, 1958). This story of the inner workings of a schizophrenic's mind is a symbolic story of the life of a person working for a business firm. The story-teller calls the extra-personalities who control her "operators," and people are "things" that are being manipulated. Her "operators" have their real counterparts in the business world.

ORNITZ, SAMUEL BADISCH, 1890-1957
Haunch, Paunch, and Jowl (Boni, 1923). A record of the process of becoming rich and politically powerful. The main characters are Jewish, and there is discussion of the Jews' place in America.

PARSON, ALICE BEALE, 1886-
John Merrill's Pleasant Life (Dutton, 1930). A penniless, clever, and promising young engineer becomes manager of a factory on the Hudson River; he ends up a successful leading citizen, comfortable, conventional, prosperous, but spiritually frustrated.

PAYNE, WILL, 1865-1954
The Money Captain (1898). The central story is the struggle between the gas king of Chicago, aided by corrupt aldermen, and a fighting, muckraking editor. A thoughtful, realistic novel that presents the case for and against industrial captains.

PHILLIPS, DAVID G., 1867-1911
The Master Rogue: the Confessions of a Croesus (1903). A clerk in a dry-goods store becomes a millionaire. A sordid and brutal story of success and unhappiness.
Light-Fingered Gentry (1907). Of the inner workings of great insurance companies.
The Second Generation (1907). Of a self-made man who does not provide for his children, wishing them to be hardened by struggle.

RICE, ELMER, 1892-
A Voyage to Purilia (Cosmopolitan, 1930). A satire on the motion-picture industry told in terms of the emotionally standardized types who inhabit the planet of Purilia. Contains some pointed social criticism.

ROBINSON, HENRY MORTON, 1898-
Water of Life (Simon, 1960). Long detailed story of three generations
of whiskey-makers. The time, 1864 to 1920. Of the start, rise, and
decline of the whiskey industry—tracing the development through
United States hearings leading up to passage of the Eighteenth Amendment and the rise of the bootlegger. Witty and wordy.

ROY, GABRIELLE, 1909-
The Cashier (Harcourt, 1955). About a Montreal bank cashier, the
tedious white-collar job that is wearing him out, his sad, average-man
life of required politeness, liberal conscience, and tensions. Good
on the attitudes toward him of a doctor, a priest, and associates.

RUCKER, HELEN (BORNSTEIN)
The Wolf Tree (Little, 1960). The story of a lumbering family of San
Francisco and the Northwest, and of a transition in their thinking from
being predators to being interested in conservation and human values.

SEIFERT, ELIZABETH, 1897-
A Great Day (Dodd, 1939). A detailed account of what was to have
been the greatest day in the life of a self-made millionaire who had
made his money on fake advertising and doped patent medicines. An
effective indictment of corrupt careers but an artificial plot.

SHIEL, MATTHEW P., 1865-1947
Contraband of War (1899). High finance and politics during the
Spanish-American War (1897-1899).

SINCLAIR, UPTON B., 1878-
A Captain of Industry (1906). A Sinclair indictment of the capitalistic
system.
The Money Changers (1908). An attack on the methods used by Wall
Street to refinance steel companies and railroads.
Oil! (Boni, 1927). Picture of the oil industry of southern California,
based on the oil scandals during the Harding administration, the brib-
ery of public officials, class antagonism, and the rivalry of big business. Glimpses of Senators, oil men, and a Los Angeles evangelist
who remind the reader of people actually living at the time of the
story.
"Co-op" (Farrar, 1936). Here Sinclair attacks the capitalistic system
only by implication. Positively, he shows the case for consumer and
producer co-operatives.

SPRAGUE, JESSE RAINSFORD, 1871-1946
The Making of a Merchant (Morrow, 1928). The rise of a large de-
partment-store merchant.
The Middleman (Morrow, 1929). Social history in fiction form of the
wholesale-hardware business.

SULLIVAN, OSCAR MATTHIAS, 1881-1955
The Empire Builder (Century, 1928). A novel based on previous studies of James J. Hill, on newspaper files, and on other firsthand materials. Glorifies the methods and attitudes of the railway builders,
and argues for the development of monopoly in the railway field.

SWIGGETT, HOWARD, 1891-
The Durable Fire (Houghton, 1956). The main character finds that he
is impelled by his own character to be ethical in spite of pressures
from above, but others too approve of his attitudes. An interesting
study of family mores of the mid-twentieth century and their impact
on a big business enterprise.

TARKINGTON, BOOTH, 1869-1946
Growth (Doubleday, 1927). This is a trilogy on the growth of a Middle
Western city, including *The Magnificent Ambersons, The Midlander,
The Turmoil.*

TRUMBO, DALTON, 1905-
The Remarkable Andrew (Lippincott, 1941). Of a young clerk who is at
outs with the corrupt business world about him, is accused of embez-
zlement, and is visited by the shade of General Andrew Jackson, who
gives him practical advice.

TURNBULL, AGNES SLIGH, 1888-
Remember the End (Macmillan, 1938). A young Scot arrives in Pennsylvania with only a few dollars and stern determination. By ignoring
the welfare of his fellowmen and by suppressing his artistic instincts
and human emotions, he becomes a millionaire in the steel and railway business.

WAKEMAN, FREDERIC, 1909-
The Hucksters (Rinehart, 1946). A satire, with some of the thinness
of its subject, on radio advertising. Laid in Radio City, it depicts aspects of life and manners among the rich business class.

WALLACH, IRA JAN, 1913-
The Absence of a Cello (Little, 1960). Excellent persiflage regarding
business and business methods.

WARREN, ROBERT PENN, 1905-
At Heaven's Gate (Random, 1943). Centers on the struggle of a young
woman to escape from her high-powered business-driven father. The
man to whom she is engaged follows her father's pattern. She becomes
the mistress of an artist, and then of a labor leader. At the end of the
story she is murdered and her former fiance loses his money; but the
father proceeds with further financial schemes.

WEEKS, JACK
Some Trust in Chariots (McGraw, 1963). The story of the man who

invented the "Wayne" automobile, and how he created an empire to leave to his son. The turmoil of the thirties is an integral part of the story.

WHITE, THEODORE HAROLD, 1915-
View from the Fortieth Floor (Sloane, 1960). A man who sees people as statistics learns to appreciate individual people as he presides over the liquidation of two large magazines, victims of the competition of television advertising. Insight into the problems of big business and of magazine publishing.

WIENER, NORBERT, 1894-1964
The Tempter (Random, 1959). This book by the distinguished mathematician explores the processes by which a large corporation manipulates people to serve its own ends. The "tempter," who tells the story, buys the person his company wants to credit with the development of a new process, but fails to corrupt the research scientist who has really done the basic work.

YAFFE, JAMES, 1927-
What's the Big Hurry? (Little, 1954). About an expedient businessman who was an accountant until the crash of '29 and after that "never stayed in one business long enough to lose too much money." Characterizes him in his family and social environment, in Chicago and elsewhere.

3. CITY LIFE

City life is a twentieth-century theme, begun in this country by Henry B. Fuller's *The Cliff Dwellers* (1893). The second important work dealing with city life directly was Stephen Crane's *Bowery Tales* (1900), which included his two masterly stories, "George's Mother" and "Maggie, A Girl of the Streets." Although the subject matter of books on this list overlaps that of those on labor, immigrants, leisure class, etc., the emphasis here is on how people live in the city and the peculiar folkways, attitudes, and problems that have grown up as a consequence of urban life in contrast to the rural-life pattern of the nineteenth century. While some writers draw pleasant or admiring pictures of American cities, a majority of novelists are strikingly in agreement in their insistence on seaminess, vice, crime, brutality, ugliness, frustration, mental illness, or poverty of spirit and culture. In some books, as in Rice's *Imperial City* and Bromfield's *Twenty-four Hours*, the multiplicity of city life itself is the sociological theme. Later books more commonly emphasize psychological themes.

ADAMS, SAMUEL HOPKINS, 1871-1958
Tenderloin (Random, 1958). A story of the relationships between underworld, police, reformers, and politicians around 1890. Vivid.

ALGREN, NELSON, 1909-
The Neon Wilderness (Doubleday, 1947). Naturalistic stories of Chicago slums, mostly of prostitutes, thugs, and dope addicts.
The Man with the Golden Arm (Doubleday, 1949). Of a gambler who hangs out in a Chicago tavern in the Polish district. A book rich in reportage on jail life, the underworld, and city life with its palliatives and frustrations.

ALMAN, DAVID, 1919-
World Full of Strangers (Doubleday, 1949). The scene is a grim section of New York City inhabited largely by immigrants and their children. A documentary treatment of fatigue, defeat, and corruption.

APPEL, BENJAMIN, 1907-
Brain Guy (Greenberg, 1936). A study of the murderous stupidity of gangsters and of their hopes and motivating ideas.
Runaround (Dutton, 1937). A story of the vote-getting racket in the melting-pot of Hell's Kitchen, New York City.
The Power House (Dutton, 1939). Vivid, realistic, melodramatic picture of the politically protected underworld rackets of New York City. Close-ups of fixers, mondaines, machine bosses, judges, ward-heelers, mobsters.

ASCH, SHALOM (SHOLEM), 1880-1957
East River (Putnam, 1946). A moving story of modern New York, of Jews and Catholics and the twentieth-century factory system. Excellent in portraying the motivations of factory owners as well as workers. The religious life of the main characters is given emphasis.

AUCHINCLOSS, LOUIS STANTON, 1917-
Pursuit of the Prodigal (Houghton, 1959). A story of the interrelationships of various suburbanites. In particular the story of one man who migrated from the suburbs to the city. The story of his attempts to understand himself and of his frustrations as he tries to follow an ethical line.

BASSO, HAMILTON, 1904-1964
Days Before Lent (Scribner's, 1939). Story of a young scientist in New Orleans during the week of Mardi Gras. He has to decide whether to go to India to do research or to stay at home and marry the girl he loves. Realistic details of New Orleans night life.

BELL, THOMAS
All Brides Are Beautiful (Little, 1936). A realistic story of life in the Bronx. Shows a wholesome young married couple solving their economic problems.
Till I Come Back to You (Little, 1943). Of a typical family of the "plains of Brooklyn" east from Borough Hall. Presents typical attitudes at the beginning of World War II.

BELLOW, SAUL, 1915-
The Adventures of Augie March (Viking, 1953). A long, rich, picaresque narrative about a young man trying to adapt himself to life—to other people—in Chicago, in Mexican towns, and elsewhere during the 1930's and 1940's. Catches the central ethical issues of modern times, notably "just how many new adaptations I was going to have to try to make."
Herzog (Viking, 1964). A year or so in the life of a college professor just after the ending of his second marriage. Of his endless mental meanderings, seemingly leading nowhere. Perhaps meant to reflect the confusion of city life in the 1960's. New York and Chicago.

BERCOVICI, KONRAD, 1882-1961
Against the Sky (Covici, 1932). Story of gypsy life on the East Side in New York City; a gypsy's love for a member of an old New York family.

BRACE, GERALD WARNER, 1901-
Winter Solstice (Norton, 1960). Of the love of a twenty-nine-year-old girl for her married neighbor, a social worker. Upon his death, she takes upon herself much of the work he had been doing. Good writing and good presentation of habits of thought of suburbanites and of youth in Boston in the 1950's.

BRADLEY, MARY HASTINGS
Old Chicago (Appleton, 1933). Four novelettes showing the life of Chicago from the War of 1812 to the opening of the Chicago Fair of 1893.

BRINIG, MYRON, 1900-
May Flavin (Farrar, 1938). The story of a young woman who comes to New York in the early 1900's with her husband. This couple is forced to live in the slums; and, in the surrounding of saloons, thieves, gambling houses, and prostitutes, one of May's sons becomes a gangster. Shows the various strata of life in a big city.

BROMFIELD, LOUIS, 1896-1956
Twenty-four Hours (Stokes, 1930). Traces the lives of six people for twenty-four hours after they attend a dull dinner party given in a beautiful New York apartment. The following twenty-four hours bring a crisis to each of these six society figures. Suggests the dramatic contrasts in New York life.

BURNETT, WILLIAM RILEY, 1899-
Little Caesar (Dial, 1929). The first highly successful novel of Chicago gangsters, told from the point of view and in the language of a gangster. "Little Caesar" bosses his gunmen until he kills a cop during a night-club holdup; the gang then breaks up, several becoming squealers.
Nobody Lives Forever (Knopf, 1943). Careful characterizations of

crooks, con-men, gangster leaders, "babes," and cheap racketeers make this a good crime-and-sex novel.

The Asphalt Jungle (Knopf, 1949). A rattling good tale of the underworld of a large Midwestern city and of how the honest police commissioner runs down a notorious criminal.

Little Men, Big World (Knopf, 1951). A fast-moving yarn of crooked politicos, gamblers, and hoodlums in a Midwestern city that Chicago gangsters are moving in on.

It's Always Four O'Clock (Random, 1956). Told by a young guitar player who is caught up in the personal and professional life of cocktail parlor musicians in Los Angeles and Beverly Hills. Catches vulgar, sensual, commercial, and sentimental aspects of life in the jazz business, including its "hipster" fringe.

CALDWELL, JANET TAYLOR, 1900-
There Was a Time (Scribner's, 1947). This recounts the story of an artist struggling to emerge from the midst of the frustrations and illusions of life in a northern New York city.

CAMERON, LOU, 1924-
The Block-Busters (McKay, 1964). A novel of racial tensions in Brooklyn and of the real-estate racketeers who exploit them. The hero helps to expose and prosecute the block-busters.

CARROLL, LOREN, 1904-
Wild Onion (Dodd, 1930). Of the career of a Chicago bootlegger and gangster. He becomes wealthy and powerful and meets death at the hands of a rival mob.

CATHER, WILLA SIBERT, 1876-1947
Lucy Gayheart (Knopf, 1935). Lucy Gayheart desires to live in Chicago away from those she knows, so that she may have time to think. A pathetic story.

CHILD, NELLISE, 1901-
If I Come Home (Doubleday, 1943). A study of a marriage between a rich southern California girl and a poor slum-raised boy. Contrasts the wealthy and the pauperized, Fascist and democratic, intolerant and sympathetic that can be found in Los Angeles. Implies the need for social reorganization in postwar America.

CLAD, NOEL, 1924-
The Savage (Simon, 1959). Plot story of a man hired to commit a murder, but who protects the victim from the crime syndicate instead. Makes organized gangs seem very powerful. Setting, New York City.

COATES, ROBERT M., 1897-
The Farther Shore (Harcourt, 1955). A story centering on the loneliness and frustrations incident to living in New York City in the

mid-twentieth century, with the main characters caught up and controlled by mores and morals far from life-sustaining.

COZZENS, JAMES GOULD, 1903-
By Love Possessed (Harcourt, 1957). A story centering on a smug, self-complacent man who thinks of himself as the embodiment of integrity and other virtues. The outcome shows his fallibility.

CRANE, STEPHEN, 1871-1900
Bowery Tales (1900). Contains "George's Mother" and "Maggie, A Girl of the Streets." Among our earliest naturalistic stories. Uses the language of the people. Realistic and full of pathos.
Twenty Stories (Knopf, 1940). Contains "Maggie" and "An Experiment in Misery."

CROY, HOMER, 1883-
Headed for Hollywood (Greenberg, 1934). An account of the struggles of a young small-town girl who came to Hollywood to find success and met only disillusionment and heartbreak. Shows Hollywood as the city of pain—those who are already set strive to maintain their status and those who are not yet in strive futilely to be acclaimed.

DAHLBERG, EDWARD, 1900-
From Flushing to Calvary (Harcourt, 1932). Realistic picture of slum life around Calvary Cemetery, New York.

DAVENPORT, MARCIA (GLUCK), 1903-
East Side, West Side (Scribner's, 1947). New York shortly after World War II. Mostly on the West Side.

DELL, FLOYD, 1887-
The Briary Bush (Doran, 1921). Deals with the early married years of a young couple in postwar Chicago. Suggests some of the Bohemian art life of the time and dramatizes the contemporary concern with sex and marriage.

DE VOTO, BERNARD AUGUSTINE, 1897-1955
We Accept with Pleasure (Little, 1934). A satire on the so-called "educated gentleman." A history teacher returns from the war shell-shocked but has too much pride to accept charity. All the characters strive for happiness but are so confused by habit and convention that they fail to find it. A detailed picture of people and events in Chicago and Boston after the war of 1914-1918.
Mountain Time (Little, 1947). Two Westerners by birth and New Yorkers by transplantation overcome emotional conflicts by returning to their native city and by gaining insight into each other's problems. A romantic story using modern speech and customs.

DOBIE, CHARLES C., 1881-1943
Portrait of a Courtesan (Appleton, 1934). San Francisco in the late

1890's. A picture of economic unrest, ethnic contrasts, Bohemian art life, whore houses, practical politics.

San Francisco Tales (Appleton, 1935). Eighteen romantic short stories of the foreign quarter, of Chinatown, and of Nordic Americans in San Francisco. Psychological overtones.

San Francisco Adventures (Appleton, 1937). Nine short stories of foreigners in San Francisco, from the point of view of a Bohemian baker. Impressionistic local color.

DOS PASSOS, JOHN, 1896-

Manhattan Transfer (Harper, 1925). Good on new folkways. Episodic, with diverse characters being brought together by the chaotic, unplanned happenings of the early 1920's. Catches the seething vitality and enormous variety of the city.

DREISER, THEODORE, 1871-1945

Sister Carrie (1900). Of the adventures or the mishaps of an eighteen-year-old girl in Chicago. Considered a shocker at the time of its publication.

Jennie Gerhardt (1911). A story of a girl who retains admirable qualities, even though she violates some of our "sacred conventions." Regarded as a good example of the naturalistic attitude.

The "Genius" (1915). A long, careful account of a painter who ultimately finds himself as an artist after succeeding in journalism and advertising. Sheds much light on manual work, love, marriage, business in the Midwest and New York at the end of the Victorian period.

FARRELL, JAMES T., 1904-

Studs Lonigan: A Trilogy (Vanguard, 1937). The three stories are *Young Lonigan, The Young Manhood of Studs Lonigan, Judgment Day.* A realistic, forceful presentation of the life of a boy growing up in the culturally impoverished middle-class district of Chicago. A stenographic report on the speech of streets, playgrounds, and pool halls. Excellent for characterization, motivation, and implication.

Father and Son (Vanguard, 1940). Story of an Irish youth on Chicago's South Side. Continues *A World I Never Made* (1936) and *No Star Is Lost* (1938).

Ellen Rogers (Vanguard, 1941). Interprets "an emergent man of ill will." Of an ill-educated, shrewd jackal, Ed Lanson, who preys on others via deceiving, cheating, and debauchery.

Bernard Clare (Vanguard, 1946). Shows a young Chicago Irish-American trying to get started as a writer in New York City. He works as a cigar-store clerk and an advertising salesman, seeks love and self-discovery, sympathizes with Sacco and Vanzetti, and is "wildly rebellious."

The Face of Time (Vanguard, 1953). Presents the central character of *Father and Son*, Danny O'Neill, at the age of five, among a variety of

O'Neills, O'Flahertys, and other Irish-Americans on Chicago's South Side.

FAST, HOWARD MELVIN, 1914-
Place in the City (Harcourt, 1937). Vivid, realistic pictures of a few people and their intimate lives. Presents the commoner types of New York's East Side, including Jews and Irish.

FERBER, NAT J., 1889-
The Sidewalks of New York (Covici, 1927). Story of the life of a Russian boy who came to America with his foster parents and grew up on the East Side of New York. Shows the life of the ghetto and its effect.

FULLER, HENRY B., 1857-1929
The Cliff Dwellers (1893). Dwellers in a large building in modern Chicago. Satirizes social ambitions. Our first important novel with city life as its central theme.

GORHAM, CHARLES O., 1911-
The Future Mister Dolan (Dial, 1948). A naturalistic, straightforward, and brutal account of a ruthless G.I., product of an Irish slum in New York City, who returns home and sets out with "savagery and sadistic meanness" to work up the scale of money and power.

HALPER, ALBERT, 1904-
Union Square (Viking, 1933). An episodic novel of the people who live around Union Square. These episodes are united in a Communist riot and the burning of a firetrap tenement house.

HALSEY, MARGARET, 1910-
This Demi-Paradise (Simon, 1960). Some intelligent and witty comments on present-day Suburbia in the form of a novelette. The forces making for conformity are much in evidence.

HARNDEN, RUTH PEABODY
I, a Stranger (Whittlesey, 1950). A subtle presentation of a misunderstood child growing up amid the society of Beacon Hill.

HAYDN, HIRAM COLLINS, 1907-
The Hands of Esau (Harper, 1962). The life story of a man who loses his job with a large philanthropic agency in 1953. Some of his former associations are suspect in this McCarthy era. The major plot revolves about his relationship with his wife and their difficulty in staying together.

HECHT, BEN, 1894-1964
Erik Dorn (Putnam, 1921). A realistic novel of the successful empty life of a brilliant journalist.

HERLIHY, JAMES LEO, 1927-
All Fall Down (Dutton, 1960). The story of a shy, sensitive adolescent

boy in an impossible family including a drunkard father, a wayward older boy, and a neurotic mother.

HOWELLS, WILLIAM DEAN, 1837-1920
A Modern Instance (1882). The story of a marriage which ended in divorce. The psychological elements make this truly "a modern instance" in nineteenth-century terms as the relationships of the major characters are explored.

HUNEKER, JAMES, 1860-1921
Painted Veils (1920). A story of a girl's rise to success as a singer in New York City. A candid, sex-emphasizing picture of hard-drinking, wise-cracking Bohemians of the Greenwich Village variety.

HUXLEY, ALDOUS, 1894-1963
After Many a Summer Dies the Swan (Harper, 1940). A satire on Los Angeles and on man's search for comfort and immortality as conducted by many Angelenos.

JACKSON, CHARLES REGINALD, 1903-
The Lost Weekend (Farrar, 1944). A sustained, realistic study of an alcoholic. Takes the reader into bars, Bellevue Hospital, and apartment houses; explains a chronic drinker's behavior in the urban civilization often labeled as "neurotic."

JANEWAY, ELIZABETH, 1913-
Leaving Home (Doubleday, 1953). Of two sisters and their brother as they all come of age between 1933 and 1940. Objective observation of everyday emotions of middle-class persons in a big city.

JONAS, CARL, 1913-
Lillian White Deer (Norton, 1964). A story of the stresses four people —two brothers and their wives—undergo in their familial and sexual relations. Lillian White Deer, the wife of the younger brother, has a more complete understanding with her brother-in-law than with her husband, whom she loves. A novel with good psychological perception.

KANTOR, MacKINLAY, 1904-
Diversey (Coward, 1928). Story of the underground world of Chicago and its cabaret life, City Hall politics, bootleg feuds, etc. Shows the effect of this city on a "dreamy" country boy.
Signal Thirty-two (Random, 1950). Good on the training, routines, practical procedures, excitements, and temptations of patrol-car policemen in New York City. Lively reporting, limited to the 23rd Precinct, of life in the city and in the police force.

KARIG, WALTER, 1898-
Lower Than Angels (Farrar, 1945). A realistic and unsparing account of the life story of one Marvin Lang, whose father ran a delicatessen shop on Staten Island. A tale of poverty and drabness.

KARP, DAVID, 1922-
Leave Me Alone (Knopf, 1957). An analysis of the suburbanite. The
leading character, who is an intellectual, has to bow to the mores of
his community, although various members of the community show an
appreciation of his independent point of view. The story amounts to an
indictment of our developed "instinct for conformity."

KENNEDY, JAY RICHARD
Short Term (World, 1959). A middle-aged man, a rich playboy, marries Laurie Dugan, poor girl. She coerces him into being a high-powered financier. Dramatic; successful plotting.

KEROUAC, JACK, 1922-
On the Road (Viking, 1957). A picaresque novel of some "mad ones,
the ones who are mad to live, mad to talk, mad to be saved, desirous
of everything at the same time," who race back and forth across the
continent from one city to another in the late 1940's—"digging" sex,
jazz, wild parties, and amorphous ideas; wearing out cars, loves, and
lives. A tumbled transcription of the zany activities of quasi-literary
bums who are "beat" and "hip" and are on the lunatic fringe of the
popular arts and outside the pale of middle-class conventions. Much
on raffish nighttime doings in New York, Denver, San Francisco, and
Chicago.

KEYES, FRANCES PARKINSON (WHEELER), 1885-1957
Crescent Carnival (Messner, 1942). Covers three generations in the
lives of two families, one of them Creole, in and around New Orleans,
1890-1940.
Joy Street (Messner, 1950). A long, expert women's novel about
present-day Beacon Hill and liberals' attempts to bring together members of old families and members of new Italian, Irish, and Jewish
families. Scenes centered on law, Society, love, and marriage.

KRAMER, DALE, 1910-
The Heart of O. Henry (Rinehart, 1954). A "dramatic narrative" with
invented conversations that fictionalizes the life of William Sydney
Porter, the Southerner-Westerner who ends up in Manhattan and makes
much use of its materials in writing his popular short stories.

KRECH, HILDA SIDNEY (GRUENBERG)
The Other Side of the Day (Knopf, 1958). On the plight of the intel-
lectually trained, bored housewife and her struggle to properly adjust
her life to part-time work and to family duties. A fair psychological
study. Setting: Berkeley, California.

LAMBERT, GAVIN, 1924-
The Slide Area (Viking, 1959). A minor novel, by an Englishman, of
people in and near the movie industry. Catches many true and bizarre
details of "westside" Los Angeles in the 1950's. Makes a symbol of

the landslides of the Pacific Palisades. "People should be a little careful and not live too near the edge, that's all."

LARDNER, RING W., 1885-1933
You Know Me, Al (1916). The letters of a semi-literate ballplayer. Lardner captures the psychology of a lowbrow and reproduces his language in a manner at once accurate and amusing.

LEVIN, MEYER, 1905-
The Old Bunch (Viking, 1937). Set in Chicago, the book traces the activities of a bunch of Jewish high-school graduates from 1921 to 1934, giving an idea of the "justice" of this city and the education, racketeering, business, and politics of the time.

LEWIS, SINCLAIR, 1885-1951
Ann Vickers (Doubleday, 1933). The story of one woman's adjustment to modern life. She represents the most advanced notions as to prison reform, charity work, and personal morality.
Cass Timberlane (Random, 1945). A story of modern marriage, centering on the psychological problem of a middle-aged judge and his wife, who is seventeen years his junior. Satirizes the country-club set. Partly commentary instead of story, in the usual Lewis style.

LONG, MARGARET, 1911-
Louisville Saturday (Random, 1950). Parallels the lives of eleven girls and women of various ages during one afternoon and evening in 1942. Shows the impact of the war on various types of city women who illustrate Genesis 3:16.

McCARTHY, MARY, 1912-
The Group (Harcourt, 1963). The story of eight graduates of Vassar, class of '33, covering about ten years after graduation. Some echoes of major problems of the thirties, but emphasis on marital difficulties, sexual affairs, and the "woman's world."

McINTYRE, JOHN T., 1871-1951
"Slag" (Scribner's, 1927). Of "the refuse of the melting-pot," the immigrant poor, their hard lives, their amusements, and their difficulties with the police. Realistic and dramatic.
Steps Going Down (Farrar, 1936). A realistic novel of the underground world in an American city. The very amiable hero manages to keep ahead of the police for the several months which cover the time of the story.

MILLER, HENRY, 1891-
Tropic of Capricorn (Paris, Obelisk Press, 1939). Life of an absolute dissident in New York City. First quarter of twentieth century. Vivid, revolting, physiological details, showing his feelings about megalopolitan humanity.

MILLER, WARREN
The Way We Life Now (Little, 1958). A story of one pathetic man, caught in an impossible situation, divorced from his wife, separated from his child, and unable to attain marriage with the married woman he loves. Smart talk. Seemingly an authentic picture of the younger adult generation of the 1950's.

MOFFETT, LANGSTON, 1903-
Devil by the Tail (Lippincott, 1947). A well-written, detailed novel of alcoholism. Excellent detail in regard to effects, attempted cures, and final rehabilitation.

MOLL, ELICK, 1907-
Seidman and Son (Putnam, 1958). An appealing story of the differences between a father and son. The son wishes to serve suffering humanity, but finally subscribes to his father's idea that he must first succeed in business in order to be able to help the distressed.

MOTLEY, WILLARD, 1912-1965
Knock on Any Door (Appleton, 1947). A naturalistic novel about an Italian-American boy in Chicago, tracing his gradual descent into a world of crime. Cause and effect relationships of an environmental study are all present, but human motivations are unconvincing.
We Fished All Night (Appleton, 1951). A disillusioned picture of disillusioned Chicagoans—laborers, strikers, members of minority groups, veterans of World War II—persons who fancy themselves to be in a cheap, betrayed world. "Lord, we fished all night and caught nothing." Heavily reportorial and naturalistic.

MURRAY, DONALD MORISON, 1924-
The Man Who Had Everything (New American Library, 1964). A super-salesman, "who had everything," becomes a quadraplegic. His adjustment, and his wife's, to their new way of life make up the story. He had to learn the value inherent in having "a very little."

MYRER, ANTON, 1922-
The Intruder; a Novel of Boston (Little, 1965). A proper Bostonian through a series of events including the rape of his wife and a confrontation with the rapist learns that there are human beings in Boston in addition to the old Brahmin class. An interesting presentation of the class system and the psychological conditioning of various strata of society.

NORRIS, FRANK, 1870-1902
McTeague: A Story of San Francisco (1899). A masterpiece of early American naturalism, interesting for its use of symbols to develop the thesis that greed ruins personality and character. Studies the degeneration of a stupid ex-dentist through unemployment, loveless wedlock, and insensate lust for gold.

O'HARA, JOHN, 1905-
Butterfield 8 (Harcourt, 1935). A very realistic tale of New York during the early 1930's, when speakeasies were in their last years. A bitter account of a young girl who led a rather fast life.

PARKER, DOROTHY, 1893-
Here Lies (Viking, 1939). A collection of two dozen skillful short stories, epigrammatic, with suggestive dialogue. Full of insight into modern urban types and social levels, and also into the human heart.

PAUL, LOUIS, 1891-
Breakdown (Crown, 1947). Story of a female alcoholic, finally cured by psychoanalysis and exposure to the group therapy of Alcoholics Anonymous.

PORTER, WILLIAM SYDNEY (O. HENRY, pseud.), 1862-1910
The Four Million (1906). Stories about New York's common people (a contrast to "the 400"). Twenty-five short stories, including many of O. Henry's best.

RICE, ELMER L., 1892-
Imperial City (Coward, 1937). A kaleidoscopic story of a New York financial family and the various people of all classes related to it through business, social circles, professional relations, and casual contacts. One of our finest books on the city.

RIESENBERG, FELIX, 1879-
East Side, West Side (Harcourt, 1927). A fine picture of New York City, of both its East and West sides after 1900. Story of a man who rises from the slums of the East Side, goes to Columbia, becomes a civil engineer, and cracks the West Side.

ROSENBERG, ETHEL, 1915-
Go Fight City Hall (Simon, 1949). A humorous novel of Brooklyn, showing the provincial customs of a subregion with characters restricted by place and by their cultural and ethnic backgrounds. Centers on a Jewish family. Excellent for speech and dialect.

ROTH, HENRY, 1906-
Call It Sleep (1934; republished by Pageant Books, 1960). A sensitive story of a boy (from age six to eight) in an immigrant family in the slums of New York, early in the twentieth century.

RUBINS, HAROLD (HAROLD ROBBINS, pseud.), 1912-
79 Park Avenue (Knopf, 1955). A literary case history of a prostitute and madam that dramatizes the call-girl racket in New York City and shows its tie-in with the police and the gangsters.

RUSSELL, RUTH
Lake Front (Rockwell, 1931). Traces an Irish family from its arrival

in Chicago in 1835 through the presidential campaign of 1840, the Civil War, the Haymarket riots, the railway strike of 1894.

SALINGER, J. D., 1919-
Catcher in the Rye (Little, 1951). An adroit study of shams in school and society as seen by a perceptive adolescent boy who is fiercely honest in his hate for phonies. Notable for the idiomatic style of the narrator.

SCHULBERG, BUDD, 1915-
What Makes Sammy Run? (Random, 1941). A sharp, realistic picture of many-sided Hollywood, focused on a Jew who rises from childhood in a New York slum to power and prominence as a movie producer.

SCOTT, NATALIE ANDERSON, 1900-
Story of Mrs. Murphy (Dutton, 1947). Story of a man "married to booze." A study of the folkways of modern city life.

SHULMAN, IRVING, 1913-
Velvet Knife (Doubleday, 1959). An exposé of the way things are done in Hollywood. Everyone practices selfishness at high speed. An oft-repeated theme, but better done than most.

SLADE, CAROLINE, 1886-
Sterile Sun (Vanguard, 1936). Story of the economic conditions that forced four young New York girls into becoming prostitutes.
Margaret (Vanguard, 1946). The story of a sixteen-year-old delinquent girl, whose mainsprings of action were fear, hatred, and greed. Society, which has failed to reach her through church or school, fails also in its repair services, leaving nothing for Margaret but an institution.

SLESINGER, TESS, 1905-
The Unpossessed (Simon, 1934). A group of short stories, loosely connected, about the life of a group living in Greenwich Village: a novelist, a weary radical, a society matron who is a little too romantic, etc.

SMITH, BETTY, 1904-
A Tree Grows in Brooklyn (Harper, 1943). Portrays the varied life among the Irish and others in Williamsburg, Brooklyn, in the years leading up to World War I. The pain and poetry of tenement life as seen by an adolescent girl.

STREETER, EDWARD, 1891-
Daily Except Sundays (Simon, 1938). A light satire on the modern suburban commuter. Full of sharp observations.

VIDAL, GORE, 1925-
The City and the Pillar Revised (Dutton, 1965). A changed but not improved version of the 1948 story of a tennis-playing homosexual in Hollywood, New York, and elsewhere, often in luxurious surroundings.

By intent a thesis novel about "normality." Appends an essay, "Sex and the Law."

WALLOP, DOUGLASS, 1920-
Ocean Front (Norton, 1962). A first-class psychological study of a man whose wife was raped and who is pursued by the feeling that he should have done more to protect her. The analysis comprehends a study of the environmental conditioning of the man and the very different conditioning of his father-in-law. An excellent presentation.

WARNER, CHARLES D., 1829-1900
A Little Journey in the World (1889). Of the spiritual disintegration of a girl who marries a financier.
The Golden House (1894). Of the complexity and heartlessness of city life, the financial ruin of some characters and the villainy of others. Continues *A Little Journey in the World*.
That Fortune (1899). The main characters of *The Golden House* are in conflict with the next generation.

WAUGH, EVELYN, 1903-1966
The Loved One (Little, 1948). Satirizes the American standard of dying, specifically, the prolific—and profitable—funeral business in metropolitan Los Angeles.

WEIDMAN, JEROME, 1913-
I'll Never Go There Any More (Simon, 1941). A young man from Albany goes to New York City, where he lives among some very undesirable people from whom he finally escapes to return to Albany. Good character delineation.
Word of Mouth (Random, 1964). In collaboration with a group of theatrical people, a prominent lawyer delves into the past to find the true story of his father, who left the United States in disgrace. In the process he is forced to reconsider his own past and his responsibility for the death of his stepmother and his father. Excellent plot and presentation.

WELLMAN, PAUL ISELIN, 1898-
Jericho's Daughters (Doubleday, 1956). A novel set in a small Kansas city in mid-twentieth century. The folkways are those of city dwellers in any part of the country, with only faint echoes of a more Puritanic past. Competent writing.

WEST, NATHANAEL
The Day of the Locust (Random, 1939). A sensational picture of the lunatic fringe in Hollywood. A psychological study of suppressed violence and spiritual emptiness.

WILSON, EDMUND, 1895-
Memoirs of Hecate County (Doubleday, 1946). Six stories, mostly about sophisticated business and artistic people, in New York City and

the rich rural suburbs. Notable for "The Princess with the Golden Hair," which contrasts rich and poor, and "The Milhollands and Their Damned Soul," which satirizes the literary racket. Time: the 1920's and '30's. Excellent realism on sexual folkways.

ZARA, LOUIS, 1910-
Dark Rider (World, 1961). A 500-page novel based on the life of Stephen Crane. Emphasis is placed on the restrictions of his early life, on his various liaisons with women, and on his relationships with other writers of his time.

4. THE LEISURE CLASS

The novel of the social climber and the novel of the idle rich have both been prominent and persistent since the 1880's. Among the earliest books of this type are William Dean Howells' *A Hazard of New Fortunes* and Henry James's *The American.* . The most popular writers about society folk at the turn of the century were Gertrude Atherton and David G. Phillips. Since that time Edith Wharton, Booth Tarkington, F. Scott Fitzgerald, and later J. P. Marquand, Paul Horgan, and Helen Huntington Howe have been among the most popular, with a host of younger writers making their contributions since the late 1920's. The prevailing tone of most of this writing is satiric. The settings of many of these stories are in other countries, as Americans with money travel about.

ATHERTON, GERTRUDE, 1857-1948
Aristocrats (Lane, 1901). Satirizes the affectations of the overrefined, emasculated, "most exclusive" American society.

AUCHINCLOSS, LOUIS STANTON, 1917-
House of Five Talents (Houghton, 1960). A glimpse of the lives of four generations of a family that became wealthy in the Gilded Age. Emphasis on the women of the family, their intrigues and pretensions.

BASSO, HAMILTON, 1904-1964
In Their Own Image (Scribner's, 1935). Story of the effect of a textile strike and the death of a worker on a group of social and superficial individuals vacationing in the neighboring winter resort. Gives a good insight into the lives of the bored and idle rich.

BEER, THOMAS, 1889-1940
Sandoval: A Romance of Bad Manners (Knopf, 1924). Covers a few days in the life of a seventeen-year-old son of a Civil War profiteer. New York in the 1870's.

BRACE, GERALD WARNER, 1901-
The Garretson Chronicle (Norton, 1947). Often reading like an autobiography, this traces the conflict in ideas through three generations

of a Massachusetts family, from the Victorian period to the 1940's. Shows in clear portraits the admirable—and the stuffy—in the Brahmin.

BURT, MAXWELL STRUTHERS, 1882-1954

The Diary of a Dude Wrangler (Scribner's, 1938). About the wealthy and fashionable who disport themselves on a Wyoming "guest" ranch.
Along These Streets (Scribner's, 1942). A slow-paced but amply filled novel of the life of the well-bred (and well-heeled) society folk in Philadelphia. Excellent reporting on kindly and brainless aristocrats—noble traditions, wasted opportunities, clubs, cuisines.

CATHER, WILLA SIBERT, 1876-1947

A Lost Lady (Knopf, 1923). A lady lost between the nineteenth century and its values and the hurly-burly and changing modes of the twentieth century. In an age when woman's life consisted of dependence on man, she would have been a lady; in the twentieth century, she was scarcely that.

CHURCHILL, WINSTON, 1871-1947

A Modern Chronicle (1910). Dealing with marriage and divorce. Reflects our changing social pattern.

CONNELL, EVAN S., 1924-

Mrs. Bridge (Viking, 1959). Mrs. Bridge, a female Babbitt, leads a singularly unproductive life, in rather complete unawareness of many things that go on around her. Her name is somewhat symbolic of her nature. One wonders if she ever won a game. The reader is glad as her children escape one by one.

DAVENPORT, MARCIA (GLUCK), 1903-

Constant Image (Scribner's, 1960). An American divorcée carries on a lively love affair with a married Italian businessman. Although it was the one great (!) love affair for each, he follows European custom and stays with his family. Some play on the idea that Americans fail to see the splendor of such extra-marital affairs.

FINLETTER, GRETCHEN

The Dinner Party (From the Journal of a Lady of Today) (Harper, 1955). A light, clever treatment of parties, home decoration, socialite visits to army bases, official decorum, child rearing, and so on.

FITZGERALD, F. SCOTT, 1896-1940

Flappers and Philosophers (Scribner's, 1920). Eight stories of socialites, who range from small-town elite to yacht-owning millionaires. Clever tales of the early Jazz Age.
This Side of Paradise (Scribner's, 1920). A picture of well-to-do youth before and after World War I. Shows sensitive and intelligent young people reacting to new sex customs, new literary ideas, and prosperity. A sensation in its day, the book now seems both "dated" in content and inexpert in construction.

The Beautiful and Damned (Scribner's, 1922). Of an aristocratic, subsidized, Harvard graduate and his beautiful wife, before, during, and after World War I. A readable picture of high life in the early Jazz Age.

Tales of the Jazz Age (Scribner's, 1922). A group of eleven stories ranging from broad burlesque to somber tragedy.

The Great Gatsby (Scribner's, 1925). A polished Fitzgerald story about love and bootlegging in fashionable Long Island society.

Tender Is the Night (Scribner's, 1934). Of wealthy, sophisticated Americans in Paris, in Swiss towns, and especially on the French Riviera. A story of progressive despair and psychological deterioration. Fitzgerald's revision, with the chapters rearranged, appeared in 1951.

FOSTER, HANNAH WEBSTER, 1759-1840

The Coquette, or, the History of Eliza Wharton (1797; Columbia University, 1939). A dramatic narrative, "founded on Fact," of the seduction of a gay, "volatile," well-bred young woman of good family. Intended as a warning to virtuous young ladies, the book is also a mirror of eighteenth-century notions of the conflict between sensibility and passion.

GRANT, ROBERT, 1852-1914

Unleavened Bread (Scribner's, 1900). The story of a social climber and her three marriages in attempts to reach "high society."

GRONDAHL, KATHRYN

The Mango Season (Morrow, 1954). Of American diplomatic representatives and their wives in Bangkok, Thailand, showing them more interested in their personal relationships, intrigue, and leisure-time activities than in serving the U.S.A.

HAM, ROSWELL GRAY

A Peak in Darien (Putnam, 1960). Of the love of a middle-aged widower and his twenty-two-year-old neighbor and the messy lives of her parents and other neighbors. Carries on the pattern of the country-club set.

HERGESHEIMER, JOSEPH, 1880-1954

Tropical Winter (Knopf, 1933). A collection of ten short stories about the inhabitants of an exclusive winter colony near Palm Beach. Tells what these people--whose only reason for living is their immense wealth--do, say, drink, wear, and think.

HORGAN, PAUL, 1903-

The Fault of Angels (Harper, 1933). Social comedy of a wealthy American and the community he endowed with an opera, a symphony orchestra, and a school of music.

No Quarter Given (Harper, 1935). Social satire on the sophisticates of Santa Fe, New Mexico.

Give Me Possession (Straus, 1957). A young man from a wealthy family in San Francisco grows up in the 1930's believing that he is above ethics and ordinary human emotions. The war and a bit of suffering bring him around to more satisfactory attitudes.

HOWE, HELEN HUNTINGTON, 1905-

We Happy Few (Simon, 1946). A satire on the cultivated upper ranks of society in Cambridge, Massachusetts. Cruelly dissects the nature of a sophisticated woman and also the conversation of Harvard literary coteries.

The Success (Simon, 1956). The major character, a woman, climbs to success in the radio-TV world, succeeding in making two husbands and her daughter miserable in the process. Glimpses of the social set in Boston, New York, and Hollywood.

The Adversary (Random, 1957). A novel of leisure people living or visiting in a small village in southern California. These characters break the pattern of the usual "leisure class" novel by doing some serious thinking about their personal responsibilities.

Fires of Autumn (Harper, 1959). A middle-aged woman, contemplating separation from her husband, learns much from "the summer ladies" in a small town in Maine. In particular, she comes to understand the facts about the relationship between her husband and his first wife and consequently to understand her own situation.

HOWELLS, WILLIAM DEAN, 1837-1920

A Hazard of New Fortunes (1890). A social-climber novel in which a couple come to New York and rise steadily in society.

ISHERWOOD, CHRISTOPHER, 1904-

The World in the Evening (Random, 1952). Glibly told story of a man who associated closely with homosexuals without becoming one (or did he?). He marries a woman twelve years older than himself. After her death, he marries a younger woman—and is soon divorced. The novel consists mainly of his speculations and thoughts while waiting for the divorce.

JAMES, HENRY, 1843-1916

The American (1877). A self-made American goes to Europe to enjoy his wealth and to essay entrance into the upper stratum of French society.

Daisy Miller: A Comedy (1878). The story of an American girl who scandalizes Rome society by her defiance of conventions.

The Portrait of a Lady (1881). A subtle psychological novel of an American girl being wooed among the elite of international society. Scene laid mostly in Europe. An artistic masterpiece but for most persons quite slow reading.

Washington Square (1881). Of a fortune hunter in wealthy New York society. Artistic and ironical. By a very genteel realist.

The Ambassadors (1903). A careful, subtle, ironic, and convincing study of the interplay of American and French civilizations on the sensibilities of Massachusetts gentlemen, one young and one old, one more open to personal growth than the other, in a Parisian setting. A masterpiece of characterization and thematic development.

LA FARGE, CHRISTOPHER, 1897-1956
The Wilsons (Coward, 1941). A deft account of the rise of a pretty, semipoisonous, relentless social climber.

LINCOLN, VICTORIA, 1904-
Celia Amberley (Rinehart, 1949). Laid in a Rhode Island town and a women's college in Cambridge, this is a picture of a girl's growing up in the 1910's and 1920's—the development of her personality and her capacity for love.

MARQUAND, JOHN PHILLIPS, 1893-1960
The Late George Apley (Little, 1937). The story of a simon-pure Bostonian, from 1866 to 1933. Brings out in detail the code of family integrity, public responsibility, and so on, of the Beacon Hill aristocrat. Subtly ironical.
Wickford Point (Little, 1939). A family chronicle depicting a self-satisfied but inefficient family at Wickford Point, north of Boston.
H. M. Pulham, Esquire (Little, 1941). A humorous, satirical picture of present-day Boston, contrasting its prevailing folkways with those of New York.
So Little Time (Little, 1943). Clever writing of high society in America as the country drifted into the war against the Axis. Of a writer whose life was disrupted by World War I and whose son faces the same situation of "so little time." Biting, timely.

NIN, ANAÏS, 1903-
Ladders to Fire (Dutton, 1946). A strange psychological study of the "confused and twisted nature" of women in the artistic leisure class, in Hollywood, New York, and Paris. Poetizes the psychiatric data on sexual sophisticates.

O'HARA, JOHN, 1905-
Appointment in Samarra (Harcourt, 1934). Of a fast-moving, country-club set in a Pennsylvania town. A ruthless and sardonic presentation of social leaders.

PHILLIPS, DAVID G., 1867-1911
The Great God Success (1901). A realistic picture of the luxuries, follies, and sins of the upper class.
The Fashionable Adventures of Joshua Craig (1909). A blatant, self-made politician marries a refined lady of the highest Washington society. Realism in character drawing.

PINCKNEY, JOSEPHINE, 1895-
Three O'Clock Dinner (Viking, 1945). Built around the making and
breaking of a marriage between the scion of an old Charleston family
and the daughter of relative newcomers to South Carolina. Interesting
for contrasts of the old and new, for drama and wit, and for the careful
literary texture of the style.

RINEHART, MARY ROBERTS, 1876-1958
A Light in the Window (Rinehart, 1948). A chronicle of the events in
several generations of a wealthy and prominent family during the
years 1919-1945. Illuminates the publishing world, modern marriage,
the conflicts between conservatives and liberals, and the problems of
leading the good life.

STAFFORD, JEAN, 1915-
Boston Adventure (Harcourt, 1944). A psychological novel of Boston
bluebloods, their virtues and errors, as seen by the daughter of an immigrant. In the tradition of Marcel Proust, the book reads slowly like
an elaborate reminiscence.
The Catherine Wheel (Harcourt, 1952). Analytical study of a woman in
love with her friend's husband. She seems to think herself a martyr,
but to regret her martydrom at the last.

STEGNER, WALLACE EARLE, 1909-
A Shooting Star (Viking, 1961). An analytic story of a thirty-five-year-
old woman, bored with marriage and adventuring in the field of extra-
marital relations. The mores of her family, wealthy New Englanders
transplanted to California, cause her to become a somewhat snooty do-
gooder by the end of the story.

TARKINGTON, BOOTH, 1869-1946
Alice Adams (Doubleday, 1921). The unsuccessful "social climbing" of
a small-town American girl.
The Plutocrat (Doubleday, 1927). An American artist, very prissy,
goes to Europe and North Africa on a tour. He feels very superior to
a Midwest *nouveau riche* family on the same tour but ends by marry-
ing the daughter: Americans are alike after all, and different from
those "bad old Europeans."
The Heritage of Hatcher Ide (Doubleday, 1941). A comedy of manners
that shows a young man, his family, and their neighbors, all once well-
to-do, bungling through the maladjustments and disillusions of the
Great Depression and its aftermath.

VAN VECHTEN, CARL, 1880-1964
Peter Whiffle (Knopf, 1922). Biography in fiction of a versatile, restless, and curious boy born in Ohio in the 1880's. He travels to Paris
and amuses himself with his group of New York friends on the money
he inherits from his uncle. Mentions numerous literary personalities.

WHARTON, EDITH NEWBOLD (JONES), 1862-1937
The House of Mirth (1905). Of a woman who belongs to the leisure class in New York. Shows the emptiness of society life and the need for money to keep up appearances.
The Custom of the Country (1913). An account of a beautiful but unscrupulous social climber and her sequence of marriages.
The Age of Innocence (Appleton, 1920). New York society in the 1870's. A pale and restrained picture of an emotion-denying, code-bound elite.
Twilight Sleep (Appleton, 1927). New York's "fast set." The main character is a woman who follows an incessant routine of important trifles.
The Buccaneers (Appleton, 1938). A story of American families trying to "crash" society in New York and London.

WILLIAMS, WIRT, 1921-
A Passage of Hawks (McGraw, 1963). Laid in Mississippi in the 1950's, centering on a spoiled, promiscuous, rich woman, who owns a cotton farm and a husband, and on a ruthless gigolo blackmailer from New Orleans.

WINSLOW, ANNE GOODWIN, 1875-1959
The Springs (Knopf, 1949). The place is a resort hotel in the country near Memphis that draws planters from the Delta. The time is around 1900. The subject is the psychic growing-up of a lovely, literate girl. A quiet, subtle story of emotional coming-of-age.

WISTER, OWEN, 1860-1938
Lady Baltimore (1906). A sympathetic picture of the life of Charleston and its urbane society with roots deep in the past.

5. MODERN WAR

The Spanish-American War, World War I, and World War II, and subsequent military invasions in Asia and Latin America are so much a part of the modern industrial world that books about them appear here. Though novels about the Spanish-American War are scarce, there was a steady stream of fiction about World War I from 1917 to 1940. Few among the writers were apologists for entry into that war, or for the war itself. Many accepted Scott Nearing's definition, "war, organized destruction and mass murder by civilized nations." After V-E and V-J days, participants in World War II wrote a great many interpretations of their wartime and postwar experiences. Novels of recent was have followed the armed forces of the United States to outposts at many places in the world, including the slaughter grounds of Korea and Vietnam. More and more the bulk of war novels deviate from tales of actual combat to stories about other matters like mine sweeping, peacetime duty in Hawaii, or assignments to supply depots and airfields in Europe, North Africa, or the Middle East as part of the "defense system" against "aggressors."

ALLEN, HERVEY, 1889-1949
It Was Like This (Farrar, 1940). Two stark and realistic stories of World War I: "Report to Major Roberts" and "Blood Lust."

ANDERSON, THOMAS, 1929-
Your Own Beloved Sons (Random, 1956). About an artillery company trapped while on a dangerous mission during the Korean War. Excellent for reportage, characterization, and dialog.

APPEL, BENJAMIN, 1907-
Fortress in the Rice (Bobbs, 1951). Story of an American who is married to a Filipina wife and who joins the guerrilla forces in the Islands during World War II.

BEACH, EDWARD LATIMER, 1918-
Run Silent, Run Deep (Holt, 1955). Built around the anxiety and danger of four patrols of a submarine in the Pacific during World War II. Lacks psychological depth but is sturdy in plot and in reporting the details of work, life, and terror in a submarine.

BEKESSY, JEAN (HANS HABE, pseud.), 1911-
Off Limits (translated by Ewald Osers; Fell, 1956). Set in the U.S. zone of Western Germany, 1945-1951, and concerned with the interactions among Germans—pro- and anti-Hitler—and a variety of American soldiers and officers. By an informed "German" writer with a broad European and American background.

BELLAH, JAMES WARNER, 1899-
Ward Twenty (Doubleday, 1946). A frank and unexpurgated picture of "clipped" veterans (maimed ones and amputees) in a military hospital. Stresses their problem of social and sexual acceptance. Reproduces their language and records their acts. An indictment of our thinking on rehabilitation.

BINNS, ARCHIE, 1899-
The Laurels Are Cut Down (Reynal, 1937). Of two brothers sent to Russian Siberia after 1918. One is killed; one returns embittered to an America which seems to have lost its ideals.

BLACKER, IRWIN ROBERT
Kilroy Gambit (World, 1960). An independent government agency smuggles guns and supports guerrilla warfare in a foreign country. Parallels the American invasion of Cuba under President Kennedy and raises certain ethical questions.

BOWEN, ROBERT O., 1920-
The Weight of the Cross (Knopf, 1951). A highly personal story of a

man committed to the hospital as a psycho. He is captured by the Japanese and regains sanity and a satisfactory religion of his own as he helps take care of the helpless. Psychologically excellent. Well written.

BOYD, JAMES, 1888-1944
Roll River (Scribner's, 1935). Compares the 1914-1918 generation with the one immediately preceding it.

BOYD, THOMAS, 1898-1935
Through the Wheat (Scribner's, 1923). A realistic picture of war. Called the "least partisan and most brilliant of doughboy reminiscences." Very accurate day-by-day description of the way an average man, a very real character, takes part in a war.
Points of Honor (Scribner's, 1925). Eleven stories of American soldiers in France, showing how insufferable World War I appeared to the average man.

BOYDEN, FREDERICK, 1924-
The Hospital (Farrar, 1951). Vivid story of three disfigured airmen and their hospital life after the war. The various psychological effects of their situation are well handled.

BROWN, HARRY, 1917-
A Walk in the Sun (Knopf, 1944). A brief, poetic, evocative tale of the landing of one platoon on a dangerous Italian beachhead. Pictures ordinary privates in the presence of death.

BURNS, JOHN HORNE, 1916-1953
The Gallery (Harper, 1947). Reports on Italians and Americans in Naples and North Africa. A powerful and ruthlessly realistic version of hospitals, dives, hotels, city streets. A bitter novel of the conquerors and the conquered.

BUTTERFIELD, ROGER, 1907-
Al Schmid, Marine (Norton, 1944). The biography of a marine who fights at the battle of Tenaru. Almost completely blinded, he struggles for reintegration into the society he left.

CAMPBELL, WILLIAM E. MARCH, 1894-1954
Company K (Random, 1933). A unique story of one company. Short sketches of many individuals in the company, telling what happened to each and his reactions. Structure similar to that of Evelyn Scott's *The Wave*.
Some Like Them Short (Little, 1939). A collection of twenty short stories concerned chiefly with the experiences of the unhappy and unfortunate; expresses the author's hatred of war.

CARSE, ROBERT, 1903-
Deep Six (Morrow, 1946). An American vessel is sunk off the African coast, and the survivors are marched into the desert by a German-

commanded bank of Vichy French. The novel describes their experiences and those of a group that escape.

CATHER, WILLA SIBERT, 1876-1947
One of Ours (Knopf, 1922). A young man oppressed by the frustrations and restrictions of Nebraska farm life prefers the life of a soldier in France, where he dies, full of illusions. Like Edith Wharton's *A Son at the Front*, this presents an "old-fashioned" view of war, unlike that in Dos Passos, Hemingway, and others.

COCHRELL, BOYD
The Barren Beaches of Hell (Holt, 1959). A good straight narrative of a young Spokane man who enlists in the marines and endures the "realities" of Tarawa, Saipan, Tinian, Okinawa, and the landing in Nagasaki. Notably free of romantic or naturalistic formulas. Good also on United Service Organizations (USO) in the marine's home town.

COZZENS, JAMES GOULD, 1903-
Guard of Honor (Harcourt, 1948). Of World War II as it related to officers and their friends in an air training camp in Florida. A careful and intense picture of interrelationships, including a Negro officer. An analysis of forces at work in American society.

CRANE, STEPHEN, 1871-1900
Wounds in the Rain (1900). A collection of stories of the Spanish-American War.

CUMMINGS, E. E., 1894-1962
The Enormous Room (Boni, 1922). An excellently written narrative of a man held in a huge camp for those suspected of being spies and traitors. The prison was an "enormous room," the nave of an old church. Realistic and subtle analysis of a kind of Pilgrim's Progress through shock and horror.

DOS PASSOS, JOHN, 1896-
Three Soldiers (Doubleday, 1921). Gives the military history of three men of dissimilar backgrounds, from their days at training camp through to the end of fighting and to disillusionment. Told from the point of view of common soldiers and full of indignation and hatred toward army life and war.

EMPEY, ARTHUR GUY, 1883-
Over the Top (Putnam, 1917). Gives some of the details of war. Glorifies America's part.
Helluva War (Appleton, 1927). Light-headed novel of the war. Presents the slapstick-comedy antics of a brawny Irish-American private.

FAULKNER, WILLIAM, 1897-1962
Soldier's Pay (Boni, 1926). Of the homecoming of a mutilated soldier. How he was received by his father, his fiancée, and others.

FISHER, DOROTHY CANFIELD, 1879-1958
The Deepening Stream (Harcourt, 1930). About a woman and her husband doing war work in France.

FOX, PAUL
Four Men (Scribner's, 1946). Follows the destinies of four members of a submarine crew in World War I through the next quarter of a century. An illuminating commentary on American civilization.

FRANK, PAT, 1908-1964
Hold Back the Night (Lippincott, 1952). Well-written story of one company of marines as they fight on until cut down to a mere handful of men.
Alas, Babylon (Lippincott, 1959). A competent projection of present knowledge about nuclear warfare into a future in which most of the northern hemisphere is made uninhabitable. The setting is Georgia, with local customs adeptly used.

FRANKEL, ERNEST
Band of Brothers (Macmillan, 1958). About a company of marines during the retreat south from the Yalu River during the Korean War. A realistic, objective, honest account of the confusion and brutality of war and the ignorance of the men as to why they are fighting. Fine on the details of men facing danger and death.

GELLHORN, MARTHA, 1908-
The Wine of Astonishment (Scribner's, 1948). A strong novel about American infantrymen in the final winter of war, 1944-1945, in the campaigns from the Luxembourg border to Munich and eastward. Studies the effect of war on men's inner lives.

HAGEDORN, HERMANN, 1882-
The Rough Riders (Harper, 1927). Contains candid details of the mismanagement, disorder, and waste which characterized America's entrance into the struggle with Spain in 1898.

HAINES, WILLIAM WISTER, 1908-
Command Decision (Little, 1947). A fast-moving adventure story of World War II, of the struggle between the believers in red tape and the believers in "command decision." Points up the problems a brigadier general faces, including how to conduct operations so as to get good newspaper coverage.

HEINLEIN, ROBERT A., 1907-
Starship Troopers (Putnam, 1959). A specimen of militaristic science fiction: a tale of an infantryman in the twenty-second century during an "interstellar" war, in an era of no natural rights and of all duty to the state, with the franchise limited to discharged veterans. A book more important for ideas than for fantastic armaments. "War and moral perfection derive from the same genetic inheritance."

HEGGEN, THOMAS, 1919-1949
Mister Roberts (Houghton, 1946). Moving and hilarious sketches of life in the Pacific on a drab Navy cargo vessel that never sees action. Tales of young men who are victims of frustration, and particularly boredom—one of the chief conditions and horrors of war.

HELLER, JOSEPH
Catch-22 (Simon, 1961). Deals with fliers in World War II during the northward invasions of Italy and France. A light, garrulous satire on the military leaders of American civilization—on their regulations, wartime rituals, problems in communication, endless circular thinking, and their crazy ways in love and heroics. If a man flew missions he was loony and didn't have to, but it he didn't want to fly he was sane and had to.

HEMINGWAY, ERNEST, 1899-1961
In Our Time: Stories (Boni, 1925). Vivid vignettes of World War I and the later fighting between Greeks and Turks, together with early Hemingway stories of Nick Adams and others in Europe and Michigan, told in the early vigorous Hemingway realistic impressionism.
The Sun Also Rises (Scribner's, 1926). Of frustrated men and women, subsidized for carousing but poor in psychic resources, who drift about and drink in France and Spain. Subtly meaningful as a symbolic study of postwar society.
A Farewell to Arms (Scribner's, 1929). A notable love story set against a sharply realistic background of fighting and war tension in northern Italy. Centers on an American volunteer.

HERSEY, JOHN, 1914-
Into the Valley: A Skirmish of the Marines (Knopf, 1943). Vividly and tersely reports one small battle on Guadalcanal. Shows the reality of war at close quarters.
A Bell for Adano (Knopf, 1944). A journalistic sketch of the important work of Allied Military Government in occupied territory. Set in an Italian town, the story shows the problems faced by both American officials and native Italians as the idea is applied that government is the servant—not the master—of the people.
The War Lover (Knopf, 1959). A psychological analysis of a man devoted to the business of death who is a hero because he wants death for himself and others. He is a contrast to the man who hates war but fights because he loves life and its values, which presumably the war preserves. An awkward plot.

HETH, EDWARD HARRIS, 1909-
Told with a Drum (Harper, 1945). A story of the effect of World War I on the mayor of a German-American city. Pathetic and appealing.

ILYIN, BORIS
Green Boundary (Houghton, 1949). Love story of a Russian-American

and a Russian girl during the cold war. Explores mental attitudes of displaced persons and escapees from Russia.

JONES, JAMES, 1921-
From Here to Eternity (Scribner's, 1951). A long account for the non-squeamish about empty living—Army life, Army love-life—at Pearl Harbor in the months leading up to the bombing in 1941.
The Pistol (Scribner's, 1958). A short yarn about gun fetishism in the regular Army just after the bombing of Pearl Harbor, among a guard detachment in the mountains. A morality on what men will do to be safe or to have the illusion of safety.

LEE, MARY, 1891-
It's a Great War (Houghton, 1929). Praised by Löhrke in *Armageddon* as one of the two best war novels written in America in the 1920's, the other being Dos Passos' *Three Soldiers*. From the standpoint of an American Y.M.C.A. hostess. Realistic and interesting.

LOWRY, ROBERT JAMES, 1919-
Casualty (New Directions, 1946). A story of savage boredom and the mean injustices suffered by men in a photo reconnaissance wing stationed in an Italian town. A bitter indictment of officers.

MAILER, NORMAN, 1923-
The Naked and the Dead (Rinehart, 1948). Of the capture of a Japanese island in the Pacific by amphibious assault and jungle fighting. Studies the relationship of the individual soldier within the Army organization, shows what the act of fighting does to character, and explores the forces and philosophies that create men's fates.

MATTHEWS, ALLEN R.
The Assault (Simon, 1947). By one of three survivors of a thirteen-man squad during the first twelve days of assault on Iwo Jima, this is an account of the marines in a war of attrition. A picture not of highly mechanized war but of close personal fighting with rifle, machine gun, and hand grenade. Painfully authentic details of the "desperate little confusions" of war. The author says he finds combat to be "completely unglamorous, a foul business full of fear and loneliness, and misery."

MERRICK, GORDON
The Strumpet Wind (Morrow, 1947). A story of World War II during the invasion of southern France. About an Intelligence officer who is spying on Vichyite activities. A competent treatment of sensitive, idealistic men drafted into the business of killing.

MICHENER, JAMES A., 1907-
Tales of the South Pacific (Macmillan, 1947). Nineteen stories of a trouble shooter in aviation maintenance on atolls and islands. Shows nurses, Seabees, Marines acutely and adroitly.

The Bridges at Toko-ri (Random, 1952). Well-told action story about the bombing of the bridges. Good psychological handling of character.

MILLER, MERLE, 1918-
That Winter (Sloane, 1948). A skillful, honest account of combat soldiers, their social and personal adjustments. In the background is a magazine organization similar to that of *Time*. In the foreground are credible people. A novel with both artistic skill and important contents.
Reunion (Viking, 1954). Eight members of an army company hold a reunion eight years after World War II. A picture of after-the-war effects of war on each, as well as analysis of present-day society.

MORRIS, EDITA, 1902-
The Flowers of Hiroshima (Viking, 1959). A simply told and deeply moving story of a young American who lives with a Japanese family in Hiroshima in the 1950's and gradually comes to see the lasting and terrible effects of the bomb on the lives of people.

MURPHY, DENIS, 1933(?)-
The Sergeant (Viking, 1958). Goes into the personal lives of men, especially the life of a master sergeant, stationed at a dull petroleum depot near Bordeaux, seven years after World War II. Clear, controlled writing.

NABLO, JAMES BENSON, 1910-
The Long November (Dutton, 1946). A grim, realistic portrayal of what a private thought as he lay wounded in an Italian house. Traces his life of hard work and disillusion in Illinois and Canada, and the realizations and convictions he gained during the war.

NASON, LEONARD H., 1895-
Chevrons (Doran, 1926). A clear picture of World War I—battles, states of mind of the soldiers, etc. Written in an amusing, familiar style.
A Corporal Once (Doubleday, 1930). A colorful and lively study of a representative American doughboy in the trenches. Little of the glamor of war; only the experiences of boys behind the line.
The Fighting Livingstons (Doubleday, 1931). About two brothers' activities at the front. The one wishing action is sent to a French instruction camp; the other, who joined the militia to dodge the draft, is called on for active service at once.

NEWHOUSE, EDWARD, 1912-
The Iron Chain (Harcourt, 1946). Contains twenty-one short stories, most of them about the iron chain of circumstances in modern war. Sad, ironic, artistic accounting of what war does to civilians and also to the professionals in disaster.

ROSHWALD, MORDECAI, 1921-
Level 7 (McGraw, 1959). A science fantasy on push-button atomic
soldiers 4,000 feet underground before the last of wars, during
the few minutes of bombing, and during the weeks of survival until the
last of men is dying. Good on the details planned—in vain—for human
survival underground for 500 years.

ROSS, JAMES E.
The Dead are Mine (McKay, 1963). An infantryman's view of the Allied landings at Anzio behind the German lines. Straight, simple,
soldierly realism about patrols, fights, killings, bombings, and the
motives and behavior of GI's.

SCANLON, W. T.
God Have Mercy on Us (Houghton, 1929). Story of the part the submarine played in adding to the horror of World War I. Presents the
psychology of a good soldier getting pleasure in serving.

SINCLAIR, UPTON B., 1878-
100%: The Story of a Patriot (Regan, 1920). Of a man who becomes a
spy upon Communist and Socialist groups during World War I. The
Mooney case is part of the background.
Between Two Worlds (Viking, 1941). Continues *World's End*. Starts
with the Treaty of Versailles and ends with the crash of 1929. A long,
comprehensive study of the period. Vigorous and dramatic and fair,
despite socialistic zeal.
Dragon's Teeth (Viking, 1942). Third novel in the series, this covers
the years 1930-1934. Combines journalism and history to cover in
story form the background of Hitlerism. In terms of Lanny Budd and
the other characters, presents national attitudes, class attitudes, and
personal attitudes toward world-shaking events.
Wide is the Gate (Viking, 1943). Continues the *World's End* series,
with Lanny Budd engaging in anti-Nazi activities during the beginning
of the Popular Front and through part of the Spanish Civil War. A
stirring, adventurous novel enriched (or slowed up) by editorializing
and social philosophy. An unquestionably honest book.
Dragon Harvest (Viking, 1945). Lanny Budd marches on through European history from Munich to the fall of Paris, while an apprehensive
world watches Europe yield to the German war machine.

STALLINGS, LAWRENCE, 1894-
Plumes (Harcourt, 1924). The story of a family who have fought in all
the American wars. The hero departs from family tradition in his revolt against the pseudo-patriotism rampant in postwar America.

STEVENS, JAMES, 1892-
Mattock (Knopf, 1927). A clever satire about a soldier who wanted to
remain a "Christian American gentleman" but fell from grace in

France. Upon his return to Kansas, he embraces the Klan, marries the deacon's daughter, and again becomes pure.

THOMASON, JOHN WILLIAM, 1893-1944
Fix Bayonets (Scribner's, 1926). An account of the actual fighting man in World War I. Shows how wars can make brutes of the best of men. *A Few Marines* (Scribner's, 1943). A Kiplingesque collection of Thomason's stories from World War I to 1939.

TOWNER, WESLEY, 1907-
The Liberators (Wyn, 1946). Shows what happens when American occupational forces move in on a small German city. Shows human frailty triumphing over the effort "to punish constructively." Important for contents rather than artistry.

TRUMBO, DALTON, 1905-
Johnny Got His Gun (Lippincott, 1939). Vivid story of a boy who lost his sight and hearing and his limbs in the war, and who lies in bed and thinks over the events of his life.

WHARTON, EDITH NEWBOLD (JONES), 1862-1937
A Son at the Front (Scribner's, 1923). Told from the point of view of those at home and written for the parents of American boys who died at the front. Though the picture of wartime Paris has validity, the version of the fighting front is wishfully false, as is evidenced by the novels of American ex-soldiers or the British "Private 19022" (Frederick Manning) in *Her Privates We* (Putnam, 1930).

WILLIAMS, WIRT, 1921-
The Enemy (Houghton, 1951). A simple, unadorned account of the work duties and emergencies aboard a ship that is part of a carrier-destroyer group looking for submarines in the Atlantic in 1943, between Norfolk and Casablanca. Details of zigzagging to avoid German subs and of dropping depth charges during the long hunt for an enemy never seen and perhaps never destroyed.

POLITICS AND INSTITUTIONS

Fiction dealing with politics in the United States has appeared off and on throughout the life of the Republic. Most of the writers have been idealists, believers in republican and democratic forms, in "the American dream" and in the Bill of Rights. They have supported the cause of the common man in his rightful search for security, happiness, and self-respect. Their writing, aside from that on the Revolution and the Civil War, has tended to expose or satirize conditions that abuse the average citizen and corrupt his political life. The ideals of the writers, then, have often been indirectly expressed in protest against unintelligent democracy, "practical politics," or minority control of government.

Subjects widely treated in the nineteenth century were Jacksonian democracy, the abolition movement, the Civil War, and Reconstruction.

The Progressive Era, 1901-1917, produced a large school of writers about politics, who wrote of the proposed or attempted reforms of the period and of the colorful political leaders and their followers, and who raked the mud of corruption. The decades since 1920 have produced a miscellaneous crop of satires, realistic studies, and historical re-examinations of the "founding fathers" and their era. A number of novelists have shown concern over the rise of native Fascists.

In this section we also include books about hospitals, schools, and other institutions dealing with segments of the general public.

1. COLONIAL AND REVOLUTIONARY AFFAIRS

The Revolution has been abundantly used in fiction for a century and a half. Almost always, until the mid-1920's, the treatment was heroic and romantic. Since then the tendency is toward researched realism, as in the work of James Boyd and Kenneth Roberts. Increasingly, too, novelists have shown that there is a case for the Tories and the English.

In addition to the Revolution, early frontier democracy and the Hamilton-Jefferson controversies have been standard subjects.

ATHERTON, GERTRUDE, 1857-1948
The Conqueror (1902). A fictionalized biography, one of the first of its type, glorifying Alexander Hamilton.

BELLAMY, EDWARD, 1850-1898
The Duke of Stockbridge (1879, 1900). A fictionalized account of Dan Shays' Rebellion, an uprising of oppressed farmers in Massachusetts, in 1786, against unbearable taxes and inadequate justice.

BOYD, JAMES, 1888-1944
Drums (Scribner's, 1926). An epoch-making book, breaking the steady

tradition of romantic treatment of the Revolution. Makes people and events real. Shows that the Revolution was an economic civil war.

BRACKENRIDGE, HUGH H., 1748-1816
Modern Chivalry (1792, 1815). A rollicking but wordy satire on the overexuberant democracy of the frontier in western Pennsylvania.

BRICK, JOHN
The Raid (Farrar, 1951). Vivid well-told story of one pioneer and his wife, and his adventures in helping to fight Butler's Rangers.
The King's Rangers (Doubleday, 1954). The usual old-fashioned treatment of the Revolution, but in this one the heroes are Loyalists, including Walter Butler.
The Strong Men (Doubleday, 1959). About men enduring the winter of 1777-1778 at Valley Forge. Well researched, with a seven-page bibliography.

CHURCHILL, WINSTON, 1871-1947
Richard Carvel (1889). A stereotyped romance, very popular in the early 1900's, against the background of society in eighteenth-century Maryland and London. Introduces Charles Fox and John Paul Jones.
The Crossing (1904). Of the conquest of the Northwest Territory by George Rogers Clark and his band, in an early extension westward of "manifest destiny." The plot is old-fashioned.

COOPER, JAMES FENIMORE, 1789-1851
The Spy (1821). A romantic tale of a patriotic peddler who masquerades as a British agent in order to get information for the Revolutionary cause. A fairly good portrait of Washington himself, and realistic hints as to the political struggle between rebels and Tories. This book established the formula for treatment of the Revolution.
The Pilot (1823). Contains stilted Cooper love scenes, also a narrative of adventure on a frigate. The mysterious pilot is John Paul Jones.

DEGENHARD, WILLIAM
The Regulators (Dial, 1943). Of Shays' Rebellion in Massachusetts in 1786 and its political significance.

EDMONDS, WALTER DUMAUX, 1903-
Drums Along the Mohawk (Little, 1936). See above, p. 24.

FAST, HOWARD MELVIN, 1914-
Conceived in Liberty (Simon, 1939). Realistic story of the Revolution, told from the viewpoint of a private from the Mohawk Valley, of the incredible hardships of the American army during the winter spent at Valley Forge.
The Unvanquished (Duell, 1942). A story of George Washington, covering the time from August 1776 to the defeat of the Hessians at Trenton on Christmas night. Good characterization.

Citizen Tom Paine (Duell, 1943). Vivid montage of scenes from the life of Tom Paine. A debatable interpretation of Paine's character.

The Proud and the Free (Blue Heron, 1950). Story of a Pennsylvania regiment in revolt against their officers. Good detail about men of various cultures working together in what was called a Foreign Regiment.

April Morning (Crown, 1961). A brief recounting of the Battle of Lexington.

FEUCHTWANGER, LION, 1884-1958

Proud Destiny (translated by Moray Firth; Viking, 1947). Unfolds a panorama of pre-Revolutionary France and the rebellious American colonies. A broad, flowing narrative dominated by such characters as Franklin, Beaumarchais, and Marie Antoinette.

FLETCHER, INGLIS, 1888-

Raleigh's Eden (Bobbs, 1940). A crowded, romantic novel of Revolutionary days in North Carolina. Gives a picture of Colonial society, plantation life, and—with some historical inaccuracies—the doings of such notables as Nathanael Greene and Lord Cornwallis.

Toil of the Brave (Bobbs, 1946). Set in the Albemarle district of North Carolina. Begins with the spring of 1779 and comes to a climax with the Battle of King's Mountain. The hero is a staff officer in the Continental Line.

FORBES, ESTHER, 1894?-

Johnny Tremain (Houghton, 1943). Boston at the outbreak of the Revolution. Of a teen-age boy who rode for the "Committee of Safety." Alive and realistic.

FORD, PAUL LEICESTER, 1865-1902

Janice Meredith (1899). A standard romance set against a realistic background of the times, making clear the selfish motivation of many American "patriots."

GESSNER, ROBERT, 1907-

Treason (Scribner's, 1944). A vigorous cynical novel about the American Revolution. Arnold's treason made understandable. Pointed and effective parallel to contemporary America.

GRAVES, ROBERT, 1895-

Sergeant Lamb's America (Random, 1940). Historical novel from the point of view of a British soldier who came here in 1776. A good picture of the British army and a commentary on the causes of the Revolution.

Proceed, Sergeant Lamb (Random, 1941). Sergeant Lamb, British soldier, escapes from prison camp, goes from New England to Virginia, and serves under Cornwallis.

HARRIS, CYRIL, 1891-
Trumpets at Dawn (Scribner's, 1938). Shows the conflicting loyalties of a New York family. Set during the American Revolution, demonstrates how it destroyed the old society, disrupted families, and changed conventions of the soldiers and the civilians. There is the conflict between the newer and poorer people and the older and wealthier families.

HERGESHEIMER, JOSEPH, 1880-1954
Balisand (Knopf, 1924). A vivid story of Federalists fighting Jefferson's new Democratic-Republican party.

HOUGH, FRANK OLNEY, 1899-
Renown (Carrick, 1938). A sympathetic picture of Benedict Arnold is given in this fictionalized story of his career.
If Not Victory (Carrick, 1939). Psychological study of a farm boy in the Hudson Valley campaigns of the Revolution.
The Neutral Ground (Lippincott, 1941). A nonpartisan narrative of the events of the war in Westchester County, New York. An exciting plot.

JOHNSTON, MARY, 1870-1936
Lewis Rand (Houghton, 1908). A vivid and entertaining narrative of Jefferson's time, involving Aaron Burr as a character.

KARIG, WALTER, 1898-   , and BIRD, HORACE
Don't Tread on Me (Rinehart, 1954). An old-type, swashbuckling-hero-type story about the Revolution, capably written.

KENNEDY, JOHN P., 1795-1870
Horseshoe Robinson (1837). A romantic tale of bravery and patriotism in the Southern forests. One of the most popular of the early treatments.

LANCASTER, BRUCE, 1896-1963
Guns of Burgoyne (Stokes, 1939). Deals with the expedition and defeat of Burgoyne's expedition at Saratoga from the viewpoint of a Hessian officer of the English army. The story is an old formula, but the history is fresh and vigorous.

MASON, F. VAN WYCK, 1897-
Three Harbours (Lippincott, 1938). A study of confusion and conflicting interests before the American Revolution in 1774-1775. Set in Norfolk, Virginia, Boston, Bermuda, and a few other places. Concerned with seacoast merchants.
Stars on the Sea (Lippincott, 1940). A romantic tale of privateering during the American Revolution. Set in Rhode Island, South Carolina, and the Bahamas.
Rivers of Glory (Lippincott, 1942). Of events of the fourth and fifth years of the Revolution, occurring on the Hudson, Montego, and Savannah rivers. A competent brew of romance and historic realism.

MELVILLE, HERMAN, 1819-1891

Israel Potter (1855). Fictionalized biography of a Revolutionary soldier. Much adventure. Enlivened scenes with Franklin, Ethan Allen, and John Paul Jones. Good realistic scenes.

MITCHELL, SILAS WEIR, 1829-1914

Hugh Wynne, Free Quaker (1897). A fairly realistic story of the events of the Revolution in and about Philadelphia. Several strong characters, and considerable drama.

The Red City: A Novel of the Second Administration of President Washington (1907). A skillful dramatization of the English and French factions in political conflict during Washington's administration. A good portrait of Washington and some of the life in the Philadelphia of that time.

MORROW, HONORÉ WILLSIE, 1880?-1940

Let the King Beware (Morrow, 1936). The hero of the story is a Massachusetts Tory who returns to England because he cannot agree with the Revolution. He gains entrance to court, where he becomes the King's trusted friend. Presents a fresh interpretation of the character of George III. Gives the views of Franklin, Burke, Penn, and Lord North.

PAGE, ELIZABETH, 1889-

The Tree of Liberty (Farrar, 1939). A story of the planting and the growing of the American tree of liberty from 1750 to 1800. Contrasts Hamilton, who had no faith in the people, and Jefferson, who knew and understood the role of the masses and fought for the establishment of American democracy. Better history than fiction.

RADDALL, THOMAS HEAD, 1903-

His Majesty's Yankees (Doubleday, 1942). A carefully prepared novel, laid in Nova Scotia and New Brunswick, and dealing with the repercussions there of the struggle of American armies against the Crown. Shows that the revolution of common people in northeastern Canada against repressive authorities in Halifax became a war "of lost opportunities," the losers fleeing to New England.

ROBERTS, KENNETH L., 1885-1957

Arundel (Doubleday, 1933). A realistic and convincing reconstruction of Benedict Arnold's march on Quebec.

Rabble in Arms (Doubleday, 1933). Sequel to *Arundel*. Here Roberts continues his story of the American Revolution and of Benedict Arnold, who the author feels was misjudged. A fine account of the country and the atmosphere of the time with some fine descriptions of the Indian and navigation.

Oliver Wiswell (Doubleday, 1940). A historical novel of the Revolution as seen through the eyes of a colonel who is loyal to the Crown.

Presenting "the other side" of the story of the Revolution, showing that the revolutionaries were not always angels. Informative and challenging. *Lydia Bailey* (Doubleday, 1947). A romantic, historical novel of troubled Haiti under Toussaint L'Ouverture and of the "war" between the United States and the pirates of Tripoli. An example of popular story telling based on original, scholarly research.

SANDBURG, CARL, 1879-
Remembrance Rock (Harcourt, 1948). A bulky novel, really three novels in one, that sweeps from early Puritan days to the Civil War. A multitudinous historical pageant, strong in reiterating humane ideals.

SCRUGGS, PHILIP LIGHTFOOT, 1898-
Man Cannot Tell (Bobbs, 1942). A clear picture of Bacon's Rebellion and the causes leading thereto.

SHAFER, DONALD C., 1881-
Smokefires in Schoharie (Longmans, 1938). Fictionalized, exciting history of the border wars in New York during the Revolution. Friendly Indians as well as hostile ones.

SIMMS, WILLIAM GILMORE, 1806-1870
The Partisan (1835). A vigorous, old-fashioned tale narrating Gates's defeat at Camden and giving a picture of camp life in the Carolina swamps.
The Scout (1854). A tale of the rivalry of a Whig and a Tory, half-brothers, for the same girl, against the background of fighting in the South Carolina woods.
Woodcraft (1856). A realistic account of economic and political conditions near Charleston at the end of the war. Indicates that many common men gained nothing after undergoing the dangers of fighting.

STERNE, EMMA G., 1894-
Drums of Monmouth (Dodd, 1935). A story of the American Revolution set in New Jersey and New York and dealing with the role of the Huguenots, the Quakers, etc. Also includes some interesting comments on the role of the students at Princeton. The central character is Philip Freneau, the poet.

SWANSON, NEIL H., 1896-
The First Rebel (Farrar, 1937). Of unruly Scotch-Irish who came to Pennsylvania in the beginning of the eighteenth century and began to assert themselves before the time of the Revolution. Deals mostly with the years from 1763-1767.
The Silent Drum (Farrar, 1940). Deals with the first armed rebellion against the Crown at the time of the Stamp Act, ten years before the Revolution. Set in the backwoods of Pennsylvania and Maryland. Gives (a bit too lengthily) the conversation of the time.

THOMPSON, D. P., 1795-1868
The Green Mountain Boys (1839). One of the popular early treatments of the Revolution.

TURNBULL, AGNES SLIGH, 1888-
The Day Must Dawn (Macmillan, 1942). A light, cheerful portrayal of brave, solid people of Revolutionary days in a western Pennsylvania town. Full of movement and adventure.

VINING, ELIZABETH (GRAY), 1902-
The Virginia Exiles (Lippincott, 1955). Historical novel of a little-known Revolutionary War episode: the arrest, detention, and, upon their refusal to sign a loyalty oath, the banishment without trial of twenty Philadelphia Friends.

WEEMS, MASON LOCKE, 1759-1825
The Life of George Washington; with Curious Anecdotes, Equally Honourable to Himself and Exemplary to His Young Countrymen (Belknap, 1962). Reprints with a scholarly introduction the "ninth edition. . . greatly improved" of 1809, famous for its fictitious anecdotes such as the cherry tree story and Washington's mother's prophetic dream.

WYCKOFF, NICHOLAS E., 1906-
The Braintree Mission: A Fictional Narrative of London and Boston, 1770-1771 (Macmillan, 1957). An "if" story built around the idea of what would have happened if England had tried to establish a North American peerage. Vivid glimpses of William Pitt, John and Abigail Adams, Josiah Quincy, and of the trial of soldiers involved in the Boston Massacre. Like a play in scene and organization, and admirably brief.

2. THE CIVIL WAR AND RECONSTRUCTION

Novels about the Civil War and Reconstruction, like those about the plantation, range from the sentimental to the realistic. The sentimental and romantic portrayal has been continuous since the war. J. W. De Forest's *Miss Ravenel's Conversion* excepted—for it was unpopular when written—increasingly realistic treatment of the war begins with Crane's *Red Badge of Courage*. The centennials of Civil War events, coming in an era of fact rather than fiction, produced much good historical writing but few novels of note.

ALLEN, HERVEY, 1889-1949
Action at Aquila (Farrar, 1938). A story of the Civil War told from the standpoint of a contemporary character, centering on the frustrations and chaos of the war.

BEARD, OLIVER THOMAS, 1832-
Bristling with Thorns (Detroit News Co., 1884). Some of the major

white characters in this lively story develop sympathy for the plight of the Negro and are working at the end to prove "there is something better than prejudice."

BILL, A. H., 1879-1964
The Beleaguered City (Knopf, 1946). Of Richmond during the years 1861-1865. Presents stereotyped Negroes and Virginia masters, and is concerned mostly with the well born, but does present the maladministration of affairs by the Confederacy.

BOYD, JAMES, 1888-1944
Marching On (Scribner's, 1927). Sturdy re-creation of history, despite a standard-type love plot. Recounts the war from the point of view of a yeoman-farmer's son who is held back socially and economically by the plantation system. One of our best Southern novels.

BRICK, JOHN
Troubled Spring (Farrar, 1950). A down-to-earth treatment of a triangle which develops when a woman marries the brother of her fiancé, who has been thought killed in the Civil War. The stay-at-home brother has developed a money-making craze contrary to his brother's ideals.
Jubilee (Doubleday, 1956). A strongly plotted story, centering on an officer trained at West Point. The author has a somewhat worshipful attitude toward the Northern armies and General William T. Sherman.

BRIER, ROYCE, 1896-
Boy in Blue (Appleton, 1937). Set in the Cumberland Valley. Climaxed in the Battle of Chickamauga. Story of an ordinary Union private, giving a picture of the actual men who fought the battles—their thoughts, emotions, and desires.

BRISTOW, GWEN, 1903-
The Handsome Road (Crowell, 1938). Continues the story of *Deep Summer*. In this book the family history is carried through Civil War times. Strong in traditional themes—the "lost state" of the gentleman class, the emergence of the poor white, the villainy of Yankees.
This Side of Glory (Crowell, 1940). Continues the story of *The Handsome Road*.

CHENEY, BRAINARD
Lightwood (Houghton, 1939). A novel of farmers in the pine barrens of southern Georgia and of the Yankee lumber company which evicts them from their lands during "Reconstruction days." Realistic and dramatic.

CHURCHILL, WINSTON, 1871-1947
The Crisis (1901). The Old South of Missouri and its defeat during the Civil War. Makes clear the part German immigrants played in saving the Union.

COOKE, JOHN ESTEN, 1830-1886
Surry of Eagle's Nest (1866). A pro-Southern account of the early campaigns in Virginia. Re-creations of Stonewall Jackson, Jeb Stuart, and other Confederate leaders. A liberal interpretation of McClellan. Interesting to read along with the nonfiction *I Rode with Stonewall* by H. K. Douglas (University of North Carolina, 1940).
Mohun: or the Last Days of Lee and His Paladins (1869). A rather realistic account of Richmond during the last days of the war, including sketches of unpatriotic blockade runners.

CRABB, ALFRED LELAND, 1884-
Supper at the Maxwell House (Bobbs, 1943). The characters of *Dinner at Belmont* struggle with the problems of Reconstruction and carpetbag rule. Effective romance.
Breakfast at the Hermitage (Bobbs, 1945). Of Tennessee after the war and a poor boy who realizes his life's ambition—to build beautiful houses.
Lodging at the Saint Cloud (Bobbs, 1946). Of Nashville harassed by the Yankees. A lively adventure story concerned with three daring young musketeers detached from the army of General Nathan Bedford Forrest and annoying the Union authorities.

CRANE, STEPHEN, 1871-1900
The Red Badge of Courage (1895). A sensitive account of the psychological effect of battle on a Northern boy. Often called the first realistic American war novel.
Twenty Stories (Knopf, 1940). Contains four of Crane's Civil War sketches—the same emphasis on the pictorial and on psychology as in *The Red Badge of Courage*.

DE FOREST, JOHN WILLIAM, 1826-1906
Miss Ravenel's Conversion from Secession to Loyalty (Harper, 1869, 1939). A vigorously realistic account of the war, honestly portraying the carnage of battle, political chicanery, and sexual immorality. The principal scenes are laid in Connecticut and Louisiana, which are effectively contrasted. Notable for the characterizations of Colonel Carter, a Virginian Loyalist, and Mrs. Larue, his Creole mistress.

DIXON, THOMAS, 1864-1946
The Leopard's Spots (1902). Violent pro-Southern and anti-Negro propaganda. A melodramatic tale of Reconstruction in South Carolina during the rule of "Black Republicans."
The Clansman (1905). An apology for the K.K.K. and an attack on Negroes. Important as the basis for David W. Griffith's famous motion picture, *The Birth of a Nation*.
The Traitor (1907). A sequel to *The Clansman*. Shows the dissolution of the Klan.
The Southerner (1913). Presents a wordy description of Abe Lincoln

and the antagonism toward him during the Civil War. The romantic interest is furnished by a woman who is loved by two brothers, one fighting for the North, the other loyal to the South.

DOWDEY, CLIFFORD, 1904-
Bugles Blow No More (Little, 1937). Richmond defends itself for years against the campaigns of McClellan and Grant, and finally falls, taking with it a way of life. Vividly impressionistic.

FAST, HOWARD MELVIN, 1914-
Freedom Road (Duell, 1944). An answer to Reverend Thomas Dixon's books, this is partisan historical fiction of Reconstruction. It gives an anti-Southern-white version of the South Carolina Constitutional Convention, post-bellum plantation life, and the Klan. A much less balanced view of Reconstruction than *Gone with the Wind*.

FOX, JOHN W., 1862-1919
The Little Shepherd of Kingdom Come (1903). Perhaps the most widely read love story of a mountain boy during the Civil War who proves himself to be just as good as "those down below"--a traditional theme.

GLASGOW, ELLEN, 1874-1945
The Voice of the People (1900). Life in Virginia during Reconstruction.
The Battle-Ground (1902). Shows how the Virginia plantation realized the "American dream" for the aristocratic owners, fostering love, gallantry, comfort. Pictures noncombatants during the war until the fall of Richmond.

HARRIS, JOEL CHANDLER, 1848-1908
Free Joe and Other Sketches (1887). Tales of Northerners and Georgians during and after the war.
Gabriel Tolliver: A Story of Reconstruction (1902). A reasonably dispassionate version, by a Southern writer, of the post-bellum South under military rule, and of the struggle for power between the Union League of the Freedman's Bureau on one side and the Klanlike Knights of the White Camellia on the other. Old-fashioned story telling, more like an essay than like the present-day historical novel.

HARRIS, L. F., 1922-   , and BEALS, F. L., 1881-
Look Away, Dixieland (Robert Speller, 1936). Study in Mississippi local color and problems during Reconstruction. The hero returns from the war to find his wife dead and his plantation wasting. It takes his daughter to make the necessary adjustments to the new industrial age.

JOHNSTON, MARY, 1870-1936
The Long Roll (1911). A vivid picture of the Civil War from a Virginian's point of view. Very careful sketches are given of Stonewall Jackson. Deals mostly with a Confederate captain who not only must

fight for the "cause" but also for the hand of the woman he loves. A fine picture of the Southerners during Reconstruction.

Cease Firing (1912). Picture of the hideous and inglorious side of the Civil War and of sacrificing individuals.

KANTOR, MacKINLAY, 1904-

Long Remember (Coward, 1934). The Battle of Gettysburg as seen by a resident pacifist.

Arouse and Beware (Coward, 1936). A tale of the hunger, destruction, and brutality of the Civil War. Effective realism.

Andersonville (World, 1955). A striking job of presenting the horrors of existence for Northern prisoners at Andersonville Prison, Georgia. Hundreds of incidents portray a shocking native-American concentration camp in the great tradition of inhumanity.

KIRKLAND, JOSEPH, 1830-1894

The Captain of Company K (1891). A strongly realistic account of camp life and of haphazard military strategy in the attack on Fort Donelson and the Battle of Corinth.

KREY, LAURA, 1890-

And Tell of Time (Houghton, 1938). A detailed and convincing picture of the problems of Texas whites during the decades of Yankee military control.

LANCASTER, BRUCE, 1896-1963

The Scarlet Patch (Little, 1947). About the service of the foreign-born volunteers who fought on the Union side. Good in action but not in characterization.

Night March (Atlantic-Little, 1958). Based on research, as the foreword notes, into certain events of 1864. Depicts the Kilpatrick-Dahlgren raid on Richmond; the life of Northern prisoners in Libby Prison; the experiences of escapees who travel southwest behind Confederate lines.

MITCHELL, MARGARET, 1900-1949

Gone with the Wind (Macmillan, 1936). See above, p. 52.

NOBLE, HOLLISTER, 1900-

Woman with a Sword (Doubleday, 1948). A solid fictionalizing of the life of Anna Ella Carroll, who was a spy, an adviser to Lincoln, a political and military mastermind, and a charming Victorian woman. Presents the men and events of the Civil War from a fresh point of view.

PAGE, THOMAS NELSON, 1853-1922

Red Rock (1898). Constituting one of the solider old treatments of Reconstruction.

PERENYI, ELEANOR SPENCER (STONE), 1918-
The Bright Sword (Rinehart, 1955). A careful historical novel built
around Confederate General Hood from his victory at Chickamauga to
his defeats at Nashville. Much on politics and social life in Richmond.

ROBERTSON, CONSTANCE (NOYES)
Fire Bell in the Night (Holt, 1944). A historically accurate account of
the Underground Railroad in Syracuse, New York, just before the Civil
War. Better as history than as creative literature.
The Unterrified (Holt, 1946). Concerned with the bitter struggle between Northerners who supported the war and the Copperhead Demo-
crats, who favored a negotiated peace. Tells a story of the political
conflicts that led to the bloody draft riots in New York City in 1863.
Makes clear the political roles of farmers, laborers, and merchants.

SCOTT, EVELYN, 1893-
The Wave (Smith, 1929). A unique story of the Civil War, showing how
"the wave" passed over all sorts of conditions of people and how it affected their lives.

STERN, PHILIP VAN DOREN (PETER STORME, pseud.), 1900-
The Drums of Morning (Doubleday, 1942). Of a young man who joined
the abolitionists and fought through the Civil War. "The conflicting and
tragic elements" leading to the war are well presented.

STONE, IRVING, 1903-
Love is Eternal (Doubleday, 1954). The love story of Mary Todd and
Abraham Lincoln, emphasizing the strong character traits of each and
the enduring nature of their love. A sympathetic portrait.

STREET, JAMES HOWELL, 1903-
Tap Roots (Dial, 1942). Centers on a group of Southern abolitionists in
Jones County, Mississippi. Skillful romance.

STRIBLING, THOMAS SIGISMUND, 1881-
The Forge (Doubleday, 1931). The Civil War affects a representative
Southern family, the Vaidens.

THOMASON, JOHN WILLIAM, JR., 1893-1944
Gone to Texas (Scribner's, 1937). Presents the struggle for readjust-
ment in Texas after the Civil War. Shows the problems of reuniting
the North and South. Mentions the dream of Sam Houston, the work of
Juarez, the Mexican raiders, and the conditions of army life.
Lone Star Preacher (Scribner's, 1941). A chronicle of the acts of
Praxiteles Swan, a Methodist preacher from Texas in the Army of
Northern Virginia, a he-man parson who engaged in many battles.

TODD, HELEN, 1912-
A Man Named Grant (Houghton, 1940). Fictionalized biography of an
enigma who was a failure before Shiloh and after Appomattox.

TOURGEE, ALBION W., 1838-1905

A Fool's Errand (1879). A story of a Northerner who settles in the South after the war and tries to solve some of the problems of Reconstruction. An interesting political discussion that criticizes both North and South.

Bricks Without Straw (1880). A propaganda novel, containing much social history, which makes clear that the Negroes needed aid from the North and tolerance from the South. Scenes of Negroes adjusting during the period of the Freedman's Bureau and the Ku Klux Klan. Concisely sums up the aspirations of Negroes and the fears of Southern whites.

The Invisible Empire (1883). Of the carpetbagger period and the Ku Klux Klan.

TUCKER, NATHANIEL BEVERLEY, 1784-1851

The Partisan Leader (1836; Knopf, 1933). A love-and-war story full of patriotic propaganda for Virginia. For Calhoun, and against Jackson and "King Martin the First" Van Buren. Expresses the states' rights doctrine in extreme form and shows disdain for democracy, industrialism, and Yankees. Prophesies secession and civil war.

WARD, SAMUEL, 1814-1884, supposed author

The Diary of a Public Man (1879). Part fiction, part facts about high life in Washington during the winter of 1860-1861. Famous for his Lincoln stories. See F. M. Anderson: *The Mystery of "A Public Man"* (University of Minnesota Press, 1948).

WILLIAMS, BEN AMES, 1889-1953

House Divided (Houghton, 1947). A solid and complicated novel about the war as seen from a Virginian point of view. Concerned with major political and military events between 1859 and 1865. Combines much historical research with some standard romantic trappings, and glosses over the evils of slavery.

The Unconquered (Houghton, 1952). A Reconstruction novel set in New Orleans. The major characters are a Southern officer who co-operates with the occupation forces and a Northern major who marries the Southerner's daughter. Various points of view adequately presented.

3. THE NINETEENTH CENTURY

Nineteenth-century political matters, other than those concerning the Civil War, which have received wide treatment in fiction, are the Jacksonian era; political corruption of the seventies, eighties, and nineties; the rise of the robber barons; the agrarian crusade; the feminist and other reform movements; and the political maneuvers surrounding the Spanish-American War.

ADAMS, HENRY, 1838-1918
Democracy: An American Novel (1880). A cold satire on Congress, where an issue is "not one of principle but of power" and the lobby, where democracy is "the government of the people, by the people, for the benefit of Senators." A well-planned thesis novel told by an intrusive author.

ADAMS, SAMUEL HOPKINS, 1871-
The Gorgeous Hussy (Houghton, 1934). On Andrew Jackson and Peggy O'Neale.

ATHERTON, GERTRUDE, 1857-1948
Senator North (1900). Shows American politics in Washington while affairs in Cuba were making possible the build-up for the Spanish-American War.

BURNETT, FRANCIS H., 1849-1924
Through One Administration (1883). A solid account of political corruption in Washington.

CHURCHILL, WINSTON, 1871-1947
Coniston (1906). Combines romance and muckracking. A study of a village boss in New Hampshire who sells political control to the highest bidder. Laid in the time between Jackson and Grant.

CLEMENS, SAMUEL LANGHORNE (MARK TWAIN, pseud.), 1835-1910,
   and WARNER, CHARLES D., 1829-1900
The Gilded Age (1873). A sharp, entertaining satire on corruption in Washington during the Grant administration. The book, which is a gallery of American types, including the Western land boomer and the boondoggling Senator, gave the name "Gilded Age" to the seventies and eighties.

COOPER, JAMES FENIMORE, 1789-1851
The Redskins (1846). Attacks Puritanism and the agrarianism of the Anti-Rent Party.

DE FOREST, JOHN WILLIAM, 1826-1906
Honest John Vane (1875). A strong satire on fraud in Washington in 1871-1872, this shows a well-intentioned man becoming a prosperous, vulgar rogue.

DONNELLY, IGNATIUS, 1831-1901
Caesar's Column: A Story of the Twentieth Century (Belknap, 1960). Reprints with an introduction the first edition of 1890 of this "prophetic," radical, didactic melodrama laid in the year 1988 and later, when a war of the classes destroys Western civilization. Criticizes the plutocracy of the 1890's from the viewpoint of a Populist leader and makes Utopian proposals for reform.

DUNNE, FINLEY PETER, 1867-1936
Mr. Dooley in Peace and in War (1898). Humorous sketches giving the ideas expressed by Mr. Dooley to his friend, Mr. Hennessey, on a variety of political and social subjects at the time of the war with Spain. *Mr. Dooley in the Hearts of His Countrymen* (1899). A satirical account of the political and social events around 1900. Shows some of the failings of our democracy and gives a picture of home life of the times. *Mr. Dooley at His Best* (Scribner's, 1938). A posthumous selection from the numerous Dooley papers, immensely popular in their day and very readable and pertinent even now.

FAST, HOWARD MELVIN, 1914-
The American: A Middle Western Legend (Duell, 1946). A fictionalized biography of John Peter Altgeld, the governor of Illinois, who pardoned the Haymarket anarchists. Dramatizes his political career, especially his conflicts with big business and President Cleveland. Skips eleven crucial and formative years of Altgeld's life.

FORD, PAUL LEICESTER, 1865-1902
The Honorable Peter Stirling (1894). Deals with a Harvard graduate who starts his political career in the East Side of New York and in sixteen years is elected governor by popular acclaim. He wins the people's faith by bettering the poor's milk supply. A sympathetic study of a good "boss."

GARLAND, HAMLIN, 1861-1940
A Spoil of Office (1892). A picture of the rise of the Grange and the Farmers Alliance against the Republican party.

KANE, HARNETT T., 1910-
New Orleans Woman: A Biographical Novel of Myra Clark Gaines (Doubleday, 1946). Of a woman's long legal fight (1832-1896) against the city of New Orleans to reclaim her lost inheritance. Parallels the nonfiction in Nolan B. Harmon, Jr., *The Famous Case of Myra Clark Gaines* (1946).

LEWIS, ALFRED HENRY, 1842-1914
The Boss (1903). A clear account of the Tammany machine and its tie-in with corporations. Shows how a man gets to be a boss.

LIPSKY, ELEAZAR
Lincoln McKeever (Appleton, 1953). Story of a highly ethical lawyer fighting the cause of the Spanish-Americans in New Mexico when one of them is accused of murder. Well-written and appealing.

McSPADDEN, JOSEPH WALKER, 1874-
Storm Center: A Novel About Andy Johnson (Dodd, 1947). Shows a homespun politician, one interested in the welfare of farmers and workingmen, rising in a vigorous and fruitful career, in Tennessee and

national politics. Especially rich in its treatment of life, politics, and the Civil War in East Tennessee.

SHIEL, MATTHEW P., 1865-1947
Contraband of War (1899). Of high finance and politics during the Spanish-American War.

STONE, IRVING, 1903-
Immortal Wife: The Biographical Novel of Jessie Benton Frêmont (Doubleday, 1944). This fictionalized life gives substantially reliable pictures of Senator Benton of Missouri and his daughter and an effective interpretation of John C. Frémont as explorer, businessman, general, and presidential candidate.
The President's Lady (Doubleday, 1951). A biographical novel based on the lives of Andrew and Rachel Jackson, making them both very heroic. Interesting plot which makes their marital affairs central in the lives of both.

TROLLOPE, ANTHONY, 1815-1882
The American Senator (1877). A long Victorian novel of a Senator who spent a winter on a landed estate in England and had some sharp things to say to the English on their economic and political usages. Pedestrian in style but somewhat interesting. Senator Gotobed of Mikewa is incredible.

WILLIAMS, BEN AMES, JR., 1915-
"Mr. Secretary" (Macmillan, 1940). A fictionalized biography of Edwin M. Stanton, showing his desire, all through the war, to utterly crush the South. Not a convincing portrait.

4. THE TWENTIETH CENTURY

In the twentieth century, major topics in the area of politics and institutions have been socialism, liberalism, communism, progressivism, fascism, conservatism, graft, capitalism, and the causes of modern war. In the twenties, gangsterism and the revival of the Ku Klux Klan were subjects for several novels. Later came novels about rabble-rousers of the Bilbo-Huey Long type. The New Deal, McCarthyism, atomic research, and Congressional investigations have all been common topics since the forties. In the fifties and sixties, interest has centered on the use of public relations men by politicians and on ultra-right pressure groups.

ADAMS, SAMUEL HOPKINS, 1871-1958
Revelry (Boni, 1926). A novel about the grafting in Washington during Harding's administration. Details of the oil scandals and the graft of the Veterans' Bureau, giving an inside picture of dishonesty in government.

BARRETT, LAURENCE I.
The Mayor of New York (Doubleday, 1965). A plain, non-sensational report on the complications of merely running the mayor's office and then the extra difficulties of trying to take constructive steps to prevent race riots and push worthwhile reforms in social welfare. An instructive book.

BASSO, HAMILTON, 1904-1964
Sun in Capricorn (Scribner's, 1942). Revolves around a Louisiana demagogue who resembles Huey Long. Expert local color and a clear delineation of a politician with personal magnetism, lust for power, and genius for self-dramatization.

BIENVENU, HAROLD
The Patriot (St. Martin's, 1964). On a southern California capitalist (who owns authentic recreations of Western towns typical of the 1880's) who uses patriotic and religious organizations to help him get ahead, and on the gimmicks of his public relations man, founder of American Patriots, Inc. Real names are thinly disguised.

BOK, CURTIS, 1897-1962
I Too, Nicodemus (Knopf, 1946). About a judge, by a judge. A fantasy in which a judge rebels against the decree that makes him an administrator of the law, when humanity needs a dispenser of justice.
Star Wormwood (Knopf, 1959). Judge Bok briefly details a young man's crime, trial, and execution; also, in direct non-fiction the judge pointedly and quotably comments on legal and judicial procedure, on "our vindictive penal system."

BOTEIN, BERNARD, 1900-
The Prosecutor (Simon, 1956). The author, a New York City trial judge, has much to say about municipal politics, the legal profession, and the duties and staff of the New York district attorney. His story is intended to be a warning against the "ruthless, resourceful prosecutor, indifferent to the rights of defendants," who can himself "with little risk win headlines or fame."

BOURJAILY, VANCE NYE
The Hound of Earth (Scribner's, 1954). An Oak Ridge scientist, who deserted the army on Hiroshima day because of his feeling of guilt, is finally apprehended. A strikingly critical picture of present-day U.S.A. "wanting to punish the impulse of decency. . .to [praise] the crime." Man's own humanity is "the hound of earth."

BRAMMER, WILLIAM
The Gay Place (Houghton, 1961). About a Texas governor who resembles Lyndon B. Johnson and Sam Rayburn and Earl Long, and who manipulates and wheedles on a pragmatic level of politics and yet

"was incorruptible. . .hadn't a selling price; he sold things. . .people
. . .but never himself."

BURDICK, EUGENE, 1918-1965

The Ninth Wave (Houghton, 1956). Despite irrelevancies (which are
interesting) and an incredible ending, an insightful novel on managed
politics in the Age of IBM. On a Los Angeles boy, out to win, indifferent to human values, who goes to Stanford, works his way up in law
and marriage, and becomes an astute manipulator of blocs of votes in
California.

The 480 (McGraw, 1964). The story of the promotion of an honest non-
political man as a candidate for the Republican nomination for President, in 1963-1964, up to the Cow Palace convention.

BURNETT, WILLIAM RILEY, 1899-

King Cole (Harper, 1936). The story of six closing days of Governor
Read Cole's "honest" campaign for re-election, including a riot planned
for publicity.

CHEVALIER, HAAKON, 1902-

The Man Who Would Be God (Putnam, 1959). Thinly disguised autobiography and history dealing with "Communistic" professors at the
University of California, university blacklists, the Federal security
agency during World War II, the harrassment of scientists, and what
the physicist's responsibility for the bomb and for national safety did
to his integrity. Deals in an important way with an important subject.
The author gives a non-fiction version in *Oppenheimer: The Story of a
Friendship* (Braziller, 1965).

CHILDS, MARQUIS, 1903-

The Peacemakers (Harcourt, 1961). By a seasoned newspaperman,
this novel pictures an international conference in Geneva concerned
with tensions in the Middle East and Africa. Shows pressures, complications, frustrations, dilemmas of cliché-ridden diplomats and
news reporters. The United States Secretary of State has to try "to
reconcile interests that profoundly and terribly conflict."

CHURCHILL, WINSTON, 1871-1947

Mr. Crewe's Career (Macmillan, 1908). A study of a boss's absentee
control of a state legislature and the idealistic revole of a younger
generation.

CLUNE, HENRY W., 1892-

The Big Feller (Macmillan, 1956). About an upstate New York boss,
early in the century, with "greed" for power, women, and alcohol.

COFFIN, TRISTRAM, 1912-

Not to the Swift (Norton, 1961). An angry thesis novel about an American
President, Malcolm Christiansen (who resembles Dwight Eisenhower),
and the cynical, selfish, calculating, manipulators that surround him.

COHEN, LESTER, 1901-1963
Coming Home (Viking, 1945). Of a young marine, wounded in the battles of Guadalcanal, who returns to his native city, Pittsburgh, and fights hard against political corruption.

COLBY, MERLE ESTES, 1902-
The Big Secret (Viking, 1949). A very satisfactory satire on bureaucratic Washington of 1950. Many recognizable pictures of Congressional investigators, bumbling cabinet officers, etc.

COTES, SARA JEANNETTE (DUNCAN), 1862?-1922
The Imperialist (1904). Set in a growing, conventional, middle-class trading and manufacturing town in Ontario, with much on the politics involving Liberals and Conservatives and the problems of making a policy that steers between American and English business overtures.

COZZENS, JAMES GOULD, 1903-
The Just and the Unjust (Harcourt, 1942). The story of a three-day trial of two gangsters, exposing the ways of legal justice and the life of a Connecticut village.

DARROW, CLARENCE, 1857-1938
An Eye for an Eye (1905). The circumstantial monolog of a Chicago wife killer who tries to escape into the South but is captured and condemned to die. Exhibits the poverty and the ward politics that lead to a brutal crime. Intended to indict capital punishment.

DAVIS, CLYDE BRION, 1894-1962
The Great American Novel (Farrar, 1938). An unpartisan, human review of the United States over the past forty years, written by a fictionary person who records the events of presidential elections, political machines, and views of the development of five cities—Denver, Kansas City, San Francisco, Cleveland, and Buffalo. Also records the events in his personal life. Interesting episodes about Teddy Roosevelt, Taft's administration, and the suffragettes.
Follow the Leader (Farrar, 1942). An analytical study of a Babbitt from "Pabuloma" who makes good in World War I and later in politics, and goes to Washington in 1942 as a dollar-a-year man with his eye on the presidency.

DINNEEN, JOSEPH F., 1899-
Ward Eight (Harper, 1936). Story of the old Irish colony of Boston. Gives much of its local color and shows why this little part of American society is run undemocratically by a boss.

DOS PASSOS, JOHN, 1896-
Adventures of a Young Man (Harcourt, 1939). A young American becomes a Communist and dies in Spain in the Loyalist army. A story of an idealist's betrayal by the groups he served.

Number One: A Novel (Houghton, 1943). A fictional biography based
on the life of Huey Long, this novel is a documentary study of how a
sleek hypocrite builds a powerful political machine. The main character powerfully dramatizes the central problem of democracy: how to
select good leaders in an age when public opinion is swayed by radios
and chain newspapers.
The Grand Design (Houghton, 1949). A picture of liberals and radicals
in Washington during the New Deal as its ideals decline into "expedi-
ency, cynicism, and war." This and the preceding two novels appear
as a trilogy in *District of Columbia* (Houghton, 1952).

DRURY, ALLEN, 1918-
Advise and Consent: A Novel of Washington Politics (Doubleday, 1959).
Built around the Presidential and Senatorial politics involved in action
on a nomination for Secretary of State. Contains a strong non-fictional
element and reveals a great deal about the inner working of Washington pressures and motivations. Too much of the conversation is like
taped transcripts.
A Shade of Difference (Doubleday, 1962). Centers around episodes involving the problems of new African Negro nations in the United Nations, which is pictured as being far from representative of the spirit
of brotherhood.

DUNNE, FINLEY PETER, 1867-1936
Mr. Dooley Says (1910). Humorous dialogue between Mr. Dooley and
his friend, Mr. Hennessey, about public affairs.

FAIRBANK, JANET A.,   ?-1951
The Lion's Den (Bobbs, 1930). Of a "radical" Wisconsin farmer, a La
Follette Progressive, who goes to Congress and gets tangled up in
practical politics.
Rich Man, Poor Man (Houghton, 1936). A plump, realistic novel which
tells the story of an ambitious young man and gives pictures of Theodore Roosevelt's Bull Moose campaign, political and economic troubles
during World War I, national party machinery, and the fight for woman
suffrage.

FERGUSSON, HARVEY, 1890-
Capitol Hill (Knopf, 1923). A shrewd version of Washington, D. C. A
story of an opportunist that gives one a notion of patronage, wire-pull-
ing, pressure groups, Washington society, and the conflict between
liberals and vested interests.

FIELD, FRANCIS T.
McDonough (Duell, 1951). A long novel about politics in New Jersey
in the early fifties. The story of a political boss who knows all the
tricks, but loses his beautiful wife, who has more humanitarian stand-
ards than he.

150 POLITICS AND INSTITUTIONS

FISHER, DOROTHY CANFIELD, 1870-1958
Seasoned Timber (Harcourt, 1939). Presents the struggle between democracy and Fascism in the symbolic story of a poor academy in rural Vermont. A wealthy graduate leaves the school a million dollars provided some very undemocratic policies are adopted. The whole town takes sides on this important question, and finally a broad-minded policy is accepted.

FRANK, WALDO D., 1889-1967
The Bridegroom Cometh (Doubleday, 1939). Of a girl who escapes from her New England home, works her way through college, makes an unsuccessful marriage, is divorced, and finally becomes a Communist. Theme: economic and political factors that hinder individuality in the United States today.

FRANKEL, ERNEST
Tongue of Fire (Dial, 1960). A fictional, newspaperlike reworking of the rise and fall of Senator Joseph McCarthy, here become Kane O'Connor of Manton, North Carolina. Oppenheimer appears under a fictional name.

FREDE, RICHARD, 1934-
The Interns (Random, 1960). Life and labor in a city hospital as experienced by seventeen interns during their final year of study.

GREENE, GRAHAM, 1904-
The Quiet American (Viking, 1956). Laid in Saigon and on the war front to the north during the final fighting between the French and Indo-chinese factions. Centers on the character, personality, and action of a New Englander attached to an American economic mission. Critical of the dangerous innocence of American foreign policy.

HACKETT, FRANCIS, 1883-1962
The Senator's Last Night (Doubleday, 1943). Through the fictional device of a day in a Senator's life, the author introduces rich talk on government, the conduct of the war, and the grave problems of postwar planning. Scathing judgment of society in general and the power-loving Senator in particular.

HALPER, ALBERT, 1904-
Union Square (Viking, 1933). See above, p. 106.

HIMES, CHESTER B., 1909-
Cast the First Stone (Coward, 1952). A psychological portrayal of men in prison. The major character is a college-trained man who fights to keep a friend away from homosexual activity and is himself misunderstood by others.

HOBSON, LAURA Z.
First Papers (Random, 1964). Of two Socialist families in New York

before World War I, one family Russian Jewish, the other New England
Unitarian. Slow-paced but good for discussions of war, pacifism, and
domestic politics.

HOUSE, EDWARD, 1858-1938
Philip Dru: Administrator: A Story of Tomorrow 1920-1935 (1912).
A crude novel, by the Texas politician who ran errands for President
Wilson, but a summing up of many Populist and other reform ideas
that became legislative acts during the first Wilson administration.

HUMMEL, GEORGE FREDERICK, 1882-
Joshua Moore, American (Doubleday, 1943). The stories of five
Joshua Moores, stretching from the setting of the first story in 1640
to the last in 1940. Indian wars, the Civil War, and other dramatic
events are involved, including recent political events.

HUSTON, McCREADY, 1891-
Dear Senator (Bobbs, 1928). A Midwesterner starts humbly as a lawyer with high ideals and legitimate ambition, rises to senatorial position, and thereafter declines in integrity as he grows more ambitious.

KARP, DAVID, 1922-
All Honorable Men (Knopf, 1956). Of the liberal head of a conservative
foundation who finds himself caught between his democratic beliefs
and the demands of his governing board when loyalty investigations of
prospective employees are being made.

KIMBROUGH, EDWARD, 1918-
From Hell to Breakfast (Lippincott, 1941). Less a skillful novel than
an excellent job of reporting on the methods and campaign promises of
a Southern demagogue. Laid in Mississippi, it is an exposé of hypocrisy, dishonesty, and ruthless egotism. Shows a new element in
Southern politics, the C.I.O. union.

KNEBEL, FLETCHER, and BAILEY, CHARLES W., II
Convention (Harper, 1964). A lively suspense story of the Republican
Convention of 1972, when the leading candidates are the governor of
California and an Eastern Senator, and the major issue is money for
nuclear weapons.

LANGLEY, ADRIA LOCKE
A Lion is in the Streets (Whittlesey, 1945). Based on the life of Huey
Long, a story of a Southern politician who rises from peddler to state
governor by using the tricks and slogans of a demagogue, including
"Divide the Riches." The novel shows appreciation of the man's ac-
complishments without condoning his ruthless methods.

LAWRENCE, JOSEPHINE
Hearts Do Not Break (Harcourt, 1960). Informed, compassionate so-
ciology in story form, written from the point of view of a social

worker. About the work of a foundation and of public agencies concerned with foster-home care and with the gray market in illegitimate babies in the new world of "the modern unwed mother."

LEDERER, WILLIAM J., 1912-   , and BURDICK, EUGENE, 1918-1965
The Ugly American (Norton, 1958). A thesis novel that is poor art but successful propaganda. Shows where the State Department fails in southeast Asian countries and suggests how it could succeed. A nonfiction epilog reinforces the thesis that the cocktail party, linguistic ignorance, and racial snobbery are losing the world to Communism.
Sarkhan (McGraw, 1965). Laid also in a southeastern Asian nation. Gives reasons for the humiliating failures of many American ambassadors in the modern age of power politics and bloody cold war.

LEMELIN, ROGER
In Quest of Splendor (Barker, 1956). A quiet melodrama that sheds light on the inside workings of family power in Quebec, the educational system, the conflict between Marxists and capitalists, and the homogeneous but divided culture of the province.

LEVIN, MEYER, 1905-
Compulsion (Simon, 1956). A study of the Loeb and Leopold case, with emphasis on the analyses made by psychiatrists. Good in picturing the attitudes of college youth toward sex in the 1920's and in recapitulating the successful plea made by Clarence Darrow against capital punishment.

LEWIS, SINCLAIR, 1885-1951
Arrowsmith (Harcourt, 1925). Built around the life of a doctor who practices in a small town, becomes a public health officer in a small city, and ends up in a large research organization similar to the Rockefeller Institute in New York City. An exposé of the politics of institutionalized research and a tribute to men who unsparingly search for truth. Authentic in scientific detail.
It Can't Happen Here! (Doubleday, 1935). Predicts in startling detail what America would be like under a Fascist dictatorship. Suggests the dangerous decay of old-style political idealism in the United States.

LONDON, JACK, 1876-1916
The Iron Heel (1908). A story of the remaking of America into a type of collective society which London calls a "plutocracy." A forerunner of books on the coming of Fascism to America, such as *It Can't Happen Here!* Perhaps more accurate in picturing how Fascism actually could come.

LOSTUTTER, MELVIN SIMMONS, 1895-
High Fever: A Novel of the Sales Promotion Decade (Harper, 1935). Of a mountain preacher and those who used him to promote an organization like the Ku Klux Klan.

LUMPKIN, GRACE, 1898-
A Sign for Cain (Furman, 1935). Story of certain happenings in a small
town in the South which involves the deterioration of the former ruling
family—and the organization of the Negroes by Denis, a Negro Communist returned from the North.

MacLENNAN, HUGH, 1907-
Barometer Rising (Duell, 1941). A reworking of the *Odyssey* laid in
Halifax during World War I. Takes up the rising sense of identity
among Canadians. "A man has to think he hasn't got a country before
he knows what having one means."
The Watch That Ends the Night (Scribner's, 1959). Dramatizes the
social idealism of the 1930's, its creative and destructive aspects, in
eastern Canada. Shows great interest in the changes in Canada during
World War II and in differences between Canada and the United States.
Pictures many parts of Canada and many activities.

MANCHESTER, WILLIAM RAYMOND, 1922-
The City of Anger (Ballantine, 1953). A story of political corruption in
a northeastern seaport. Central characters are a "numbers" king and
an incorruptible police commissioner.

MANKIEWICZ, DON M., 1922-
Trial (Harper, 1955). Communist exploitation of the trial of a young
Mexican in a West Coast city. Good glimpses of the prejudices and
"way of life" in southern California. Place names are fictitious.

MASTERS, DEXTER
The Accident (Knopf, 1955). The accident is the death by radiation of
a scientist at Los Alamos. The book is a live discussion of the problems arising out of our production and use of the atom bomb. The various attitudes of scientists, military men, and politicians are well stated.

MASTERS, JOHN, 1914-
Fandango Rock (Harper, 1959). A yarn that tells of a love affair between a matador and an American girl on a Strategic Air Command
base in Spain. The affair involves United States public relations, the
Church, the cost of living in Spain, American gaucheries, and the differences between "life, liberty, the pursuit of happiness" and the
Spanish "death, discipline, the acceptance of sorrow."

MILLER, MERLE
The Sure Thing (Sloane, 1949). The story of thirty-six hours in the
life of a young member of the State Department in Washington. During
that period he is subjected to an unjust investigation which eventually
costs him his job.

O'CONNOR, EDWIN, 1918-
The Last Hurrah (Little, 1956). Excellent portrayal of an old-time

political boss, his associates and campaign tactics in a Boston-like
city. Explains how the New Deal ended an era of bosses. Good on the
Irish and rich in talk.

PAUL, ELLIOT HAROLD, 1891-1958
The Governor of Massachusetts (Liveright, 1930). A pleasant satire
showing an honest, simple-minded organ manufacturer as governor of
the state and as a victim of graft and political scheming. Nineteenth-
century style.

PEARSON, WILLIAM, 1922-
A Fever in the Blood (St. Martin's, 1959). An inside story on cam-
paigning in a state that resembles Illinois, where an ambitious down-
state district attorney uses a murder trial and all standard political
tricks in a drive to become governor. Creates no believable characters but reports much on the last-minute shenanigans of office-seek-
ers.

PHILLIPS, DAVID G., 1867-1911
The Plum Tree (1905). Public-utility bosses in a small town make a
political career for a young lawyer.

RAND, AYN
The Fountainhead (Bobbs, 1943). In a strong, adroit story, crammed
with irony and ideas, the author defends the philosophy and morality of
individualism and attacks mass-oriented, "humanitarian" institutions.
Atlas Shrugged (Random, 1957). A political parable, a piece of science
fiction, a dialog on ethics, a celebration of man as a heroic being.
Again the author attacks the leviathan state and politicians who, as she
sees them, are looting the rich in order to give to the mediocre.

RYLEE, ROBERT, 1908-
The Ring and the Cross (Knopf, 1947). Of a Senator who is the dictator
in a seaboard Texas metropolis. Sheds light on the political significance of acts by members of A.F.L. unions, the Klan, conservative
churches, and industrialists' associations. A counterattack on books
that defend economic Fascism.

SANDOZ, MARI, 1907-1966.
Capital City (Little, 1939). See above, p. 86

SHIRER, WILLIAM LAWRENCE, 1904-
Stranger, Come Home (Little, 1954). One of the best books about
McCarthyism. In a 1949-1950 setting, the story of a commentator
called before a Senate committee and accused of Communist activity.
Follows the pattern of actual hearings quite closely.
The Consul's Wife (Little, 1956). Deals with a plot connived in by the
spouse of the American consul in a small Asian country controlled by

Britain. Interesting comments on Americans and British amid the Asian scene.

SINCLAIR, UPTON B., 1878-
Boston (Boni, 1928). A fictionalized report on the Sacco-Vanzetti case in Massachusetts, one of the famous civil liberties cases of the 1920's. Contrasts the psychology of the needy worker with the desire of the rich to retain power. Shows the different application of justice for the two classes.
Presidential Agent (Viking, 1944). The fifth volume in the series, this novel deals largely with events immediately preceding the opening of World War II.

STONE, IRVING, 1903-
Adversary in the House (Doubleday, 1947). A fictionalized life of Eugene V. Debs. The historical parts are quite accurate. The relationship with his wife, to which the title refers, seems overdrawn.

STRIBLING, THOMAS SIGISMUND, 1881-
The Sound Wagon (Doubleday, 1935). An exciting and provocative satire on practical politics, including gangster rackets.
These Bars of Flesh (Doubleday, 1938). The story of a Southern politician who goes north to Megapolis to school. Satirizes politics, political groups, and educational institutions.

SYLVESTER, HARRY, 1908-
Moon Gaffney (Holt, 1947). A slice-of-life novel of Irish Catholics in New York City in the 1930's. Shows a young politician torn between the spiritual and materialistic forces in his cultural complex. Exhibits the struggle of an idealist to adjust himself during strife between Fascists and anti-Fascists. Attacks religion only in so far as it attacks those religious leaders who betray the human spirit.

TARKINGTON, BOOTH, 1869-1946
The Conquest of Canaan (1905). Of a small town and an idealized young lawyer of the lower class who becomes its mayor. A Progressive Era political novel.

TRAIN, ARTHUR, 1875-1945
Yankee Lawyer; The Autobiography of Ephraim Tutt (Scribner's, 1943). The story of an American lawyer's seventy-five years up to 1943. Mr. Train's pictorial character in a full-length portrait. Humorous.

TWERSKY, JACOB, 1920-
Face of the Deep (World, 1952). The author, who is blind, traces the lives of six blind people from early adolescence until each is in his twenties. A real glimpse into the lives of the blind, and of the institutions that work with them and for them.

UPDIKE, JOHN, 1932-
The Poorhouse Fair (Knopf, 1959). Of a special day at a New Jersey poorhouse. Shows the psychic plight of the inmates and the plight of the idealistic administrator who has to institutionalize old people who have been individualized by their past and are now capable of violence because "Boredom is a ter-rible force."

WALKER, MILDRED
Medical Meeting (Harcourt, 1949). Excellent account of a young doctor doing research on a mold used in the cure of tuberculosis. He has to choose between security in a good institutional job and going on with his research. Well written, compelling.

WALLACE, IRVING, 1916-
The Man: A Novel (Simon, 1964). A readable tale, well plotted, about the first Negro President and the problems he faces, an impeachment trial included.

WARREN, ROBERT PENN, 1905-
All the King's Men (Harcourt, 1946). Concerns the governor and boss of a Southern state, his urge to power, and his relations with two men and a woman who become attached to him. Follows in part the story of Huey Long's life. Shows the boss rising to supply a local need and then falling victim to his own power over voters and women. The book ignores Negroes but gives crisp views of cynical politicos.

WELLMAN, PAUL ISELIN, 1898-1966
The Walls of Jericho (Lippincott, 1947). Story of a young lawyer's struggle against political corruption—Old Guard politicians and "piratical utilities and the money power"--in a Kansas town in the early twentieth century. A dramatic picture of the close-knit relationships of the small town and of folkways on the High Plains. Sympathetic to farmers and common people.

WHITE, W. L., 1900-
What People Said (Viking, 1938). See above, p. 78.

WHITLOCK, BRAND, 1869-1934
Big Matt (Appleton, 1928). A generally realistic novel which shows the sense of honor of a state boss and also a governor's inner conflict between the need to serve the state and his desire for re-election.

WILDER, ROBERT, 1901-
Flamingo Road (Putnam, 1942). Of Florida in the bootleg era, exposing state and local politics.
The Wine of Youth (Putnam, 1955). An oil town in Texas, especially before and after the crash in 1929. Much on Mexico and Mexican-Americans. Built around political corruption and a Mexican-American boss. Good style.

WILLIAMS, BEN AMES, 1889-1953
Time of Peace (Houghton, 1942). A swift-moving historical novel of American life from 1930 to 1941. Mainly of anti-Roosevelt Bostonians and their changes of opinion as to foreign policy and the war. A propaganda novel, but written with "Galsworthian impartiality."

WILLIAMS, WIRT, 1921-
Ada Dallas (McGraw, 1959). A melodrama, properly set in Louisiana, with much reportorial detail on how politics works at the state level. Taking place after World War II, telling of a call girl who becomes governor, the novel exploits sex and also the old struggle between New Orleans and the rural part of the state.

WILSON, CHARLES M., 1905-
Rabble Rouser (Longmans, 1936). Tells of local politics in Arkansas before 1914. Shows the rise of a sincere man of the people who sides with underdogs and becomes governor. Plot somewhat improbable.

WILSON, MITCHELL A.
Meeting at a Far Meridian (Doubleday, 1961). Fictional journalism based on research in the Soviet Union, about the problems faced by American and Soviet physicists as they strive toward international co-operation. Though cluttered by a love story, the book personalizes the space race and the cold war.

5. SCHOOLS AND COLLEGES, PUBLIC AND PRIVATE

During the cold war and the hot wars of the 1950's and 1960's, with the rise of education to new national importance, novelists have given much attention to the activities of faculty members, administrators, students, and non-students in high schools, colleges, and universities of all sorts. As a genre, academic novels, which are generally the work of teachers, are thin, unreal, waspish, and stereotyped—written for insiders. They are at their best when their main emphasis is not on academic life as such but on something else like finding oneself or finding another person to love, as in Malamud's *A New Life* or Bassing's *Home Before Dark*.

The nation-wide problem of segregated schooling, touched on in many novels about city life, the South, religion, and ethnic groups, is central in books such as those listed under "The Negro" by Mrs. Worth Hedden, Bucklin Moon, William Owens, and Saunders Redding.

ALDRIDGE, JOHN WATSON
The Party at Cranton (McKay, 1960). Very literary, with some experimentation with writing, this book mercilessly pictures certain social and intellectual aspects of faculty life in a university. For insiders.

AUCHINCLOSS, LOUIS
The Rector of Justin (Houghton, 1964). Pictures the headmaster of a New England private school, 1939-1947, as stuffy and Puritanic.

BAKER, CARLOS H., 1909-
A Friend in Power (Scribner's, 1958). Explores the minds and motives of a faculty committee that is looking for a new president. Stodgy, stiff conversations. Some accurate summing up of faculty types.

BARR, STRINGFELLOW, 1897-
Purely Academic (Simon, 1958). A somewhat ironic presentation of present-day college life. Centers on a social science professor and his colleagues. More exposition than story, with many situation clichés, but a truer delineation of college than most books give.

BASSING, EILEEN JOHNSTON, 1908-
Home Before Dark (Random, 1957). Essentially a psychological story of a wife's intense attempt to "come back" after years in an insane asylum and win from her husband (a professor) a love he has never had for her, but also by indirection a good academic novel, for it shows how her husband's critical attitude toward her is much conditioned by his ambition to rise conventionally in the campus hierarchy.

BRACE, GERALD WARNER, 1909-
The Spire (Norton, 1952). A year in a New England college with its internal politics and its moralistic notions. Quite satisfactory.

CALITRI, CHARLES
Strike Heaven on the Face (Crown, 1958). Of a "sex club" at a high school. Critical of the politicking of administrators and of the immorality of parents' wishing to cover up scandal; admiring of a teacher who takes his task seriously and bravely.

CALLAGHAN, MORLEY, 1903-
The Varsity Story (Macmillan, 1948). Tells about the University of Toronto and its religious pluralism during the 1920's and the Depression. Names some actual persons, points up the conflict between the humanities and the technologies, and stresses the importance of realizing that "truth" has many facets.

FARRIS, JOHN
Harrison High (Rinehart, 1959). Reports on the vast volume of chatter and other non-academic aspects of school life, notably football, caste, "love," juvenile crime, and vandalism, as seen by youths. Close to melodrama.

FREDE, RICHARD, 1934-
Entry E (Random, 1958). Dwells on the indifference and irresponsibility and the conventional code of an IBM university generation raised

on "a helluva lot of Don't's and almost no Do's," one that can rape but won't rat.

GESSNER, ROBERT, 1907-
Youth is the Time (Scribner's, 1945). The scene is Metropolitan College, situated in lower Manhattan. A realistic close-up of a campus, and also a mirror of war-bred problems.

GUTTERSON, HERBERT
The Last Autumn (Morrow, 1958). A rich boy's suicide at a prep school brings on a crisis over telling the truth—which involves choosing between living people and new buildings that are only in the planning stage.

HERSEY, JOHN, 1914-
The Child Buyer (Knopf, 1960). Written in the form of a legislative hearing. A satire with overtones of horror on American public education, with special barbs for superintendents, school psychologists, doting teachers, PTA leaders, materialistic parents, and ignorant legislators. An exposé of the corruptible ego in each man.
Too Far to Walk (Knopf, 1966). Of the problems of undergraduates in search of intense, sensory, and meaningful experience during the 1960's, as reflected in events on the campus of an Eastern men's college.

HUNTER, EVAN, 1926-
The Blackboard Jungle (Simon, 1954). A supposedly realistic picture of a tough secondary school in New York City.

KELLY, ROBERT GLYNN
A Lament for Barney Stone (Holt, 1961). A comedy about university professors and administrators. Centers on an English professor, a bachelor *and* celibate who resembles J. Alfred Prufrock. Contrived in plot but sound in background, as on deans and professors.

KUBLY, HERBERT
The Whistling Zone (Simon, 1963). Shows a present-day dehumanized state university, somewhere west of Chicago, run like a corporation, where students and faculty alike have lost the liberal tradition and intellectual freedom and engender only such news as panty raids and gang rapes.

LIPSKY, ELEAZAR
The Scientists (Appleton, 1959). A legal drama about a university scientist and his patented discovery in the toils of the law and big business. Much on doings in classes, laboratories, and offices. And much on the campus hierarchies that make and break careers.

McCARTHY, MARY, 1912-
The Group (Harcourt, 1963). Takes eight Vassar girls, Class of 1933, and follows on in their lives. A sharp, sardonic exhibit.

MALAMUD, BERNARD, 1914-
A New Life (Farrar, 1961). At heart a tale of love and personal re-
clamation, but also a remarkably revealing account of politics and
pedagogy in the English department of a land-grant college in Cas-
cadia—a state that resembles Oregon.

MORRISON, THEODORE, 1901-
The Stones of the House (Viking, 1953). Of the trials of the acting
president of an Eastern college as he solves perplexing problems. The
book shows real understanding of college life.
To Make a World (Viking, 1957). Long and talky but knowledgeable
about academic and foundation politics. Hinges in part on ends and
means in science and ethics.

NABOKOV, VLADIMIR, 1899-
Pnin (Doubleday, 1957). A short, sharp satire on faculty social life
and on college professors—including specialists in the humanities—as
seen by an emigré Russian professor. Episodic, witty.

NEMEROV, HOWARD, 1920-
The Homecoming Game (Simon, 1957). With an improbable plot but
recognizable characters, Nemerov satirizes the overemphasis on football and the Machiavellian ethics in a small private college.

O'CONNOR, WILLIAM VAN, 1915-
Campus on the River (Crowell, 1959). Twelve stories of college people, mostly faculty members, presenting the psychology of the mis-
fits and also a believable portrait of the administrative machinery.

PERKINS, VIRGINIA (CHASE), 1902-
The End of the Week (Macmillan, 1953). Presents thirteen grade-
school teachers as they spend their time from 3:00 p.m. to midnight on
a Friday evening. None of them is happy or satisfied or intelligent
enough to seem human. They are on a perfect treadmill of semi-in-
tellectual activity.

ROGERS, LETTIE HAMLETT, 1917-
Birthright (Simon, 1957). An analytical novel, centering on a school-
teacher in North Carolina who loses her job by speaking in favor of
integration. Vivisects the families who dominate the town.

SARTON, MAY, 1912-
Faithful are the Wounds (Rinehart, 1955). A thesis novel laid at Harvard, symbol of American education at its best. Explores academic
freedom in terms of present-day conflicts between liberals on the one
hand and investigators and instigators of subversion on the other.
The Small Room (Norton, 1961). Studies a woman's college, using a
case of plagiarism as a means of analyzing the art of both teaching
and meeting the needs of students.

STILLWELL, HART
Campus Town (Doubleday, 1950). A hard-boiled novel set at a Southern state college after World War I. Much on campus politics, sports, sex, intolerance, and the Klan.

TANNER, LOUISE (STICKNEY)
Miss Bannister's Girls (Farrar, 1963). Of sixteen who graduate from an exclusive girls' prep school in New York City, 1940, and their subsequent, often scandalous, lives. Light and intended to be amusing.

SCOTT, VIRGIL, 1914-
The Hickory Stick (Swallow, 1948). Laid in a small Ohio town in 1936-1937, with many flashbacks. A bitter version of professors of education, school boards, and progressive educators, and a sympathetic picture of the hard, unrewarding work of high school teachers.

SIEGEL, BENJAMIN
The Principal (Harcourt, 1963). Realistic details of the problems a high school principal faces in gaining accreditation for a run-down school.

SULLIVAN, SCOTT
The Shortest Gladdest Years (Simon, 1962). Three hundred and eighty-one pages on the private and social life of four Ivy League students at a Yale-like university.

TIGUE, ETHEL E.
Betrayal (Dodd, 1959). The last week of the semester in an Idaho school of twenty-three teachers. Though a melodrama of sorts, makes points about school boards and "educators," and shows how schools underpay teachers, neglect the proper aims of education, and keep students busy at non-educational activities.

WILLIAMS, JOHN EDWARD, 1922-
Stoner (Viking, 1965). Built around the life of a Missouri farm boy who becomes a student and then a professor of English at the University of Missouri and struggles on, lonely and dogged, to uphold humane values.

WILLINGHAM, CALDER, 1922-
End as a Man (Vanguard, 1947). A realistic picture, told largely in dialog, of students' personal life and official discipline in a private military college in a Southern state. Catches without blinking the prejudices, the sadism, and the rule-breaking immorality of some of the cadets.

YELLEN, SAMUEL, 1906-
The Passionate Shepherd: A Book of Stories (Knopf, 1957). Ten short stories, all tenderly and adroitly told. Laid in Ohio and Indiana municipalities. Notable for several stories that go into the meanness and frustration of faculty life in a Midwestern university located in a small town.

RELIGION

Since Hawthorne began writing, there has been a steady tradition of depicting and psychoanalyzing Puritans and their descendants in New England and to the west, as for example, the Presbyterians in Nova Scotia, Virginia, and elsewhere. Evangelical religion has been treated in moods varying from the sentimentality of Lloyd Douglas to the satire of Sinclair Lewis. The various minority religions have attracted many novelists, who have produced a small library of books about Jews, Quakers, Mormons, and members of sects such as the Shakers. Since World War II, with the Catholic church making many adjustments to the American environment, Catholic novelists have been stimulated to interpret aspects of their church.

1. PURITANS AND PURITANISM (INCLUDING CONGREGA-TIONALISTS AND PRESBYTERIANS)

Stories of the Puritans and Puritanism show that Puritan thought has had an influence upon these United States in every stage of our history. There are stories of the settlers of Massachusetts and their attitudes toward Quakers and other dissenters, stories of the great witchcraft delusion, stories of Puritan fundamentalist beliefs and superstitions carried on through the eighteenth and nineteenth centuries. There are such artistic outcroppings as the works of Poe, Melville, and Hawthorne, with their probing of consciences and their obsessions with the problems of evil and retribution. There are moralistic crusaders like Harriet Beecher Stowe and mystical speculators of many sorts. Finally we come to the twentieth-century revolters against Puritanism, who center on the frustrations and unhappiness of those who are bound by too rigid a code, several of them attempting to picture "the last Puritan." And in writers like Esther Forbes and Anya Seton there are objective researchers who work as carefully as historians.

ANDERSON, SHERWOOD, 1876-1941
Winesburg, Ohio (1919). See above, p. 37.

BARKER, SHIRLEY
Peace, My Daughters (Crown, 1949). Dramatizes Salem during the witchcraft excitement—including the satanic powers that (villagers thought) invaded the town. A picture of terrorism as a means of control.
Tomorrow the New Moon (Bobbs, 1955). An interesting picture of a preacher of the early seventeenth century in New England and his rejection of the Calvinists' doctrine of the elect. His opponents in the

clerical world use accusations of sex irregularity to discredit him with the people.

BROMFIELD, LOUIS, 1896-1956

Early Autumn (Stokes, 1926). Shows a rigid aristocratic caste in present-day Massachusetts that stifles freedom of personality and action. *A Good Woman* (Stokes, 1927). The "good woman" is a domineering type who spoils her son's life.

CANNON, LeGRAND, 1899-

Come Home at Even (Holt, 1951). A story of a couple who came to Salem to live, because the husband felt God had called him to settle there. The story involves his struggle between visionary "calls" and the common sense which wins out in the end.

CARLISLE, HELEN GRACE, 1898-

We Begin (Smith, 1932). A story of one Separatist family during the years in Holland and the first years in America. Centers on the sex frustration and neurotic condition of the elder brother of the family.

DELAND, MARGARET, 1857-1945

John Ward, Preacher (1888). A mildly interesting story of a gentle but sternly Calvinistic preacher. One of the first novels to treat of the conflict between conservative and liberal ideas in religion during the great debate over evolution.
Dr. Lavendar's People (1903). A portrait of a kindly parson who tries to live by a law higher than human law and to aid distressed people in his community. Decisions made in line with Puritan tradition.

DODGE, CONSTANCE W., 1896-

In Adam's Fall (Macrae, 1946). About the Salem witch hunt. A dramatic and depressing combination of background and plot.

EGGLESTON, EDWARD, 1837-1902

Roxy (1878). A picture of southern Indiana in the 1840's, when settlers were in the path of a crusading Methodism. Shows strict attitudes of the early Middle Westerners in regard to sex. Realistic for its day, with well-developed characters.

EHRLICH, LEONARD, 1905-

God's Angry Man (Simon, 1932). A strong, intense, fictionalized biography of John Brown, nineteenth-century abolitionist. Objectifies the austere, illiberal, crusading spirit that the seventeenth-century Puritans planted in America.

FORBES, ESTHER, 1894?-

A Mirror for Witches (Houghton, 1928). Excellent ironic account of the life of one girl who became a witch. Behind the actual words of the tale the reader may see the pathetic, real story of the main character.
Paradise (Harcourt, 1937). An exciting, well-rounded presentation of

seventeenth-century Massachusetts Puritans. *Paradise* gives them flesh and blood and shows the effect of the frontier on them.

FULLER, EDMUND, 1914-
Brothers Divided (Bobbs, 1951). A well-told story of the 1930's. The main character becomes a liberal Presbyterian minister and helps to straighten out the chaos created by his Communist brother.

GLASGOW, ELLEN, 1874-1945
Vein of Iron (Harcourt, 1935). Of a Virginia Presbyterian community, in particular of a father and daughter who were strong enough to break away from the Puritanic code surrounding them.

GREY, ZANE, 1872-1940
Wanderer of the Wasteland (Harper, 1923). A melodramatic story of a sensitive boy who feels he has committed mortal sin and wanders for a number of years in the deserts of southern California, suffering miserably.

HAWTHORNE, NATHANIEL, 1804-1864
The Scarlet Letter (1850). The established literary classic about the tortures of a Puritan conscience, the psychic repercussions of living for revenge, and the educative value of sin. Laid in seventeenth-century Boston.

HOWE, EDGAR W., 1854-1937
The Story of a Country Town (1883). Of a small community in Kansas. Each major character is caught in some fashion by the Victorian sex-sin complex that leads to frustration and defeat. Perceptive and sympathetic portraits.

HUGHES, RUPERT, 1872-1956
Stately Timber (Scribner's, 1939). Describes in great detail the life of Puritan New England in the 1650's. Presents the fight for freedom in a society that denied it.

JOHNSTON, MARY, 1870-1936
The Great Valley (Little, 1926). Shows strong faith helping a Scotch Presbyterian woman through hardships during the French and Indian War.

LEWIS, SINCLAIR, 1885-1951
The God Seeker (Random, 1949). In the 1840's, a devout Congregationalist goes to Minnesota as a missionary working under a Presbyterian. Interesting treatment of the work of missionaries and various reactions thereto. Inconsistent characterization.

MacLENNAN, HUGH, 1907-
Each Man's Son (Little, 1951). Among Scots Highlanders in a village on the island of Cape Breton. A study of Calvinist guilt and conscience and of its impact on family relationships.

MARQUAND, JOHN PHILLIPS, 1893-1960
The Late George Apley (Little, 1937). See above, p. 118.

MARQUIS, DON, 1878-1937
Sons of the Puritans (Doubleday, 1939). See above, p. 42.

MELVILLE, HERMAN, 1819-1891
Moby Dick (1851). A chaotic masterpiece and a great sea romance which dramatizes the problem of evil in the conflict between Captain Ahab and the white whale. May be taken as a pessimist's reply to Emerson and the optimistic transcendentalists.

PHILLIPS, DAVID G., 1867-1911
Susan Lenox: Her Fall and Rise (Appleton, 1917). A naturalistic story, shocking to Puritans, since it pictures an "immoral" woman making a success of her life.

POE, EDGAR ALLAN, 1809-1849
Best Tales (Modern Library, 1924). Poe's stories of death, murder, and conscience, with their emphasis on the "guilt complex," should be noticed in connection with the "Puritan mind."

REES, GILBERT, 1923-
I Seek a City (Dutton, 1950). A simple, compelling story of Roger Williams as he grows up in England, and of his life in the New World.

SANTAYANA, GEORGE, 1863-1952
The Last Puritan (Scribner's, 1936). Ironical and philosophical analysis of a talented blueblood who has been suppressed by tradition to the point of futility in all of his personal relationships.

SETON, ANYA
The Winthrop Woman (Houghton, 1959). Solid, good writing and rich social history, about a group of London and Groton people who come to Massachusetts Bay Colony in 1631. Built around the rebellious niece of Governor John Winthrop who befriends Anne Hutchinson and who is a figure in Connecticut and New Netherlands during the period 1631-1655. Better researched than some history; a "re-creation and interpretation" of the original documents.

STONE, GRACE Z., 1896-
The Cold Journey (Morrow, 1934). Story of the attack by French and Indians on a Massachusetts colonial village (based on the Deerfield Raid of 1704), followed by the journey of captives and victors through the snow of Quebec. Contrasts the rigid piety of the Puritans and the acceptance of life by the French.

STOWE, HARRIET BEECHER, 1812-1896
The Minister's Wooing (1859). A detailed picture of scrupulous Calvinists with well-nurtured consciences. An important presentation of New England, some time after the Revolution, when religion was still

a powerful force in the daily lives of people. Introduces several real
people, including Aaron Burr and Samuel Hopkins.
Old-Town Folks (1869). A revealing picture of the firm place of many
Puritan ideals in the weekday life of New Englanders about 1790. A
strong interpretation of a people whose lives centered in the meeting-
house.

WHITTIER, JOHN GREENLEAF, 1807-1892
*Leaves from Margaret Smith's Journal in the Province of Massa-
chusetts Bay, 1678-79* (1849). Published anonymously. A vivid account of the second generation in New England. An imaginative piec-
ing together of old records. It gives a day-by-day picture of Puritan
life, including maltreatment of Quakers.

WINWAR, FRANCES, 1900-
Gallows Hill (Holt, 1937). Salem in the days of the witchcraft delusion.

2. THE METHODISTS, BAPTISTS, ROMAN CATHOLICS, EPISCOPALIANS, AND LUTHERANS

The place of the large church groups has been a subject for fiction
since the appearance of Edward Eggleston's popular *The Circuit Rider*
in 1874. The matters written about most commonly have been the place
of the churches in pioneer times, and the development of revivalism
and the continuance of "old-fashioned" evangelical religion in certain
groups in the South. Recent books about ministers and priests have
emphasized their troubled consciences and their contributions to the
daily life of the communities they serve. Often the discussion of Catholicism is used to accentuate the story of the struggles of Catholics to
adjust themselves in what used to be a "Protestant America." Catholic
novelists like Morley Callaghan, writing of Quebec and Ontario, and J.
F. Power, writing of Illinois and Minnesota, give fresh insight into the
activities of Catholics.

AGEE, JAMES, 1909-1955
A Death in the Family (McDowell, 1957). A poignant, immediate, poetical account of the effect of a Catholic's death on his widow, his small
children, and his relatives. A subtle study of the impact of death and
grief. Laid in Knoxville and the adjacent hill country, around 1915.

BATES, ARLO, 1850-1918
The Puritans (1898). Of two high-minded young Bostonians, both
novitiates in an Episcopalian monastic order, and their contrasting
solutions to the conflicts between the spiritual and the physical in life.
Shows the attitudes of socialites toward religion and religious cults.
Old-fashioned in technique but substantial in content.

BERLIN, ELLIN MACKAY
Lace Curtain (Doubleday, 1948). Presents the deep problems raised by a mixed marriage of Protestant and Catholic. Told against the background of a rich Irish-Catholic family living on a Long Island estate.

BONN, JOHN LOUIS, 1906-
And Down the Days (Macmillan, 1942). A novel of the life of the daughter of Maria Monk (who wrote *Awful Disclosures,* which led to anti-Catholic riots in America). The daughter becomes a Catholic but never arrives at spiritual peace.

BRADFORD, ROARK, 1896-1948
Ol' Man Adam an' His Chillun (Harper, 1928). Bible stories as told by illiterate Mississippi Negroes. Humorous yet reverent. The basis for the play, *The Green Pastures.*

BRANTLEY, RUSSELL
The Education of Jonathan Beam (Macmillan, 1962). A simply told story of a "poor white" boy, surrounded by fundamentalist religion-ists, who in his first year at college begins to see the shortcomings of his faith. Without using a critical tone, the author succeeds in poign-ant examination of the accepted mores of a small Southern community.

BUCK, PEARL SYDENSTRICKER, 1892-
The Exile (Day, 1936). Story of the author's mother, wife of a stern missionary, whose unquestioning faith she was unable to follow.

CALLAGHAN, MORLEY, 1903-
Such is My Beloved (Scribner's, 1934). On the problems of a young priest who tries to save the souls of prostitutes and is punished for his unworldliness.

CATHER, WILLA SIBERT, 1876-1947
Death Comes for the Archbishop (Knopf, 1927). Makes clear the hard-ships and accomplishments of Catholic missionaries, particularly Father Latour, in New Mexico and Arizona. The book is more pano-ramic than dramatic. Excellent writing, and appreciation of the work of the Church.

CHURCHILL, WINSTON, 1871-1947
The Inside of the Cup (1912). A product of the Progressive Era, this treats the theme of corruption within the Church. Idealism versus snobbery in the Episcopal Church.

COZZENS, JAMES GOULD, 1903-
Men and Brethren (Harcourt, 1936). An objective but slightly cynical presentation of one type of modern clergyman, the rector of a promi-nent Fifth Avenue church who is urbane, intelligent, and "liberal" in outlook.

CURRAN, DOYLE, 1917-
The Parish and the Hill (Houghton, 1948). A set of highly personal memories of an Irish-American girlhood in a New England mill town. Shows the inner conflicts of a young person adjusting to parochial narrowness on one hand and the open-opportunity system of America on the other hand.

DOUGLAS, LLOYD C., 1877-1951
Magnificent Obsession (Willett, 1929). An "inspirational novel" of a young waster who is redeemed by following a doctrine of anonymous aid to his fellow men. A fictionalized sermon that preaches a sugary doctrine
Green Light (Houghton, 1935). The story of the dean of a Midwestern cathedral in present-day America. The dean has become more understanding because of his suffering from infantile paralysis in his youth. He gives his understanding and comfort to a young surgeon much in need of it.
White Banners (Houghton, 1936). Douglas presents his sentimental philosophy—that there is material and spiritual peace only in being patient, having courage, and serving humanity—through the character of Hannah Parmalee, who by using the philosophy saved the Ward household from financial failure and brought peace to all the members of it in the twenty years of her employment.

EGGLESTON, EDWARD, 1837-1902
The Circuit Rider (1874). Shows the great part played by "Methodism" and other evangelical religions in frontier communities. Set in Ohio in the first quarter of the nineteenth century.

FANTE, JOHN, 1911-
Dago Red (Viking, 1940). Stories of Catholic Italians in a Colorado town. Shows the place of religion in their lives, in parochial schools, at communion, and so on.

FREDERIC, HAROLD, 1856-1898
The Damnation of Theron Ware (1896). A narrow young Methodist minister goes to pieces spiritually and becomes an agnostic.

GORDON, CAROLINE, 1895-
The Malefactors (Harcourt, 1956). A symbolic, difficult novel of ideas and manners; about an aging literary man who converts to Catholicism.

HEDDEN, MRS. WORTH TUTTLE
Love is a Wound (Crown, 1952). A well-told but too-long story of a Southern triangle, a Methodist preacher loved by two sisters, one of whom he marries. Puritan attitudes toward sex plus Southern romanticism lead to quite a bit of unhappiness for each of the three.

HURLEY, DORAN, 1906-
Monsignor (Longmans, 1936). Scene laid in a small New England factory town inhabited largely by Irish, French-Canadian, and Portuguese Catholics. Shows the day-by-day life of an Irish priest who is fighting a hopeless struggle against the sin of self-pride and desire for power. *The Old Parish* (Longmans, 1938). Gives a clear picture of religion in the lives of Irish Catholics in a Massachusetts village.

KENNEDY, JOHN P., 1795-1870
Rob of the Bowl (1838). A story of early days in Maryland, centering on the conflict between Catholic and Protestant in 1681. Emphasizes the struggle for religious freedom.

LEWIS, SINCLAIR, 1885-1951
Elmer Gantry (Harcourt, 1927). Biting satire on the Protestant churches in America, especially on revivalists.

MATTHIESSEN, PETER
At Play in the Fields of the Lord (Random, 1965). An adventure story of fundamentalist missionaries--shown as deceiving themselves and others—among Indians in the Amazon jungle.

MICHELFELDER, WILLIAM A.
A Seed upon the Wind (Bobbs, 1954). The story of a doctor and a nurse in a Catholic hospital and their rejection of the Church. Psychological exploration of the subject of human love and its relation to the life of the spirit.

MORGAN, AL
Minor Miracle (Dodd, 1961). A clever, sentimental tale of a priest who is victimized by a commercial hoax concerning a miracle. Kindly in depicting the duties of, and the problems faced by, a spokesman for supernatural faith living in the machine age.

MURFREE, MARY N. (CHARLES EGBERT CRADDOCK, pseud.), 1850-1922
The Prophet of the Great Smoky Mountains (1885). A tale of Tennessee superstitions and revivalism after the Civil War.

PAAP, OPAL LEIGH (BERRYMAN), 1897-
Pioneer Preacher (Crowell, 1948). A fictionalized account of the author's father, a Baptist minister in a Texas town early in the twentieth century. A tender account of a family facing hardship while the father faced saloon keepers, cattle rustlers, and other sinners.

POWER, CRAWFORD
The Encounter (Sloane, 1950). An important, careful, subtle examination of a puritanic Catholic priest in a Maryland town and later in Philadelphia—his relationships with fellow ecclesiastics, parishioners,

and a vaudeville entertainer, and his agonies of conscience over his pride, his "vice of metaphysical egomania."

POWERS, JAMES FARL, 1917-
Prince of Darkness (Lehmann, 1948). Stories about Chicago Catholics —nuns, monks, a monsignor—and also about baseball players and night-club Negroes. Good anecdotes and characterizations, especially in the title story, which is about a busy day in the life of one Father Burner.
The Presence of Grace (Doubleday, 1956). A cycle of short stories of priests, bishops, parishioners, in Illinois, the Dakotas, and Minnesota.
Morte d'Urban (Doubleday, 1962). Excellent characterization and much genial humor, in the world of Catholic orders in Chicago and rural Minnesota. Dramatizes such problems as how to "raise the *tone*" of an order, how to handle public relations, how to set up and maintain a retreat, and how to face the changing reputation of a parish.

RICHTER, CONRAD, 1890-
A Simple Honorable Man (Knopf, 1962). The life story of a Lutheran pastor who spends his time among the coal-mining towns of western Pennsylvania, turning down chances to serve in wealthier communities.

ROBINSON, HENRY MORTON, 1898-
The Perfect Round (Harcourt, 1945). A fantasy of the conflict between good and evil in modern life. A returned soldier struggles against moral evil in the postwar world and finally regains his faith in the Catholic church.
The Cardinal (Simon, 1950). A novel based on episodes from the lives of several priests. Good in exposition of Catholic ideas and attitudes.

ROHRBACH, PETER THOMAS
A Gentle Fury (Hanover, 1959). A somewhat sentimental story of a young priest who makes good in a slum parish, where he fights the narcotics traffic and wins the confidence of the neighborhood.

ROLVAAG, OLE E., 1876-1931
Their Father's God (Harper, 1931). A realistic account of the disintegration of a family chiefly as a result of the religious differences between the Catholic wife and the agnostic husband.

SHELDON, CHARLES, 1857-1946
In His Steps (1897). A statement of the social gospel, advocating that churches concern themselves with social problems rather than with individual salvation. Over 23,000,000 copies sold, in 21 languages.

SMITH, LILLIAN, 1897-1966
One Hour (Harcourt, 1959). A psychological study of a pastor in a Southern city as he wrestles with the problems that arise when one of his friends is accused of attempting to rape an eight-year-old girl.

The author awkwardly arranges her material but gives a perceptive glimpse of individual tensions in a society that seems inclined toward neurosis.

SPELLMAN, FRANCIS JOSEPH, CARDINAL, 1889-
The Foundling (Scribner's, 1951). A simply told, appealing story of a foundling brought up by the welfare agencies of the Church, emphasizing what the Church does for the unfortunate. Accepts as good, some decisions the non-Catholic reader may question.

STREET, JAMES HOWELL, 1903-
The Gauntlet (Doubleday, 1945). The story of a Baptist minister and his search to find his functional place amid church politics in a small Missouri town.
High Calling (Doubleday, 1951). Story of a Baptist pastor in a small Missouri town. Sentimental and appealing, upholding some simple religious doctrines. Sequel to *The Gauntlet*.

THOMASON, JOHN WILLIAM, 1893-1944
Lone Star Preacher (Scribner's, 1941). A collection of eight stories of a Methodist Episcopal preacher from Texas who accompanied the Texas men in the Army of Northern Virginia in the Civil War. See above, p. 141.

TURNBULL, AGNES SLIGH, 1888-
The Bishop's Mantle (Macmillan, 1947). Of a young rector of the Episcopal Church. A well-integrated study of the life and faith of a modern churchman and of the problems he must face, such as tenements in the city and the tenets of his sermons. Mature and satisfying.

WALWORTH, DOROTHY, 1900-
Nicodemus (Houghton, 1946). Begins with the Easter morning service of a fashionable Fifth Avenue church and ends there on the following Christmas Eve. A composite portrait of people in search of faith.

WELLMAN, PAUL ISELIN, 1898-1966
The Chain (Doubleday, 1949). A clever, light novel about a serious subject: a spiritually minded Episcopal minister in conflict with his comfortable, materialistic congregation. Set in a Kansas town.

WILDER, THORNTON, 1897-
Heaven's My Destination (Harper, 1934). Shows what happens to a textbook salesman who tries to live up to his religious principles in a world dominated by business ideals.

ZIEGLER, ISABELLE GIBSON, 1904-
The Nine Days of Father Serra (Longmans, 1951). About early missionary days in San Diego. Notable for vivid characterizations of Father Junípero Serra, Indians, and the military leaders.

3. THE JEWS

Although Jews have been present in North America since the seventeenth century (the earlier ones being Spanish, Portuguese, or English, the later ones being German, Polish, or Russian, mainly), a body of fiction dealing directly with Jews as a group did not develop until the turn of the twentieth century. Many books concentrate on the struggle for adjustment of various immigrant groups as they find their religious traditions in conflict with the customs and habits of the United States and Canada. As in the stories of other religious persuasions, the revolt of the young against the restrictions of their elders is a common theme.

ANGOFF, CHARLES, 1902-
Journey to the Dawn (Beechhurst, 1951). Takes the Polonsky family from a Russian village (around 1900) to Boston, where there is conflict between the orthodox and the Zionists or the moderns. Much on the good and bad features of life for Jews in America. Rich in details and phrases of life and language.
In the Morning Light (Beechhurst, 1952). Takes young David Polonsky through high school and his early errand-boy jobs, while World War I is going on. Long, even prolix, and drenched with details of Jewish life, and a great variety of personal conflicts within the family.
The Sun at Noon (Beechhurst, 1955). Follows David and his Boston family during his four years at Harvard, 1919-1923. Much on Harvard professors, including stringent comments on actual persons, and on the intellectual exposure of a student in Widener Library. Good on Russian Jews caught between European and American ways.
Between Day and Dark (Yoseloff, 1959). Very long, again, and also rich in fresh details of Jewish family life, as David works on papers in Boston and in a small town, learns about American magazines, and accepts an invitation from Harry P. Brandt (H. L. Mencken) to go to New York and work on the *American World (Mercury)*.
The Bitter Spring (Yoseloff, 1961). Takes David to Manhattan's coteries of editors, intellectuals, critics, with vivid closeups of characters clearly modeled on persons like Mencken and George Jean Nathan. A social history of New York in the 1920's, including the sophisticated fad for Negroes.
Summer Storm (Yoseloff, 1963). David and the other Polonskys during the years 1933-1935. Over-detailed, with much on state and national leaders and shifting currents of opinion as Hitler rises in Europe and Mencken declines in America.

ASCH, SHALOM (SHOLEM), 1880-1957
Uncle Moses (Dutton, 1918). Deals with Polish Jews adjusting themselves to an American environment.
The Mother (Liveright, 1930). The tragic story of a young girl who

spends her days acting as a mother to the younger members of her
family of Polish Jews that migrate to New York. She later is forced to
be a "mother" to her husband and is never allowed a normal life.
Passage in the Night (Putnam, 1953). Centers on one man's search for
spiritual peace as he attempts to right a wrong committed when he was
young. His struggle is with his son, who puts family prestige above his
father's sense of ethics. Quiet and forceful writing.

BARKER, SHIRLEY
Strange Wives (Crown, 1963). Set in Newport, Rhode Island, at the
time of the Revolution, centering on the marriage of a Jew and a Puritan girl and their gradual acceptance of each other.

BELLOW, SAUL, 1915-
Herzog (Viking, 1964). About a Russian-Jewish professor of literature
and philosophy in New York City—his memories of childhood in
Montreal, his years in Chicago, his well-informed and widely grounded
thoughts about events. The book has a richly supra-American quality
of ideas, values, foreign languages, memories, many-sided experiences.

BLANKFORT, MICHAEL, 1907-
The Strong Hand (Little, 1956). Deals with a devout American Jew, a
rabbi who is a combat chaplain. Scenes in the Philippines, Hollywood,
and New York. Stamped with reality. Gives insight into the faith and
the practices of first- and second-generation Jews for whom Judaism
is "religion, nation or culture or all of these."

BRINIG, MYRON, 1900-
Singermann (Farrar, 1929). Of a Jewish family that leaves Rumania to
settle in Silver Bow, Montana, a mining town resembling Butte. The
children all become a part of American life in various ways. The parents are pathetic in their lifelong struggle.
This Man is My Brother (Farrar, 1932). Sequel to *Singermann*, with
much stress on the sexual and other psychological problems of the
second generation.

CAHAN, ABRAHAM, 1860-1951
The Rise of David Levinsky (1917). An excellent, classic biographical
portrait of one man adjusting himself to life in America. Vivid pictures of his early life in Russia. Good presentation of Jewish social
customs and folk attitudes. Strife of orthodox versus unorthodox, and
of German-Jew versus Russian-Jew.

CASPARY, VERA, 1899-
Thicker Than Water (Liveright, 1932). A chronicle of three generations in a Jewish family in Chicago. Shows orthodox religion losing its
hold.

COHEN, HYMAN, and COHEN, LESTER, 1901-1963
Aaron Traum (Liveright, 1930). Of Slavic Jews in America. An excellent realistic picture of life among the garment workers of New York City. The hero and his friends become unionists.

COURNOS, JOHN, 1881-
The Mask (Boni, 1920). A sensitive account of Russian Jews who transplant themselves to America and find themselves trapped economically in the textile mills of the City of Brotherly Love. *A klug zu Kolumbussen,* "Woe to Columbus!"

DAHLBERG, EDWARD, 1900-
Those Who Perish (Day, 1934). A psychological novel of American Jews and their reactions to the coming of German Nazism.

FERBER, NAT J., 1889-
The Sidewalks of New York (Covici, 1927). A story of a Russian boy who grows up with his foster parents on the East Side of New York. Shows life in the ghetto and its effect on residents.
One Happy Jew (Farrar, 1934). A story of five brothers. The one who remains true to his family traditions is the "happy Jew."

FIELD, BEN, 1901-
The Outside Leaf (Reynal, 1943). About a Jewish tobacco farmer who loves his Connecticut land. This vigorous novel is a non-stereotyped account of the Jew in America.

FUCHS, DANIEL, 1909-
Summer in Williamsburg (Vanguard, 1934). A novel about the people of Williamsburg, the Jewish section of Brooklyn—a dreamer who commits suicide, a racketeer, the leader of a boys' gang, a salesman's wife.
Homage to Blenholt (Vanguard, 1936). More Williamsburg tenement characters, with good reporting on the milieu. Mostly about one family with a son studying literature and all getting ahead and coming to own a delicatessen, and so on up.
Low Company (Vanguard, 1937). Focuses on a soda parlor at "Neptune Beach," where gangsters and whoremasters compete to control a string of houses and where petty gamblers and thieves and brutal amateurish murderers appear. These three Fuchs books, all reprinted in *Three Novels* (Basic, 1961), are witty, sad, faithful pictures of Jewish Brooklyn and nearby beaches in the early 1930's.

GOLD, MICHAEL, 1894-
Jews Without Money (Liveright, 1930). The East Side of New York as Gold saw it in his youth. Pictures of crowded tenements, prostitution, dirt, and crime. Good descriptions of Jewish characters.

GOLLOMB, JOSEPH, 1881-
Unquiet (Dodd, 1935). Presents a man's life from childhood in Russia through adolescence in East Side New York tenements. Indicates the busy life of the streets. Presents the conflict of family loyalty and personal aspiration.

GORDON, NOAH
The Rabbi (McGraw, 1965). A story of a thoroughly modern rabbi, tracing his life from 1925, when he is a young boy, up to 1964 when he is middle-aged. He marries a convert, daughter of a Congregational minister, and much of the psychological impact of the story has to do with prejudice among members of the two religious groups. He serves a number of congregations, each different, and each with its own shortcomings and failures to practice a socially motivated faith. Excellent portrayal.

GRAHAM, GWETHALYN, 1913-1965
Earth and High Heaven (Lippincott, 1944). A lecture in disguise dealing with the psychological problems of a Gentile-Jewish marriage. Covers the standard arguments and basic situations. Laid in Quebec during the war years, 1939-1945. A wise book on love, marriage, and "race" prejudice.

HOBSON, LAURA Z.
Gentleman's Agreement (Simon, 1947). An outspoken novel about social anti-Semitism in America.

HURST, FANNIE, 1889-
Humoresque, a Laugh on Life with a Tear Behind It (1919). Eight stories of Jewish life in New York City. The ordinary ups-and-downs of common people in the slightly sentimental tone of the Progressive Era.

JESSEY, CORNELIA
Growing Roots (Crown, 1947). Of Russian Jews in Colorado from the 1890's on. The first half of the book is a definitive re-creation of the life of a Jewish immigrant family. The second half talks of anti-Semitism and Zionism. An able, thoughtful novel of the growth of a girl.

LAWRENCE, JOSEPHINE
Let Us Consider One Another (Appleton, 1945). The love story of a young American girl, of mixed Protestant and Catholic descent, who marries a Jewish army officer. Her reactions to unexpected discrimination that follows on their marriage and her struggles with her own family point up this study of American intolerance. Realistic, vivid, and effective.

LEVIN, MEYER, 1905-
The Fanatic (Simon, 1964). A story with many threads that reflects

life in the synagogue and in the theatrical world during the late 1940's and early 1950's.

LEWISOHN, LUDWIG, 1882-1955
The Island Within (Harper, 1928). A tragicomedy of the ingrained character of the Jew, with its ethnic pride, ambition, frustration, and compensations.
Trumpet of Jubilee (Harper, 1937). Story of the conditions of the Jew under Hitler. A young nonreligious lawyer is murdered, and his wife and son flee first to France and then to America. Here in a Midwestern city they live with their relatives, whose narrow-mindedness appalls them.

LIPTON, LAWRENCE, 1898-
Brother, the Laugh is Bitter (Harper, 1942). Of a would-be businessman, gangsterism, anti-Semitism, and also orthodox Jewish home life.

MALAMUD, BERNARD, 1914-
The Assistant (Farrar, 1957). A simply told story packed with meaning, about a poor Jewish grocer in New York and his Italian assistant, who gradually overcomes his ambivalent feeling about Jews and becomes a Jew. An appealing study of character development.

MILLER, ARTHUR, 1915-
Focus (Reynal, 1945). Dramatizes anti-Semitism on one block of a city street. A study of nightmarish fear and poisonous prejudice. Makes anti-Semitism real and comprehensible. Particularly effective because the hero, although taken for a Jew, is not Jewish.

ORNITZ, SAMUEL BADISCH, 1890-1957
Bride of the Sabbath (Rinehart, 1951). The story of a Jewish boy growing up in New York City from about 1900 to 1930. Critical of Jewish custom and religion, also of Catholic. The main character throws orthodox religion overboard.

ROSENBERG, JOSEPH D.
Kosher Americans (Associated Publishers, 1929). A detailed study of life of a Jewish-American family, once poor and now rich. Depicts customs, records speech, dramatizes troubles.

ROTH, PHILIP
Goodbye, Columbus (Houghton, 1959). Six stories of present-generation Jews. Realistically observing of the manners, speech, and attitudes of persons caught between faith and cynicism.

SCHNEIDER, ISIDOR, 1896-
From the Kingdom of Necessity (Putnam, 1935). An autobiographical novel which traces a man's life from the time he comes to America at the age of six until he reaches maturity and finds his place in the world.

SEID, RUTH (JO SINCLAIR, pseud.)
Wasteland (Harper, 1946). Shows the emotional problems of the children of Russian Jews. They dwell in a wasteland between being immigrants and being Americans. The central character "finds himself" with the aid of a psychiatrist. A strong realistic novel.

TODRIN, BORIS
Out of These Roots (Caxton, 1944). Puts into print the polyglot world of Brooklyn and shows a boy growing up. He is the son of an intellectual Jewish family from southern Russia.

WEIDMAN, JEROME, 1913-
The Enemy Camp (Random, 1958). Of a Jew married to a Gentile woman, whom he has never fully accepted, since he thinks of her as part of "the enemy camp." A domestic crisis shows him he has been wrong.

WISEMAN, ADELE
The Sacrifice (Viking, 1956). Newly arrived European Jews, in some city or other, who have a rich and varied family life. Reworks the Abraham and Isaac story and adds comedy to it, in a "butcher shop-delicatessen-kibitzarnia."

YELLEN, SAMUEL, 1906-
The Wedding Band (Atheneum, 1961). A compact, revealing, artistic analysis of the marriage of an immigrant Jew and a native American non-Jew. A detailed view of Jewish life, including some quasi-comic clashes, in the Cleveland of the 1920's.

YEZIERSKA, ANZIA, 1885-
Hungry Hearts (Houghton, 1920). Stories of the immigrant's struggles in New York's ghetto. Intense, vivid, and appealing.
Salome of the Tenements (Boni, 1923). Of a Jewess unhappily married to a Gentile. Sensational.
Bread Givers (Doubleday, 1925). Of a Jewish girl fighting her way from poverty through college and into the teaching profession. Convincing realism.
Arrogant Beggar (Doubleday, 1927). Of a girl from the tenements and her experience with organized charity. A lively style.

4. RELIGIOUS EXPERIMENTS AND SMALL SECTS (INCLUDING DISCIPLES OF CHRIST, MORMONS, QUAKERS, NAVAJOS, CHRISTIAN SCIENTISTS, AND SHAKERS)

There have been increasing numbers of novels about religious innovations, bizarre sects, communal experiments, and small but permanent groups such as the Quakers and the aboriginal Navajo tribe. Of the minor sects in the United States, the Latter-Day Saints, or Mormons, have received the most attention, probably because of the controversies they once raised and their hardy, successful settlement of Utah and nearby states. In fiction as in folklore the Mormons have appeared both noble and villainous. The Quakers have been almost as extensively treated, but have always appeared kindly and gentle, their mistreatment being the most constant theme. Novels about the Navajos show the conflict between indigenous beliefs and imported Christianity as part of an over-all clash of cultures.

ARMER, LAURA ADAMS, 1874-1963
Waterless Mountain (Longmans, 1931). Story laid among the Navajo Indians of northern Arizona today. The principal character is a sensitive young man who is training to be a Medicine Priest.

BALDWIN, JAMES, 1924-
Go Tell It on the Mountain (Knopf, 1953). The religious experiences of a fourteen-year-old Negro in the Temple of the Fire Baptized, in Harlem. Flashbacks tell of the early life of his father and others in the South. A psychologically intense study of minority Christians bitterly trapped in the world of non-Negro Christians.

BROWN, CHARLES B., 1771-1810
Wieland (1798). Portrays a religious maniac acting under the command of God. A novel of terror.

CAMERON, LESLIE GEORGIANA (ANN GEORGE LESLIE, pseud.), 1886-
Dancing Saints (Doubleday, 1943). Story of a boy's life from eight to twenty as a member of a "Shaker" group. A convincing narrative about a little-known religious group.

CAMERON, OWEN
The Antagonists (Doubleday, 1946). Of the conflicts between a farmer and a "faith healer" who has a great influence over the farmer's wife and one of his children. Gives a good analysis of the "savior" complex.

COCHRAN, LOUIS, 1899-
The Fool of God (Duell, 1958). A comprehensive novel based on the facts of the life of Alexander Campbell, founder of the Disciples of Christ. Details his beliefs and his arguments with Baptists and Presbyterians during his attempt to bring unity among Christian believers. Relates Campbell to the total life of his time, including the mid-nineteenth century struggle over slavery.

COOLIDGE, DANE, 1873-1940
The Fighting Danites (Dutton, 1934). Highly melodramatic story of plot and counterplot in the southern Mormon country along the Arizona line. Unfavorable to the Mormons.

CORLE, EDWIN, 1906-
People on the Earth (Random, 1937). Deals in large part with a Navajo boy's struggle between his own religion and that of the white man.

DELAND, MARGARET, 1857-1945
The Kays (Harper, 1926). The tale is dominated by an austerely religious "iron woman" (a member of the True Followers), who has the courage to be a conscientious objector in Civil War days, when pacifism was quite unpopular.

DREISER, THEODORE, 1871-1946
The Bulwark (Doubleday, 1946). This is a patient story of a fine Pennsylvania Quaker, a man with principles "too high for these days," who becomes a wealthy banker but never forgets the example of John Woolman or the precepts of the Book of Discipline. His children react to him in varying ways in the age of automobiles and flaming youth. Gives insight into the Society of Friends.

EGGLESTON, EDWARD, 1837-1902
The Faith Doctor (1891). Satirical treatment of early Christian Science and of the times which gave it its start.

EMERSON, ELIZABETH H.
The Good Crop (Longmans, 1946). A story of a Quaker couple who move their family of eleven children from Tennessee to Illinois in the nineteenth century. A descriptive and enlightening account of Quaker life.

ENGSTRAND, STUART D., 1905-1955
They Sought for Paradise (Harper, 1939). A fictionalized account of the Swedish immigrants who came to Bishop Hill, Illinois, under the guidance of Erik Jansson, a religious fanatic, who claimed to be a Messiah and established a communal settlement. Over-sensationalized on the subject of sex and underdeveloped psychologically.

ERTZ, SUSAN
The Proselyte (Appleton, 1933). Of Mormon missionary work in England, and the emigration of a group of converts to Salt Lake City via chartered boat, railroad, and foot. A good account of the Handcart Expedition across the plains. Details of life in Deseret. Deals with the problems raised in the minds of monogamous Mormons by the plural marriage revelations.

FISHER, AGNES ADAMS
Daylight and Dark (Funk, 1955). Latter-Day Saints in a Missouri village in the 1930's. The major character is in the process of breaking with his religious background, but his wife is torn between her religion and a more natural way of life. The younger generation seems to have "escaped." Psychologically satisfying.

FISHER, VARDIS, 1895-
Children of God (Harper, 1939). A dramatic account of troubles of the Mormons during their early history, especially in Missouri. Notable characterizations of Joseph Smith and Brigham Young. A tribute to the fanatical zeal that founded a substantial civilization in the desert.

GIBSON, JEWEL, 1904-
Joshua Beene and God (Random, 1946). A satire about an elderly Texan—Joshua—who thought he was the center of the universe and that God was made in his image. He was a member of the Church of Christ.

GILES, JANICE (HOLT)
The Believers (Houghton, 1957). Of a community set up on Gasper River, Kentucky, by the United Society of Believers in Christ's Second Coming ("Shakers"). Incidents of tyrannical goodness and of great wrongs perpetrated by gentle, innocent fanatics who refuse to countenance careful, tender marriage or sex "among God's people"—who do not "go against nature without becoming sterile." Carefully researched.

GREY, ZANE, 1872-1940
Riders of the Purple Sage (1912). Melodramatic and romantic story of Utah in 1871, in the days of Mormon authority. In part, picturing the invisible methods of pressure employed by the Church in an attempt to break the will of a faithful but independent woman member.

HAWTHORNE, NATHANIEL, 1804-1864
The Blithedale Romance (1852). A narrative of the persons taking part in the Brook Farm experiment, making clear why it failed.

HOWELLS, WILLIAM DEAN, 1837-1920
The Undiscovered Country (1880). An unsympathetic treatment of spiritualism and Shakerism; a study of the religious and emotional problems of Americans who have lost old church ties and are seeking new beliefs.
The Day of Their Wedding (1895). Two Shakers fall in love, marry, try to live in the "outside world," find adjustment impossible, and return to the colony to live as brother and sister. A mild satire.
The Leatherwood God (Century, 1916). A story of a man who claimed to be God, causing excitement in a small community.

HUGHES, LANGSTON, 1902-
Tambourines to Glory (Day, 1958). Hughes calls this story of "The Reed Sister's Tambourine Temple" "an urban folk tale set against a background of colorful independent unorthodox churches which have sprung up all over Harlem in the last decade." Shows how "Gospel racketeers" such as numbers ring operators endanger the activity of sincere religionists.

KEROUAC, JACK, 1922-
The Dharma Bums (Viking, 1958). Itinerant "Beat Generation" intellectuals, pretty much committed to the Bohemianism of San Francisco and Berkeley, climb up a West Coast mountain to search for Truth (Dharma) and Enlightenment. An odd and gusty mixture of naturalistic doings and Zen Buddhism talk. Kerouac puts more of the same in *Big Sur* (Farrar, 1962).

KIRKBRIDE, RONALD DE LEVINGTON, 1912-
Winds Blow Gently (Fell, 1945). A convincing picture of Quaker life and a dramatic exposition of the Quaker creed. About the experiences of a family of Pennsylvania Quakers, the David Jordans, who move to South Carolina.
Spring is not Gentle (Doubleday, 1949). The Jordan family start a co-operative to help their neighbors through the Depression. David and his wife are separated when he decides to be a conscientious objector in World War II.
Only the Unafraid (Duell, 1953). Third in the trilogy about David Jordan and his family. In this story David comes home from prison and helps to re-establish a rural co-operative. Differences of religious belief keep him from two women he loves.

LA FARGE, OLIVER, 1901-1963
Laughing Boy (Houghton, 1929). An excellent story of Navajos and their troubled relationships with whites. An appealing presentation of religious ideas and ideals.
The Enemy Gods (Houghton, 1937). A story centering directly on a Navajo boy's struggles with the white man's religion, and telling of his return to his own people and their ways.

LAURITZEN, JONREED
The Everlasting Fire (Doubleday, 1962). Extended treatment of the Mormons' experience at Nauvoo, Illinois, and of the basic issues it raised, such as the Constitution versus a Constitutional but industrious and unconventional sect. The siege of Nauvoo by Mormon haters, internal Mormon politics, the struggle for power after Joseph Smith was assassinated, the rise of Brigham Young, the Mormon dreamers of the good life who "build homes and temples, not saloons"—all these are here.

MARTIN, HELEN REIMENSNYDER, 1868-1939
Tillie, a Mennonite Maid: A Story of the Pennsylvania Dutch (1904). One of the popular dialect stories of the early 1900's. Thesis: the restricted life of Mennonite women.

MORRIS, HILDA, ?-1947
The Long View (Putnam, 1937). Of a Quaker family from the Civil War to 1929, in a New Jersey village and the Middle West.

NELSON, TRUMAN JOHN, 1912-
The Sin of the Prophet (Little, 1952). About Theodore Parker, the Unitarian abolitionist, and the famous case of Anthony Burns, the runaway slave in the Boston of 1854. A closely researched novel full of famous figures such as Richard Dana, Colonel Higginson, and Moncure Conway. Parker: "Though all the rulers in the world bid us commit treason against man, and set the example, let us never submit."

O'CONNOR, FLANNERY, 1925-1964
The Violent Bear It Away (Farrar, 1960). An old man in southeastern rural Tennessee claims Jonah-like prophetic powers and raises a boy "to expect the Lord's call" and be a prophet. Shows the strange, destructive—even murderous—things a Bible-obsessed person can do.

PUTNAM, NINA WILCOX, 1904-1962
The Inner Voice (Sheridan House, 1940). About the role Southern Quakers played in the abolition movement.

ROBERTSON, CONSTANCE
Seek-No-Further (Farrar, 1938). Story of an imaginary community in upstate New York in the 1860's. Presents the relationships between the community and the outside world. Awakens a sense of horror of "the machine." Story deals with the son of the founder of the community and of his struggle to rescue the girl he loves from a scheming intruder.

SCOWCROFT, RICHARD, 1916-
Children of the Covenant (Houghton, 1945). A tender and mature novel about a Mormon family in Ogden. Shows tensions in the church, the family, and individual characters. Realistic reportage on present-day Mormons, but emphasis on the universal rather than the peculiar.

SESSLER, J. J., 1899-
Saints and Tomahawks (Pyramid, 1940). A historical novel of the Moravian settlements in Pennsylvania, 1736-1760.

SINCLAIR, UPTON B., 1878-
They Call Me Carpenter (Regan, 1922). A clever satire in which Jesus comes to Los Angeles in modern times, does and says the things he did and said in his own time, only to be pronounced a freak and denied the right to become a martyr.

SNEDEKER, CAROLINE DALE, 1871-
The Town of the Fearless (Doubleday, 1931). On the socialist experiment at New Harmony, Indiana.
Uncharted Ways (Doubleday, 1935). A thoughtful story of early colonial days. Gives a picture of the persecutions of the Quakers by tyrannical and bigoted Puritans. Interprets the religious beliefs and faith that motivated the lives of the principal characters.

SNELL, GEORGE D.
Root, Hog, and Die (Caxton, 1937). A novel of an upstate New York farm boy who is inspired by Mormonism to go to the Utah paradise, where in time he becomes prosperous and influential in business enterprises. Laid against the background of the history of the Latter-Day Saints, from New York to Salt Lake City.

SORENSEN, VIRGINIA (EGGERTSEN), 1912-
A Little Lower than the Angels (Knopf, 1942). Of Mormons in Nauvoo, the main character a sensitive woman married to a Mormon.
On This Star (Reynal, 1946). Describes the tightly knit insularity of the Mormon community and the religious conflicts of one woman.

WHIPPLE, MAURINE, 1904-
The Giant Joshua (Houghton, 1941). The story of the settlement of St. George, in southern Utah, as seen by the young third wife of an old Mormon leader. A substantial picture of the Mormon settlers versus Indians, hunger, United States agents, and their own personal problems.

WYCKOFF, NICHOLAS E., 1906-
The Corinthians (Macmillan, 1960). Of a merchant and landholder who rents land to Mormons in Illinois and who carefully maintains relations with his barren Gentile wife in Illinois while reproducing with a Mormon woman in Missouri. A patient, proper, informed historical novel.

YOUNG, MARGUERITE, 1909-
Angel in the Forest (Scribner's, 1966). About two early nineteenth-century Utopian communities, the Rappites and the Owenites, at Harmony (New Harmony), Indiana. A big, rangy, imaginative book that sheds light on the origin of messianic compulsions as well as on the failure of plans for an ideal society on earth. First published in 1945.

MINORITY ETHNIC GROUPS

Next in popularity to "Farm and Village Life" and "Industrial America" as themes for fiction writers comes "Minority Ethnic Groups." The peculiarities in dress, language, and folkways of the newly arrived immigrant and such other distinct groups as Negroes and Indians have been a constant invitation to comment, and the terrible social and psychological adjustments these minorities have had to make have been a challenge to observation and analysis. Since the populations of the United States and Canada are composed of so many ethnic fragments, any nationalistic or racial group represented here could be thought of as a minority ethnic group; but *America in Fiction* is concerned only with those books which in some way point out one or more groups as distinct.

In the number of books written about him the Negro leads. We have noted more than twice as many novels about the Negro as about the Indian, who ranks second in our list. We have made a third group of the French, Spanish, Italians, and Latin Americans—since in many respects the books about these groups stress somewhat similar mores. Other ethnic groups, none of whom are represented so generously as the foregoing, are lumped together in our Section 4.

1. THE NEGRO

The Negro is the largest and most distinct minority ethnic group in the United States, since European nationalities, such as the German, which may actually outnumber the Negro in our total population, merge so completely with our basic pattern in a couple of generations that they are lost as a minority group. Several unique things are to be noted about the Negro group as compared with other minorities. First and foremost, he is the most distinct minority, because of his color, and at the same time most like the great bulk of the American population in his folkways and his beliefs, because he has been here just as long as the Puritans of Massachusetts and the Cavaliers of Virginia and the "old-timers" of the West. He is called "race problem" number one, or he faces race problem number one: prejudiced white people. Aside from fiction of the "Old South," listed elsewhere, the most noticeable subgrouping of fiction concerning him (were we to attempt division) would perhaps be into books about urban Northern Negroes and books about rural Southern Negroes. As with other subjects there has been a general progress from sentimental, romantic treatment in the nineteenth century to a realistic, analytical treatment in the twentieth century. Certain stereotyped misconceptions of Negro character have shown remarkable vitality. Like folklore, literature has been all too prone to think in terms of such types as the contented plantation "darky," the amoral creature of joy, the arrogant brute of Reconstruction, the exploited proletarian, or the civil rights rioter. Sensational matters, including sex and lynching, have been overemphasized. The daily life of most Negroes and the psychological attitudes that result from segregation have received proportionately meager treatment. So controversial is the whole "Negro question" that strong stories dealing with it are likely to be partisan or propagandistic, protesting against the way the Negro is reserved for violence, sexual exploitation, political pay-offs, and dirty work, as he is in Baldwin's *Another Country* and Wright's *The Long Dream*.

ADAMS, EDWARD C. L., 1876-
Congaree Sketches (University of North Carolina, 1927). Forceful and effective stories of Negro life in South Carolina—of prayers, wakes, farming, chain gangs, etc. Some good, nonstereotyped Negro comedy. *Nigger to Nigger* (Scribner's, 1928). Intimate folk humor but, even more, protest against the cruel ways of white folks.

ANDERSON, ALSTON, 1924-
Lover Man (Doubleday, 1959). Fifteen vignettes that range in setting from Alabama to New York and once to Germany with a GI. Told in the first person in appropriate speech by a variety of Negroes.

APPEL, BENJAMIN, 1907-
The Dark Stain (Dial, 1943). Told with detachment, an unencumbered account of the clash of white and black in Harlem. This tale of cop vs. Negro gone berserk sums up three centuries of "racial" conflict. "All the elements of a thriller and all the threat of a warning."

ATTAWAY, WILLIAM, 1911-
Blood on the Forge (Doubleday, 1941). A skillful depiction of what happens to three Negro boys who leave the Kentucky plantation to work among the slag heaps and Bessemers of Pennsylvania. Sharply drawn picture of psychological effects on the Negro of the two ways of life.

BALDWIN, JAMES, 1924-
Another Country (Dial, 1962). A bitter anti-whites document of repetitious sex, violence, perversion, and degradation in the Harlem and Greenwich Village entertainment world—"a region where there were no definitions of any kind, neither of color, nor of male and female."

BASSO, HAMILTON, 1904-1964
Courthouse Square (Scribner's, 1936). Shows the plight of a justice-loving liberal in a Southern town. Quietly demonstrates the cruel exploitation of the Negro.

BLAND, ALDEN, 1911-
Behold a Cry (Scribner's, 1947). About an urban Negro worker who

has migrated from the South, and his personal and social tensions. Laid in Chicago during World War I and the early 1920's.

BRADFORD, ROARK, 1896-1948

This Side of Jordan (Harper, 1929). Pictures day-by-day life of Negroes on a plantation in the bayou country. Involves folkways and important happenings, such as an epidemic of syphilis and a Mississippi flood.

John Henry (Harper, 1931). One of the best versions of the tall tales of a superhuman Negro stevedore in a class with Paul Bunyan, Mike Fink, and Pecos Bill. Emphasis on philandering and other attributes commonly ascribed to Negroes.

Let the Band Play Dixie, and Other Stories (Harper, 1934). A collection of twelve short stories about the everyday life of Southern Negroes. Presents also much of Negro psychology and an insight into Negro character, action, and motivation.

BROOKS, GWENDOLYN, 1917-

Maud Martha (Harper, 1953). Valid picture of colored people in Chicago through the eyes of a sensitive girl growing up and into marriage and motherhood. Written by a well-known poet.

BROWN, FRANK LONDON

Trumbull Park (Regnery, 1959). A thesis story about the first Negro families to move into a Chicago housing project. Of the terror and anxiety they endure and the self-respect they gain by staying.

CALDWELL, ERSKINE, 1903-

Kneel to the Rising Sun (Viking, 1935). The title story and others in the volume depict the Southern Negro as a member of the working class, crushed by the economic system.

CALLAGHAN, MORLEY, 1903-

The Loved and the Lost (Macmillan, 1959). A love story with good treatment of the subtleties of Negro-white and other prejudged relationships in Montreal.

CASPARY, VERA, 1899-

White Girl (Sears, 1929). Story of an ambitious girl from the South who comes to Chicago, where she easily passes as a white. But throughout her new life and new experiences she is in constant fear lest she be discovered to be a Negro. A good description of the lonely big city life and of the life of lower-class working girls.

CHESNUTT, CHARLES WADDELL, 1858-1932

The Conjure Woman (1899). Negro life as depicted by an old Negro telling stories to a white woman. Reminiscent of Joel Chandler Harris.

The Wife of His Youth; and Other Stories of the Colour Line (1900). Studies of the character and racial feeling of half-breeds.

The House Behind the Cedars (1900). Concerned with the color line. A story involving an octoroon heroine and a mulatto suitor. By the first important Negro novelist.

COOK, FANNIE, 1893-

Mrs. Palmer's Honey (Doubleday, 1946). About a St. Louis woman who evolves from being a "perfect servant" into a militant Negro leader. Covers the whole field of Northern Negro thinking—attitudes toward world wars, intermarriage, education, segregation, labor unions. The characters are stock symbols of opposing forces rather than flesh-and-blood persons.

CULLEN, COUNTEE, 1903-1946

One Way to Heaven (Harper, 1932). Presents two aspects of Harlem life, the religious, hard-working underdogs and the intelligentsia with their assumed sophistication.

DuBOIS, WILLIAM E. B., 1868-1963

The Dark Princess (Harcourt, 1928). A romantic story of the welding together of all the dark races of the earth. The hero, an American Negro, loves an Indian princess from Asia. Realistic passages about such things as the life of a Pullman porter.

DUNBAR, PAUL LAURENCE, 1872-1906

The Best Stories of Paul Laurence Dunbar (edited by Benjamin Brawley) (Dodd, 1938). Selections from Dunbar's four collections of short stories: *Folks from Dixie*, 1898; *The Strength of Gideon*, 1900; *In Old Plantation Days*, 1903; *The Heart of Happy Hollow*, 1904. Entertaining sentimental stories of Negroes throughout the nineteenth century, ranging from broad comedy to serious treatment of labor strife and lynching.

ELLISON, RALPH, 1914-

The Invisible Man (Random, 1952). A vivid, symbolic, prescient, extraordinary story of a responsible, college-trained young Southern man making his way among conflicting attitudes and exploitations in Manhattan. Excellent on the Negro's problems of personality and identity in a world of dispossession and eviction. Shows Negroes betraying Negroes. At base is a protest against the idea, North or South, "that white is right."

FAULKNER, WILLIAM, 1897-1962

Intruder in the Dust (Random, 1948). Partly a propaganda piece on the subject of the Negro and lynching; partly an intense, vivid, macabre story involving violent Mississippi hill folk and a blood-hungry town.

FAUSET, JESSIE R., 1885-1961

There Is Confusion (Boni, 1924). Of present-day, wealthy Negroes, talented and descended from honored slave families. Tells of their struggle for self-expression and social betterment.

Plum Bun (Stokes, 1929). A love triangle involving a man, who is passing as white, and two sisters, one of whom is white. Clear contrasts of Negro and white life in New York City.

The Chinaberry Tree (Stokes, 1931). Pictures middle-class Negroes in a New Jersey town as living lives quite parallel to the lives of whites of similar economic and cultural status, including snobbery and social ostracism.

Comedy: American Style (Stokes, 1933). The story of a group of young near-white Negroes in Philadelphia. Shows the life of one family embittered because of the mother's determination to pass as white and to marry her children to white people.

FEIBLEMAN, PETER S., 1930-

A Place Without Twilight (World, 1958). Told by an almost-white New Orleans girl who is caught in the racial trap of being an outsider to Negroes and whites. She is a fine, sensitive person, a virgin "stuck between the night and the day," increasingly aware of reality. Evocative touches and good dialog.

FISHER, RUDOLPH, 1897-

The Walls of Jericho (Knopf, 1928). A picture of Harlem and of the Negro's thoughts and habits. A story of the tempestuous courtship of a large piano mover and a pretty housemaid.

FLANNAGAN, ROY C., 1897-1952

Amber Satyr (Doubleday, 1932). A condemnation of Southern lynch law. Shows a community killing a splendid mulatto who repulses the advances of a white woman.

FULLER, EDMUND, 1914-

A Star Pointed North (Harper, 1946). A novelized biography of Frederic Douglass, a slave who escaped North and became a leader in abolitionism in the United States and abroad. Re-creates the days of slavery in the South and reform zeal in the North.

HARRIS, JOEL CHANDLER, 1848-1908

Uncle Remus (1881). Folk-stories in dialect as told by a "plantation Negro."

Nights with Uncle Remus (1883). More folk tales, told by Uncle Remus and others.

Free Joe and Other Georgian Sketches (1887). Contains two long stories of Negroes, old-fashioned "darkies."

HARRIS, MARK, 1922-

Trumpet to the World (Reynal, 1946). Of a Negro who is educated and loved by a white woman, and persecuted in Army and civilian life, and yet never loses his perspective. A clear-headed, constructive, unembittered book about individual and group relationships.

HEDDEN, MRS. WORTH TUTTLE
The Other Room (Crown, 1947). Of a young white Virginia woman who becomes a teacher in a Negro school in New Orleans and gradually loses most of her aversion for Negroes. Psychologically sound and satisfyingly dramatic.

HENDERSON, GEORGE W.
Ollie Miss (Stokes, 1935). An unusual story of a migratory Negro worker, a girl, who is a field hand for other Negroes. Interesting psychological study of simple-minded croppers.
Jule (Creative Age, 1946). Sequel to *Ollie Miss*. Of her son's boyhood in Alabama, his courtship, and his experiences in finding work and friendship in New York City.

HEWLETT, JOHN HENRY, 1905-
Cross on the Moon (Whittlesey, 1946). A study of bigotry, hypocrisy, and intolerance in the South, with the purpose of shocking the reader into a realization of the forces and conditions that lie behind the accounts of Southern racial violence.

HEYWARD, DuBOSE, 1885-
Porgy (Doubleday, 1925). Pathetic story of a crippled Negro in the swarming tenement quarter of Charleston.
Mamba's Daughters (Doubleday, 1929). Of three generations of Negro women and their struggles to amount to something.

HIMES, CHESTER B., 1909-
If He Hollers Let Him Go (Doubleday, 1945). Laid in the shipyards of wartime Los Angeles. A violent book about discrimination, torment, hate, and murder. Hardboiled in technique and bitter and protesting in spirit.
Lonely Crusade (Knopf, 1947). A story showing the psychological effects of fear on a union organizer in all his relationships with men and women. An angry, violent story of labor struggles, communist politics, race prejudice, and sexual aggression—among workers and employers in an aircraft plant.

HOLMES, JOHN CLELLON, 1926-
The Horn (Random, 1958). About a Negro saxophonist with an original style and the musicians he appears with, all yearners after ideal beauty. Close detail on how jazz is performed. Like jazz, the author is rhapsodic and epigrammatic.

HUGHES, LANGSTON, 1902-
Not Without Laughter (Knopf, 1930). A good, plain, realistic story of a Negro boy growing up in Kansas and Chicago. Autobiographic, seemingly. Pictures the struggles of an intelligent Negro family against discrimination and humiliation.
The Ways of White Folks (Knopf, 1934). A group of short stories told

from a Negro's point of view about the relations between the Negro and white. Artistic and class-conscious.

HURSTON, ZORA NEALE, 1901-1960
Jonah's Gourd Vine (Lippincott, 1934). Pictures country life, including religion, in the far South, with abundant Negro dialect.
Mules and Men (Lippincott, 1935). An accurate recording of Negro folk tales of store porches and turpentine camps.
Their Eyes Were Watching God (Lippincott, 1937). A story of Florida Negroes, in particular of a handsome quadroon woman.

JOHNSON, JAMES WELDON, 1871-1938
The Autobiography of an Ex-Colored Man (1912). A readable and important novel which discusses, either directly or by implication, snobbery within the Negro group, "passing," the attitude of the Southern white, and the artistic capacity of the Negro.

KELLEY, WELBOURN, 1916-
Inchin' Along (Morrow, 1932). Of an Alabama Negro and his struggle for freedom and independence from white injustice and domination.

KILLENS, JOHN OLIVER-
And Then We Heard the Thunder (Knopf, 1963). Follows the mistreatment a Negro GI receives in Georgia, California, and Australia.

KYTLE, ELIZABETH
Willie Mae (Knopf, 1958). A "true-story" fictional composite that is substantially correct, the author says, for "almost any Southern Negro." As written, is a remarkable self-revelation, told in her language, by a Georgia girl who becomes a house servant in Atlanta and Louisville and goes on to many factory or field jobs, marriage, and all the tasks of day-to-day living, before and after World War I.

LARSEN, NELLA
Quicksand (Knopf, 1928). Of a woman, part Negro, part Dane, who belongs to two ethnic groups, yet not to either, and struggles for self-realization.
Passing (Knopf, 1929). Story of a fair-skinned, beautiful Negro who passed for "white" in society and marriage.

LEE, GEORGE W., 1894-
River George (Macaulay, 1937). Of an educated Tennessee Negro persecuted by whites for trying to aid his fellows.

LEWIS, BESSIE
To Save Their Souls (Christopher, 1939). A story running from 1810 to about 1870. Shows that the Negroes gained a great deal in being brought to America. Satirizes the Northerners for trying to "save their souls," and shows that the Southerner knows best.

McKAY, CLAUDE, 1890-1948
Home to Harlem (Harper, 1928). A tale of a returned soldier's search for a girl he met in a cabaret. A picture of the home and the night life of the Harlem Negro. Shows gay abandon in speakeasies and buffet flats.

MEADE, JULIAN R., 1909-1940
The Back Door (Longmans, 1938). A sympathetic novel of a Negro couple in the South, the girl a domestic helper for a white family, and her good-looking husband, a factory worker.

MIERS, EARL SCHENCK, 1910-
Big Ben (Westminster, 1941). A fictionalized biography of Paul Robeson. Clearly presents the problems of a gifted Negro in a society which demands that a Negro "know his place."

MILLER, WARREN
The Cool World (Little, 1959). In his own language the "President of the Royal Crocadiles," a Harlem gang, tells of his activities, his code, of rumbles, murder, dope-peddling, of dirty streets, rats and roaches, even of possible redemption. A highly readable, astonishing inside view of restless youths in a world of transients.

MOON, BUCKLIN, 1911-
The Darker Brother (Country Life Press, 1943). An excellent portrait of various believable Negro characters in New York today, particularly those migrating from Florida.
Without Magnolias (Doubleday, 1949). Story centering around the president of a Negro college in Florida, his secretary, and a member of his staff. Believable incidents and psychology.

NEARING, SCOTT, 1883-
Free Born (Urquhart, 1932). Subtitle: "An Unpublishable Novel." Of a class-conscious Negro. Contains gruesome details of lynching and physical maltreatment. "The first revolutionary novel of Negro life." More indignant than literary.

OWENS, WILLIAM A., 1905-
Walking on Borrowed Land (Bobbs, 1954). A good picture of a Negro principal of a school in Oklahoma. He meets personal tragedy, but keeps his dignity, makes friends among both Negro and white, and improves the lot of his community. Good, serious realism.

PAGE, THOMAS NELSON, 1853-1922
In Ole Virginia (1887). Pictures the old-fashioned darky. One of the important books "creating" the type who loved "ol' Marster," etc.

PEEPLES, EDWIN AUGUSTUS
Swing Low (Houghton, 1945). A story of a Negro, country bred and country loving, who is persuaded by his wife to move to Atlanta.

Though he finds some friends and help there, ultimately he is defeated by prejudice and injustice, and returns to the country.

PETERKIN, JULIA, 1880-1961
Green Thursday (Knopf, 1924). Collection of stories about Negro farm life in the South. In each story there is reference to the Negroes' struggle against poverty and hunger. The book brings out their religion and superstition.
Black April (Bobbs, 1927). Stories of an isolated South Carolina plantation. Notable for catching the atmosphere and local color of Negro life, also for embodying much of what non-Negroes used to think Negroes were like.

PETRY, ANN LANE, 1911-
The Street (Houghton, 1946). A realistic novel about the struggle of a young Negro woman to make a decent life for herself and her young son in the slums of Harlem. She is good and all the other adults are bad, although she grew up in the same environment. The book shows Harlem as a ghetto exploited by unscrupulous whites and Negro collaborators.
The Narrows (Houghton, 1953). A perceptive story of a disastrous love affair between a rich white girl and a Negro. The principal setting is the Negro section of a small industrial town in Connecticut.

REDDING, JAY SAUNDERS, 1906-
Stranger and Alone (Harcourt, 1950). Fairly realistic story of a young man who works his way through college, and finally becomes a rather successful school administrator, double-crossing his racial group (Negro) in approved style.

REID, MAYNE, 1818-1883
The Quadroon (1856). A melodrama of "mixed blood." The basis for Dion Boucicault's sensational play, *The Octoroon*.

ROBERTS, ELIZABETH MADOX, 1885-1941
My Heart and My Flesh (Viking, 1927). A psychological study of the moods of a gently bred, white Kentucky girl who finds that some Negroes of the village are her half-sisters.

RYLEE, ROBERT, 1908-
Deep, Dark River (Farrar, 1935). Of a Negro who hopes to become a preacher but who kills another Negro and gets a sentence of life imprisonment. A symbolic title—the river typifies the stream of struggling blacks. The hero is happier in the penitentiary than he was outside.

SHELBY, GERTRUDE (SINGLETON) MATTHEWS, 1881-   , and
    STONEY, S. G.
Po' Buckra (Macmillan, 1930). Story of the penniless heiress to an

unproductive plantation who marries a "po' buckra," who, unknown to her, has both Negro and Indian blood. The authors exploit the most extreme doctrine of racial inferiority, showing that one with Negro blood is certain to be indolent and vicious.

SMITH, LILLIAN EUGENIA, 1897-1966
Strange Fruit (Reynal, 1944). Effective portrayal of how the Negro problem affects both white and Negro in the South, and how white discrimination affects everything a Negro says and does. Shows the ironic gap between religious theories and practices. Eloquent, yet artistically restrained.

SPIVAK, JOHN, 1897-
Georgia Nigger (Harcourt, 1932). An exposure of the convict-lease system and the tortures and cruelties of chain-gang prisons.

STRAUSS, THEODORE, 1912-
Night at Hogwallow (Little, 1937). Set in a shanty town in the South, a dramatic account of the lynching of an innocent Negro who is accused of rape.

STRIBLING, THOMAS SIGISMUND, 1881-
Birthright (Century, 1922). Story of a Harvard graduate, a mulatto, who returns to his home in Tennessee, where he again is subjected to discrimination. His hopes for changing his native home dwindle as he becomes acquainted with the economic conditions.

SUMMER, CID RICKETTS, 1890-
Quality (Bobbs, 1946). A plea for moderation in the struggle for Negro rights, set forth in the experiences of a Southern nurse who has passed for white in the North.

THURMAN, WALLACE, 1902-1934
The Blacker the Berry (Macaulay, 1929). On the plight of the very dark Negro woman who encounters in some communities a double wall of color prejudice, within and without the race.

TOOMER, JEAN, 1894-
Cane (Boni, 1923). A collection of sketches and short stories dealing with emotional and sensual characteristics of the Southern Negro. Set in Georgia and the black belt of Washington, D.C.

TURPIN, WATERS E., 1910-
These Low Grounds (Harper, 1937). Novel of four generations of Negroes from just before the Civil War until the present. Concentrates mostly on a young man who had a college education and whose plans were always for better education for his people.
O Canaan! (Doubleday, 1939). Story of one of the thousands of Negro families who came to Chicago from the South in 1916. The family prospers and becomes prominent in South Side social affairs.

VAN VECHTEN, CARL, 1880-1964
Nigger Heaven (Knopf, 1926). An early account of the abnormal conditions under which the Harlem Negro lives. A story of a graduate of the University of Pennsylvania who goes to Harlem, planning to write.

WARREN, ROBERT PENN, 1905-
Band of Angels (Random, 1955). Story of an almost purely white Negro girl, sold down the river just before the Civil War. The story deals with her psychology and her attempts to be "really free."

WHITE, WALTER F., 1893-1955
Fire in the Flint (Knopf, 1924). Of a well-educated Negro doctor who saves a sick white woman but is misunderstood by a Georgia mob.
Flight (Knopf, 1926). Describes a race riot in Atlanta and tells a tale of a New Orleans octoroon who could "pass." Shows a Negro choosing between Negro and white association.

WOOD, CLEMENT, 1888-
Nigger (1922). Pictures a Negro family from its origins in slavery to modern life in Birmingham. A careful, convincing sociological novel.

WRIGHT, RICHARD, 1908-1960
Uncle Tom's Children (Harper, 1938). A collection of four long short stories dealing with the Negro and white conflict in the present-day South and of the suppression of black by white. Wright tells in an artistic style that the children of Uncle Tom have just as much to fight today as they did in Tom's time.
Native Son (Harper, 1940). Bigger Thomas, hemmed in by the restrictions of white-dominated Chicago, commits a series of crimes, finding in them the only positive self-expression of his life. An intense, realistic novel, the best yet written by an American Negro, which dramatizes the psychology of the Negro and the problem of giving the Negro the full rights due a native son.
The Long Dream (Doubleday, 1958). Shows what growing up in the South is like for an intelligent, sensitive, even rich Negro, here the son of an undertaker. Vivid details and arresting dialog about tensions that damage varied individuals in both of the dominant races. Exhibits Uncle Toms and also defiant new forthright Southern Negroes who will no longer grin and cry, who are courageous and out to win.

YOUNG, ISADOR S.
Jadie Greenway (Crown, 1947). A sort of *Tree Grows in Brooklyn* for the colored people. An account, largely realistic and documentary, of a Brooklyn girl who slips into delinquency and then is saved and put on the right road.

2. THE INDIAN

In early fiction the Indian was either a misrepresented villain or an impossible nobleman. The white man's superior villainy was not mentioned. Now that he is on reservations, no longer a military foe, and generally not an economic competitor, the Indian is a subject of great interest. In many works of fiction he has been given central prominence, his cultural complex has been detailed, and much attention has been paid to his problems of adjusting himself to the dominating white civilization which surrounds him. Where once we had melodrama about the Indian with his bloody tomahawk, now we have clear-cut realism or affectionate ethnology.

ARMER, LAURA ADAMS, 1874-1963
Dark Circle of Branches (Longmans, 1933). Story of the removal of Navajos into exile in 1862, "the long walk."

AUSTIN, MARY, 1868-1934
One Smoke Stories (Houghton, 1934). Brief stories as told by the Indians around their campfires between their smokes of corn-husk cigarettes. Various tribes of the Southwest are represented.

BANDELIER, ADOLF F., 1840-1914
The Delight Makers (1890). A remarkable re-creation of Indian life in the Southwest long before Columbus. Abundant details of the life of cliff- and pueblo-dwellers in El Rito de los Frijoles near Santa Fe, and of their relations with other tribes. By a noted anthropologist.

BEATTIE, JESSIE L., 1896-
The Split in the Sky (Ryerson, 1960). Deals with the Iroquois of Grand River Reservation of the Six Nations Indians near Brantford, Ontario, where the way of life is changing, there are problems with the government in Ottawa, and Iroquois nationalism is on the rise. Focuses on an Indian who returns to the reservation after twenty years of integration near Buffalo.

BUFFALO CHILD LONG LANCE, Blood Indian chief, d. 1932.
Long Lance (Farrar, 1936). This fictionalized autobiography is excellent on life among the Blackfeet at the time when white pressure to go on the reservation was growing severe.

CHATEAUBRIAND, FRANÇOIS RENÉ, VICOMTE DE, 1768-1848
Atala (1801). Indians pictured as having the freedom of savages, yet the knowledge and susceptibilities of Europeans. Of the Rousseau school, illustrating the theory of "nature's nobleman."

COOKE, JOHN ESTEN, 1830-1886
My Lady Pocahontas (1879). The life of a famous character who is both historical and legendary. Virginia in the seventeenth century.

CORLE, EDWIN, 1906-
Fig Tree John (Liveright, 1935). Of an Apache Indian who left his tribe and settled on an isolated spot near Salton Sea with his wife and son. A picture of the adjustment of the Indian to the present world.
People on the Earth (Random, 1937). A modern realistic novel of Navajo life. Theme: the struggle of the young to adopt white ways and yet retain the good things of their own civilization.

DYK, WALTER, 1868-
Son of Old Man Hat (Harcourt, 1938). A Navajo biography of Left-Handed as recorded by Walter Dyk.

FISHER, ANNE B., 1898-
Cathedral in the Sun (Carlyle, 1940; Pacific Books, 1951). Of three generations of California Indians and their connection with the California missions between 1818 and 1882. Shows the missions changing during the period.

FULLER, IOLA
The Loon Feather (Harcourt, 1940). As told by Tecumseh's daughter, a tale of difficult adjustments as trappers and loggers come westward into Michigan.
The Shining Trail (Duell, 1943). A story of Indians being pushed out of the Illinois country at the time of the Black Hawk War.

GARLAND, HAMLIN, 1860-1940
The Captain of the Gray-Horse Troop (1902). An accurate presentation of life on a Montana reservation in the 1890's. Shows settlers and cowmen stupidly and cruelly abusing respectable Cheyenne Indians. A good story.
The Book of the American Indian (Harper, 1923). Contains significant short stories dealing sympathetically with reservation Indians, Cheyennes, Teton, Sioux. A mixture of careful observation, oral record, and fictional interpretation. "The Silent Eaters" is a simple, forceful story of the life of Sitting Bull.

GILES, JANICE (HOLT)
Johnny Osage (Houghton, 1960). On Osage Indians in conflict with Cherokees in the Arkansas River country in the early 1820's. Partly history with real names.

HUNT, JOHN CLINTON, 1925-
Generations of Men (Little, 1956). Laid among the "Chetopas" in Oklahoma some time after 1941. Free from clichés, a plain, modest tale of people caught between memories of the past and necessities of the present. A good deal on hounds and hunting.

JACKSON, HELEN HUNT, 1831-1885
Ramona (1884). A popular presentation of the plight of the mission Indians in California as land-hungry Anglo-Saxons swept over the state.

The significance, however, is obscured by a sentimental love story that usurps the foreground.

JAMES, HARRY C., 1896-
Red Man White Man (Naylor, 1958). A sympathetic account of the Hopis in the 1920's, especially their problem of continuing their culture in the face of biased white attitudes and institutions. While the story line and characterizations are obvious, so is the author's knowledge of Hopis and other Arizonans.

LaFARGE, OLIVER, 1901-1963
Laughing Boy (Houghton, 1929). An excellent story of Navajos, their customs, their ideals, and their troubled relationships with whites. A moving account of the plight of a minority misunderstood by the white man and forced into maladjustments.
All the Young Men (Houghton, 1935). A dozen effective short stories dealing largely with Indians—Apaches, Pahutahs, Navajos, and others.
The Enemy Gods (Houghton, 1937). Of a Navajo boy's struggle with religious adjustment.

LAURITZEN, JONREED
Arrows into the Sun (Knopf, 1943). Laid in pioneer times, the novel artistically describes Arizona scenery and a Mormon settlement. Penetrates the mind of a Navajo half-breed torn between two ways of life, his American father's and his Indian mother's. A beautiful and spirited Mormon girl helps him find his white heritage.

LIGHTHALL, WILLIAM D., 1857-?
Master of Life (1908). An "aboriginal romance" of the prehistoric Hiawatha and his founding of the league of the Iroquois. Presents the chivalrous and reverent side of the Indian.

LINDERMAN, FRANK B., 1868-1938
Morning Light (Lige Mounts: Free Trapper) (Day, 1930). Fictionalized biography, describing the fur trade on the upper Missouri a hundred years ago. Sincere and convincing. Story of a trapper who preferred Indian life to white.
Red Mother (Day, 1932). The life of Pretty Shield. Presents the Indian from a woman's point of view. Interesting stories of the buffalo days, of the Battle of the Little Big Horn, and of the death of Custer.

LOOMIS, EDWARD, 1924-
The Hunter Deep in Summer (Viking, 1961). A modest courtroom-trial novel, set in a town on the California-Nevada border, that makes use of tensions surviving in the 1950's between Piutes and non-Indians.

LOTT, MILTON
Dance Back the Buffalo (Houghton, 1959). Sympathetic to the Cheyennes near the Rosebud Agency in South Dakota, 1889-1890, who fell into the

delusion of the Messiah preaching the return of old days, danced the Ghost Dance, and were slaughtered by United States troops.

McCLINCHEY, FLORENCE E.
Joe Pete (Holt, 1929). A story of present-day life of the Ojibway Indians of northern Michigan. As the author has lived with them for years, her material is quite authentic.

McNICHOLS, CHARLES L., 1895-
Crazy Weather (Macmillan, 1944). A good local-color story of western Arizona, in which two adolescent boys, one white, one Mojave, go through strenuous events during four days of terrible heat. Through the white boy's struggle to be either "white" or "Indian," various contrasts are built up between the two ways of life.

McNICKLE, D'ARCY, 1904-
The Surrounded (Dodd, 1936). Portrays a tribe of reservation Indians in western Montana. Shows the plight of the Indian—a conflict between traditions of the tribe and desire for a wider life.

MANFRED, FREDERICK, 1912-
Conquering Horse (McDowell, 1959). The author uses a strong style to tell much of plainscraft and religious ceremonials, including the Sun Dance, in a story of the Yankton Sioux during the great days of horse culture. Excellent in the quasi-myth of how the central character proves himself by conquering a great white stallion.

MATHEWS, JOHN JOSEPH
Sundown (Longmans, 1934). Shows the Osage civilization destroyed by alien ideals and customs after the discovery of oil. Contrasts the potentialities of Indians with the decadence they have fallen into. Of an Oklahoma Indian boy who tries to be a white man and ends up a man without an ethnic group.

MORROW, HONORÉ WILLSIE, 1880?-1940
Lydia of the Pines (1917). Interest centers about grafting politicians confiscating Indian lands in Minnesota. In Progressive Era style the young hero and heroine fight for the right.

OSKISON, JOHN M., 1874-
Black Jack Davy (Appleton, 1926). Life in Indian Territory and Oklahoma before and after the land rush of 1889.

REID, MAYNE, 1818-1883
The White Chief, a Legend of Northern Mexico (London, 1855). A dramatic and satisfying adventure story of a white man who became chief of an Indian tribe and underwent various experiences fighting Spaniards who mistreated the Indians in what is now New Mexico.

RICHTER, CONRAD, 1890-
The Light in the Forest (Knopf, 1953). Story about a white boy brought

up by the Indians around the mid-eighteenth century. Contrasts Indian and white ways of living and attitudes showing certain superiorities in the Indian way of life.

RYAN, DON
The Warrior's Path (Duckworth, 1937). An anthropological novel about a captured Virginia boy who was adopted by the Lenape (Delaware Indians) and became a white Indian, fighting with Pontiac and The Prophet. Contains much reliable interpretation of social and religious life among the Ohio Valley tribes during the days of bloody fights with Braddock, Bouquet, Armstrong, and other Tulhasaga (white men).

SIMMS, WILLIAM GILMORE, 1806-1870
The Wigwam and the Cabin (1845). A volume of uneven short stories, some realistic and some silly, including considerable humane evaluation of Catawbas, Cherokees, and Choctaws.

SMITH, DAMA MARGARET
Hopi Girl (Stanford, 1931). A reliable and interesting story of changing customs in a Hopi village. Modern times.

SORENSEN, VIRGINIA (EGGERSTEN), 1912-
The Proper Gods (Harcourt, 1951). A Yaqui brought up in Arizona returns as a veteran to his ancestral home in Mexico. Contrast of two cultures. An excellently told story.

STRANGE, ROBERT, 1798-1854
Eoneguski, or, the Cherokee Chief: A Tale of Past Wars (1839). An intricate, overplotted novel à clef by a United States Senator who sympathized with the Indians duped and forced to trek from North Carolina to west of the Mississippi. Critical of white settlers in North Carolina and of frontier law court procedure.

UNDERHILL, RUTH M., 1884-
Hawk over Whirlpools (J. J. Augustin, 1940). Of the desert Indians of Arizona and the changes in their community life because of contact with Americans. A story of the conflicts of a part-Mexican boy who wishes to gain white man's power.

WATERS, FRANK, 1902-
People of the Valley (Farrar, 1941). Of a valley high in the mountains of New Mexico and of its people—part French, part Spanish, part Irish, part Indian. The main character, Maria del Valle, is half-Indian.
The Man Who Killed the Deer (Farrar, 1942). Of a young Pueblo Indian, a nonconformist in his tribe, and how he finally returned to the blanket. A pathetic struggle, vividly presented.

3. THE FRENCH, THE SPANISH, THE ITALIANS, AND THE LATIN AMERICANS

The treatment of the French, the Spanish, and the Latin Americans varies from highly romantic pictures of the old regime in California to drab pictures of present-day living conditions in parts of some Northeastern and Southwestern cities. Romances were spun about the contrasts between Spanish and Yankee customs, the peculiar customs and traditions of the Creoles of New Orleans and the Acadians of central Louisiana, and the explorations and settlements of the French throughout the St. Lawrence and Mississippi valleys. Recent stories have centered about the relation of the Latin American to the labor market, his living conditions in slums, and his religious superstitions and observances. Picaresque stories have been written about Mexican bandits of the Southwest, and pathetic stories about Mexicans, from Texas to California, who are still meeting discrimination after two hundred years of residence. Among the newer immigrant groups the Italians have rapidly become a special but integral part of the American pattern, and are generously represented in recent fiction. Puerto Ricans are beginning to appear in stories.

Although the French of Quebec have produced a literature of their own about their special part of Canada, which sees itself as almost a separate nation, few of their novels are in translation and easily available.

ATHERTON, GERTRUDE F., 1857-1948
  Los Cerritos: A Romance of Modern Times (1890). Poor whites and Mexicans settle on Los Cerritos, an abandoned ranch in southern California. The owner attempts ejection.
  The Californians (1898). The civilization of the old Spanish regime contrasted to the strenuous life of the Yankee.
  The Splendid Idle Forties (1902). Romantic tales of early California. Interesting material on folkways, religious beliefs, etc. Accepts romantic notions of the chivalry of the Spanish (also their cruelty) and the barbarism and degradation of the Indian.
  Rezánov (1906). A historical romance of Spanish California. Based on the courtship of Nicolai Petrovich Rezánov, of the Russian-American Company, and Doña Concha Argüello y Moraga, daughter of the Comandante of the Presidio in San Francisco. Once popular for its charming, sad love story.

BRIGHT, ROBERT
  The Life and Death of Little Joe (Doubleday, 1944). A sympathetic tale of a Spanish-American village in New Mexico. Pictures a poverty-stricken, dispossessed community, in which youth is torn between old and new ways. A revealing though often melodramatic account of the vanishing "native" culture in the Taos area.

CABLE, GEORGE WASHINGTON, 1844-1925
Old Creole Days (1879). A famous collection of short stories about the Creoles of New Orleans. Realistic for its day.
The Grandissimes (1880). A long, involved romance of Creoles and others in the lower Mississippi Valley.
Dr. Sevier (1884). Of New Orleans before the Civil War. Much detail on Creole customs.
Bonaventure: A Prose Pastoral of Acadian Louisiana (1888). Good in detail of country homes, country schools, etc.

CARUSO, JOSEPH, 1923-
The Priest (Macmillan, 1956). Much on the customs and attitudes, especially religious ones, of Sicilians of the West End in Boston, where an experienced priest is involved in his own crises of conscience.

CHOPIN, KATE, 1851-1904
Bayou Folk (1894). Artistic tales of Creoles, Negroes, and Cajuns along the lower Mississippi.
A Night in Acadie (1897). Additional dramatic tales of the Louisiana bayou country.

CLAD, NOEL, 1924-
Love and Money (Random, 1959). Well written and carefully checked against history (from before World War I to after World War II). About an Alsatian immigrant in the United States. He is a meticulous, formal man of inflexible principle, an investment counselor whose cultural momentum leads only to slow changes of manners in America. Excellent on his character, his wives, an Alsatian chef he knows, on the social history of the period, on "the vitality of America, the continuum of Europe, the interaction of the two."

COOLIDGE, DANE, 1873-1940
Gringo Gold (Dutton, 1939). A melodramatic tale of the adventures of Joaquín Murieta, famous bandit in California Gold Rush days. Explains Murieta's motivation and sympathetically interprets the suppressed Mexican minority in California.

CRICHTON, KYLE, 1896-1960
The Proud People (Scribner's, 1944). A Spanish-American family in Albuquerque in 1941 and their relationship to the non-Spanish community.

D'AGOSTINO, GUIDO, 1906-
Olives on the Apple Tree (Doubleday, 1940). An understanding picture of the Italians in America, seen through the eyes of a young Italian-American.
Hills Beyond Manhattan (Doubleday, 1942). Of the Americanization of a Frenchman—a struggle between New York villagers and rich interlopers from the city.

DE CAPITE, MICHAEL, 1915-
Maria (Day, 1943). The setting is the "little Italy" of Cleveland, Ohio. Lifelike characters, especially Maria, who submits to an arranged marriage and cruelty from her husband, but tries to bring up her children to be Americans.

DE CAPITE, RAYMOND, 1926?-
The Coming of Fabrizze (McKay, 1960). Lively glimpses of Italian immigrants in Cleveland during the 1920's, where the title character works his way up from day labor to stock market investment.
A Lost King (McKay, 1962). A light, lyrical approach to an Italian-American family in the Cleveland industrial section, as a boy grows up.

DERLETH, AUGUST, 1909-
Shadow of Night (Scribner's, 1943). One of the author's series of novels laid in and around Sac Prairie, Wisconsin, this shows how French and German immigrants to the Wisconsin Valley frontier slowly changed from being Europeans to being Americans.

DI DONATO, PIETRO, 1911-
Christ in Concrete (Bobbs, 1939). Of a New York Italian family—its piety, its customs, its economic helplessness. Realistic portrayal of a slum district. Makes clear the immense importance of a job.
Three Circles of Light (Messner, 1960). A solid, salty, and deeply suggestive account of family and community affairs among Italians in a village colony in West Hoboken. Much lively characterization, much on the carryover of Old World notions, much comedy, and two strong cuckold dramas. Ends with the family disaster that *Christ in Concrete* begins with.

FANTE, JOHN, 1911-
Wait Until Spring, Bandini (Stackpole, 1938). Of an Italian-American family in the West. Good realism about the children's life.
Ask the Dust (Stackpole, 1939). Story of a young ambitious Italian, who comes to Los Angeles hoping to find fame as a writer but finds only hunger and discouragement.

FERGUSSON, HARVEY, 1890-
The Conquest of Don Pedro (Morrow, 1954). See above, p. 16.

FORBES, HARRIE REBECCA PIPER (SMITH)
Mission Tales in the Days of the Dons (1909). A collection of thirteen stories and poems of the Spaniards, Mexicans, and Indians of California before the North Americans came. Preserves some of the best legends.

FORGIONE, LOUIS
Reamer Lou (Dutton, 1924). Of immigrant young men, Italian especially, and their personal adjustments, not all good for them and society, as they live and work on New York Harbor.

The River Between (Dutton, 1928). Of a prosperous Italian immigrant family living in the Italian settlement on the Hudson Palisades.

FOSTER, JOSEPH O'KANE, 1898-

In the Night Did I Sing (Scribner's, 1942). A psychological interpretation of Spanish-Americans in Taos Valley, New Mexico—their humor, religion, attitude toward Americans. A pathetic story in its realization of their present poor estate.

GARNER, CLAUD

Wetback (Coward, 1947). Tells of a Mexican who swims the Rio Grande and struggles to become a happy citizen of the United States. He suffers from thieving fellow workers, unscrupulous bosses, and properly strict immigration officials but finally becomes an expert goat breeder and then a citrus rancher. Warm in human sympathy but too synoptic to be fully artistic.

GILES, BARBARA

The Gentle Bush (Harcourt, 1947). The chronicle of a Louisiana family from the post-Reconstruction period through the first decade of the twentieth century. Emphasis on Creole folkways and social cleavages along ethnic lines.

GRAU, SHIRLEY ANN

The Hard Blue Sky (Knopf, 1958). Takes place on islands near the mouth of the Mississippi. Many incidents about Creole fishermen, mostly a mixture of French and Spanish—their work, their personal affairs, the storms they endure.

HEARN, LAFCADIO, 1850-1904

Creole Sketches (ed. by Charles Woodward Hutson) (Houghton, 1924). Sketches written, 1878-1881, for *The Item*. Literary masterpieces about Creoles of his time.

JESSEY, CORNELIA

Teach the Angry Spirit (Crown, 1949). Life in the Mexican quarter of Los Angeles. The time is during World War II, and the zoot-suit riots are the climax of the book. An appealing story of a brother and a sister caught between the two cultures.

KING, GRACE E., 1851-1932

Balcony Stories (1893). Local-color tales of Negroes, Creoles, and others in Louisiana.

LAXALT, ROBERT, 1921-

Sweet Promised Land (Harper, 1957). A simple, touching biographical account of the author's father, a Basque sheepherder in western Nevada, and his visit to his home town in the French Pyrenees.

MacLENNAN, HUGH, 1907-
Two Solitudes (Duell, 1945). A penetrating, schematic study of the conflicts of English-speaking and French-speaking Canadians on the Island of Montreal in the period 1917-1939. Analyzes all the complications in Quebec society and the basic ethnic conflict.

MADALENA, LORENZO
Confetti for Gino (Doubleday, 1959). About a courtship in the Italian fishing community in San Diego. Good as a genre study of local Italian life and of the fishing business in California and Mexican waters.

MANGIONE, JERRE, 1909-
Mount Allegro (Houghton, 1943). Humorous, sympathetic sketches of Sicilian-Americans in Rochester, New York. Anecdotes depict religion, recreation, education, and so on, among a gay, bubbling people. A kind of Italian *Life With Father*.

MELLER, SIDNEY, 1906-
Home is Here (Macmillan, 1941). Shows how Italian immigrants are slowly transformed into Americans on Telegraph Hill, San Francisco.

MOODY, ALAN B., 1900-1944
Sleep in the Sun (Houghton, 1945). Episodes in the lives of a group of poverty-stricken Mexican families living in a California canyon.

NUNN, GUY, 1915-
White Shadows (Reynal, 1947). Effectively presents a Mexican family adjusting to the United States, from their arrival as immigrants until the children have grown up and received an education.

O'DONNELL, EDWIN P., 1895-
Green Margins (Houghton, 1936). A detailed picture of the daily life of the ethnic mixtures of inhabitants of the delta country below New Orleans—their food, clothing, customs, and picturesque language. Portrait of a subregion.

PAGANO, JO, 1906-
The Paisanos (Little, 1940). Ten stories of Italians in Los Angeles. Mostly humorous and centering on folkways: eating, drinking, and talking.
Golden Wedding (Random, 1943). The story of an Italian family in a coal town in Colorado, in Denver, in Salt Lake City, and in Los Angeles.

PARSONS, VIVIAN
Not Without Honor (Dodd, 1941). Of a French-Canadian farm boy who migrates to a mining community on the Upper Peninsula of Michigan. Tells with vigor and realism of his exceptional success story and of his attempt to make all foreigners understand what the "promised land" meant to him.

PAZ, IRENCO, 1836-1924
Life and Adventures of the Celebrated Bandit Joaquín Murrieta (trans. by Frances P. Belle) (Powner, 1925). A spirited, fictionalized biography of "the most famous bandit chief who has ever lived on this earth," his assistant, Jack Three Fingers, and his persistent pursuer, Captain Harry Love.

PEREZ, LUIS, 1904-1962
El Coyote the Rebel (Holt, 1947). Humorous, informal autobiography of a Mexican who was conscripted as a boy soldier in the Contreras Rebel Army in its fights with the Moralistas and Pancho Villa, and who finally escaped into the United States. There he obtained citizenship and worked his way through the public schools. Gives a gay version of the difficulties of an immigrant ignorant of the language.

ROBERTS, MARTA
Tumbleweeds (Putnam, 1940). Traces the life of a Mexican family with six children living in California, with whom all is well until the father loses his job and the family has to go on relief. Shows the paradoxes and inadequacies of public relief.

ROY, GABRIELLE, 1909-
Where Nests the Water Hen (Harcourt, 1951). Quiet local color of settlements in remote Manitoba near Lake Winnipegosis, in the era of Buick cars. Mostly about French settlers and their Capuchin missionary. Glimpses of Icelanders, Ukrainians, and others.

ST. MARTIN, THADDEUS, 1886-
Madame Toussaint's Wedding Day (Little, 1936). A graphic local-color story of a Cajun community in Louisiana.

SHULMAN, IRVING
The Square Trap (Little, 1953). Interpretation of the home life and reactions of a Los Angeles Mexican family by a non-Mexican. The older son becomes a boxer—an exposé of the dead end at which a Mexican arrives in the fight game.

STEINBECK, JOHN, 1902-
Tortilla Flat (Viking, 1935). A pleasant fantasy about the Paisanos of Monterey. Emphasizes the carefree life of these descendants of the early inhabitants of Mexican Alta California. Humorous, with some realistic detail.

STILWELL, HART, 1902-
Border City (Doubleday, 1945). A story of racial intolerance and corrupt politics in a city on the border between Mexico and the United States. The hero is a newspaperman who first defends, then falls in love with, a Mexican girl.

STONE, ELINORE COWAN, 1884-
The Laughingest Lady (Appleton, 1940). A simple romantic story of a
schoolma'am from the East who succeeds in capturing the "most eli-
gible" male in a small New Mexican village. Much interesting detail
about her third-grade Mexican-American class.

SUMMERS, RICHARD A., 1906-
Dark Madonna (Caxton, 1937). A story of early twentieth-century
Tucson and its Mexican quarter. Emphasis on superstitions and
amatory adventures. Realistic, but partly twentieth-century folklore.
The Devil's Highway (Nelson, 1937). Concerning the work of Padre
Kino and the establishment of Mission San Xavier del Bac near Tucson.
The main character is a Spanish boy soldier, detailed to watch over
Father Kino. A dramatic story, with much on Spanish and Mexican folk
beliefs.

TINKER, EDWARD LAROCQUE, 1861-
Toucoutou (Dodd, 1928). A tale of New Orleans of the 1850's, giving
much of the local color of the time and showing the prevailing race
prejudices.

TOMASI, MARI
Like Lesser Gods (Bruce, 1949). Well-told story of Italian workers in
the granite quarries of Vermont. Good presentation of folkways and of
the merging of two cultures.

VIERTEL, PETER
The Canyon (Harcourt, 1940). A warm, appreciative reminiscence of
adolescence in Santa Monica Canyon in pre-bulldozer days and of the
relationship of an "American" boy with a "Mexican" boy and an "Indian" boy. Catches sad subtleties in "race" relations when one is
young and then when one is older.

VILLARREAL, JOSÉ ANTONIO
Pocho (Doubleday, 1959). On a Mexican-American growing up in Santa
Clara, California. Seemingly autobiographical.

WHITE, STEWART EDWARD, 1873-1946
Ranchero (Doubleday, 1933). Mexicans and Spanish in California in the
1840's. A contrast between the North American and the Spanish of
California, in which the Yankee is captivated by Spanish ways. Neat
romance.

4. OTHER ETHNIC GROUPS (INCLUDING THE IRISH, THE SCANDINAVIANS, THE GERMANS, AND ORIENTALS)

The Irish as well as other European nationalities appeared often as
comic characters in fiction throughout the nineteenth century, but writers

since 1920 have made the Irish and the others serious subjects for full-length treatment.

When the present vogue of writing about ethnic groups got under way, Middle Western Scandinavians were a group of immigrants new enough to be noticeably distinct in customs and ideas. Hence they have been extensively used as subject matter.

There are almost as many stories about Germans as about Scandinavians, though many of them go back to an earlier period of American history. Other groups dealt with in fiction include Russians, Czechoslovaks, Poles, Japanese, Chinese, Armenians, Jugoslavs, Greeks, Hawaiians, and the Dutch. Many stories of Jewish immigrants are listed earlier under "Religion."

ADAMIC, LOUIS, 1899-1951
Grandsons (Harper, 1935). Concerns a Jugoslav family in which the three sons are completely a part of American life; one is a member of the I.W.W., one a gangster, and one a wounded war veteran.

ALGREN, NELSON, 1909-
Never Come Morning (Harper, 1942). Polacks in Chicago's Northwest Side—reminiscent of James T. Farrell's "Irish." Bruno Bicek (Lefty Biceps) is the "Studs Lonigan" of the story.

ALLEN, FRANCES N., 1865-
The Invaders (1913). Of the Poles and Celts who move into a New England village, and have prejudice to overcome.

ANTHONY, JOSEPH, 1897-
Golden Village (Bobbs, 1924). Of Rumanian immigrants seeking the golden village of their dreams only to find imperfect American towns that require great adjustments.

BAHR, JEROME
All Good Americans (Scribner's, 1937). Thirteen short stories of the Jews, Poles, Germans, Irish, and Norwegians—all good Americans—who live in a small Wisconsin town.

BANCROFT, GRIFFING
The Interlopers: A Novel (1917). Presents material on the conflict between "native white" farmers in southern California and Japanese immigrants and their children. More interesting for theme than for style.

BELL, THOMAS, 1903-
Out of This Furnace (Little, 1941). See above, p. 80.

BENSON, RAMSEY, 1866-
Hill Country (Stokes, 1928). A biographical novel of James J. Hill, builder of the Great Northern Railway and, from one point of view, a potent influence in bettering the lives of early settlers in Minnesota.

Presents the Swedish settlers as almost too clean and upright to be tolerated by their American neighbors.

BOJER, JOHAN, 1872-1959
The Emigrants (Century, 1924). Written by a Norwegian about emigrants from Norway. Similar in theme to Rolvaag's *Giants in the Earth*. A good picture of the struggles of a pioneering Norwegian family.

BUDD, LILLIAN
Land of Strangers (Lippincott, 1953). Of the personal lives of two young Swedes, a man and a woman, their married life and the difficulties of adjustment in America.

CANNON, CORNELIA JAMES, 1876-
Red Rust (Little, 1928). See above, p. 45.
Heirs (Little, 1930). Of Polish immigrants supplanting "old stock" New Englanders in a New Hampshire village. Presents the problem of Americanization.

CASTLE, WILLIAM, and JOSEPH, ROBERT
Hero's Oak (Reader's Press, 1945). The setting is Vermont, the time, 1910 to 1936; the people, Polish immigrants through two generations of victory and defeat, in agriculture and the professions.

CATHER, WILLA SIBERT, 1876-1947
O Pioneers! (1913). Story of a capable Swedish-American girl running a big farm in Nebraska.
My Antonia (1918). A well-written story about a Bohemian family in Nebraska during the sod-house era.
Obscure Destinies (Knopf, 1932). Contains three short stories; notably "Neighbour Rosicky," which gives a mellow, optimistic picture of a Czech farmer in the prairie corn belt.

CHRISTOWE, STOYAN, 1898-
My American Pilgrimage (Little, 1947). Of a Macedonian who works in gangs building western railroads and catches a vision of America. A simple, eloquent testament of discovery and faith. A fictionalized version of the autobiography *This Is My Country* (Carrick, 1938).

CONWAY, BROOKE (pseud.)
The Loving Are the Daring (Prentice, 1947). Story of family life in a Midwestern German-American home, 1905-1920. The widow Kraemer and her six children are the leading figures. Similar to McLean's *Mama's Bank Account*.

DE JONG, DAVID CORNEL, 1905-
Belly Fulla Straw (Knopf, 1934). Of a Dutch family that disintegrates after settling in Michigan shortly before 1918.

DEMETRIOS, GEORGE, 1896-
When Greek Meets Greek (Houghton, 1947). Two dozen short stories, simply told, about Greeks in Macedonia or Greek immigrants in Boston.

DINNEEN, JOSEPH FRANCIS, 1897-
Queen Midas (Little, 1958). A fast, short narrative about a shrewd Irish immigrant girl who becomes a rich woman and a political power in "Boylston" (Boston), where "modernity fought stubbornly against antiquity." Time: 1896 to the 1930's.

EDMISTON, JAMES
Home Again (Doubleday, 1955). The story of one family of Japanese-American evacuees and their return to California. Good detail and good characterization.

FARRELL, JAMES T., 1904-
Can All This Grandeur Perish? (Vanguard, 1937). A collection of short stories.
Tommy Gallagher's Crusade (Vanguard, 1939). A study of the poisonous spirit and background of Tommy Gallagher, a representative of the young men who sell anti-Semitic literature on city street corners.
My Days of Anger (Vanguard, 1943). Fourth in the Danny O'Neill series, continuing *A World I Never Made* (1936), *No Star Is Lost* (1938), and *Father and Son* (1940), this tells of Danny in the mid-1920's, when he attends the University of Chicago. With tough, turbulent Chicago as the background, this is essentially the tale of a sensitive young Irish-American, whose character is complex and full of apparent contradictions. A vivid story showing what the Irish do to America and what America does to the Irish.

FREITAG, GEORGE H.
The Lost Land (Coward, 1947). August Kreitzer, a German-American, marries an Irish-American girl. The story depicts the crosscurrents of the Old World and the New, and the efforts of August, who works in a steel mill, to develop a successful farm.

GILMAN, PETER
Diamond Head (Coward, 1960). Poorly integrates fiction and chunks of Hawaiian local color, history, and geology but tells of a labor attorney who is a mixture of haole (white), Japanese, and Hawaiian, who sees the whites' years as terminating with the arrival of statehood.

GLOCAR, EMILIAN, 1906-
Man from the Balkans (Dorrance, 1942). About a Serbian immigrant and his successful attempts to adjust himself to his new American environment.

GROVE, FREDERICK PHILIP, 1872-
Settlers of the Marsh (Doran, 1925). Of Swedish immigrants and others from Europe and the United States in the bush settlements where Canadian forests are near the prairies—in "the land of the million farmsteads to be had for the asking."

HAGOPIAN, RICHARD, 1914-
The Dove Brings Peace (Farrar, 1944). A diverting series of sketches describing the life of an Armenian family in Massachusetts. Shows the attitude of older members and the bewilderment of the younger, as they try to adapt themselves to American ways.

HURLEY, DORAN, 1906-
Herself: Mrs. Patrick Crowley (Longmans, 1939). A humorous though not realistic tale of Mrs. Patrick Crowley, who won an Irish sweepstake and so left Millington, Massachusetts, and went to spend her money and see great New York City.

HURST, FANNIE, 1889-
Lummox (Harper, 1923). Of a strong girl, half-Swede and half-Slav, and her lonely, hard life as a servant girl in New York City.
A President is Born (Harper, 1928). A story of the first eighteen years of a boy born into a large Austrian family in the United States. Of a European family gradually being adjusted to American life.

IRWIN, WALLACE, 1875-
Letters of a Japanese Schoolboy (1909). Kindly humor which makes capital of the Oriental's difficulties with English idiom. Hashimura Togo comments on such things as political conventions, the third term, and the servant "problemb."
Seed of the Sun (Doran, 1921). A story with a strong anti-Japanese bias. The author sees the Japanese in California as a menace, and their methods as devious, clever, and devilish. The facts that they want land, work hard, and raise children seem to him reprehensible.

JORDAN, MILDRED A. (MRS. J. LEE BAUSHER), 1901-
One Red Rose Forever (Knopf, 1941). A semifictional account of Heinrich Stiegel, a German who arrived in Pennsylvania in 1750 and later made beautiful glass. Lusty romance ill-paired with lively history.
Apple in the Attic: A Pennsylvania Legend (Knopf, 1942). A simply told story of the home life of a Pennsylvania Dutch family.

KAZAN, ELIA, 1909-
America America (Stein, 1962). A short, script-like account, objective as a film, on the anguishing experience of an Anatolian Greek who finally achieves his desire to escape from Turkey to New York.

KEHOE, KARON
City in the Sun (Dodd, 1946). Of the tensions of Japanese-Americans

in the Maricopa relocation center, Arizona. A story of the moral degeneration of an American boy.

LA PIERE, RICHARD TRACY, 1899-
Where the Living Strive (Harper, 1941). The story of the life of a Chinese immigrant in San Francisco, 1875 to the 1930's. Informative for insight into Chinese character.

LEBEDEFF, VERA
The Heart Returneth (Lippincott, 1943). Concerns a colony of White Russians in Detroit. Good on the social life and ideas of the group.

LEE CHIN-YANG
The Flower Drum Song (Farrar, 1957). A rich old man, a refugee from central China, resists Western influences in San Francisco's Chinatown. Younger refugees are Americanizing. Good on aspects of immigrant Chinese in California.
Lover's Point (Farrar, 1958). A minor story, of loneliness and love, involving Chinese, Japanese, and Americans in San Francisco and towns on Monterey Bay.

LESLIE, FRANK
There's a Spot in My Heart (Simon, 1947). Of a young Irish boy growing up in a "west side" New York house, living with his humorous grandfather and devout grandmother.

LIN YU-TANG, 1895-
Chinatown Family (Day, 1948). A calm novel about the life and difficulties of a Chinese immigrant family in New York City. Full of sidelights on American civilization as seen through oriental eyes.

LINDBERG, WALTER
The Winding Road (Lutheran Literary Board, 1933). An autobiography in story form. The tale of an immigrant who runs into all manner of difficulties.

LION, HORTENSE, 1898-
The Grass Grows Green (Houghton, 1935). Of a Bavarian girl who comes to America determined to live a peaceful life but is greatly upset by World War I. Scene laid in New York's German colony.

McLEAN, KATHRYN (ANDERSON) (KATHRYN FORBES, pseud.), 1909-1965
Mama's Bank Account (Harcourt, 1943). Simple story of a Norwegian mother in San Francisco and how she took care of her family, in the words of one of her daughters. Ironic, sentimental, amusing, satisfying.

McSORLEY, EDWARD, 1902-1966
Our Own Kind (Harper, 1946). A portrait of an Irish-American

212 MINORITY ETHNIC GROUPS

iron-worker's family living in a Providence tenement in the early twentieth century.

MARCHAND, MARGARET
Pilgrims on the Earth (Crowell, 1940). Of Irish-Americans in a steel town near Pittsburgh. Of labor strife, religious ideas, and folkways.

MEANS, FLORENCE CRANNELL, 1891-
The Moved Outers (Houghton, 1945). Story of a young Japanese-American girl and the year her family spent in a relocation camp before she went away to college.

MICHENER, JAMES A., 1907-
Hawaii (Random, 1957). Centers on the various ethnic groups making up the state of Hawaii, beginning with the Polynesians who arrived in the ninth century. Interesting explorations of the cultural patterns of Hawaiians, Chinese, and Japanese, and their relationships with North American missionaries, sailors, businessmen, planters, and others.

MOBERG, VILHELM, 1898-
The Emigrants (translated by Gustaf Lannestock; Simon, 1951). Based on research and first-hand experience. Laid in period of heavy Swedish emigration to America, 1840-1890. Book ends with family's arrival in New York City, 1850. Makes clear why Swedes left Europe. An earthy novel; artistic.
Unto a Good Land (Simon, 1954). See above, p. 6.

MULDER, ARNOLD, 1885-
Dominie of Harlem (McClurg, 1913). Dutch peasants in twentieth-century America trying to struggle against change or progress.
Bram of the Five Corners (McClurg, 1915). A story of Michigan Hollanders. The protagonist is a minister of high ideals who must solve his problem of being betrothed to a moron.

NICHOLS, EDWARD J., 1900-
Hunky Johnny (Houghton, 1945). About a second-generation Slovak-American, raised in Gary, who goes to Chicago and has to face the problems of the Depression and of love for a "white girl."

O'CONNOR, EDWIN, 1918-
The Edge of Sadness (Atlantic-Little, 1961). A cross-section view, full of humanity, of the break in middle-class generations, the gulf between the old-time Irish-Americans and their grandchildren—as seen by a chatty priest relegated to an apathetic, crumbling, melting-pot parish in Boston.

ORMONDE, CZENZI, 1913-
Laughter from Downstairs (Farrar, 1948). A series of sketches about a Bohemian family in a town in the Pacific Northwest. A happy picture of the melting-pot bubbling well from the very first generation on.

PAPASHVILY, GEORGE, 1895-   , and PAPASHVILY, HELEN
Anything Can Happen (Harper, 1945). A pleasant, humorous autobiographical story of a Russian (from Georgia) who works at many
jobs between Ellis Island and Hollywood.

PETERSON, ELMER T., 1884-
Trumpets West: An Epic of America (Sears, 1934). About a Swedish-
American in the Middle West.

PINE, HESTER
The Waltz is Over (Farrar, 1943). Careful presentation of "Germanic
traits," in a picture of three generations of German-Americans from
1845 to 1942.

ROLVAAG, OLE E., 1876-1931
Peder Victorious (Harper, 1929). Sequel to *Giants in the Earth.*. A son
of the Norwegian family marries an Irish-Catholic girl. The melting-
pot theme.
Boat of Longing (Harper, 1933). Seemingly autobiographic. An excellent portrait of a Norwegian immigrant, his homesickness, his struggles to get along in the United States, where he expected to gain wealth.

ROSTEN, LEO CALVIN (LEONARD Q. ROSS, pseud.), 1908-
The Education of Hyman Kaplan (Harcourt, 1937). An amusing story of
an Americanization class in a New York City night school.
Return of Hyman Kaplan (Harper, 1959). More stories about students
and their teacher at American Night Preparatory School. In the preface the author says the stories "are all true—but they never happened."

RUESCH, HANS, 1913-
Top of the World (Harper, 1950). Simply told story of an Eskimo family, emphasizing the differences in custom and moral beliefs between
the Eskimo and the white man.

SAROYAN, WILLIAM, 1908-
My Name is Aram (Harcourt, 1940). Tales of an American-born Armenian growing up in California. Boy's experiences set in Armenian
background and told with a combination of naïveté and cynicism.

SCHERMAN, KATHARINE
The Long White Night (Little, 1964). The leader of an Eskimo village
resents the intrusion of whites into his area and partly succeeds in a
conflict with them. Well written, with a plot that grows out of character.

SEIDE, MICHAEL, 1910-
The Common Thread (Harcourt, 1944). Ten stories about the adjustment of immigrants and the children of immigrants in Brooklyn. All
men are bound by a common thread, the same hopes, the same capacity
for joy and sorrow.

SHAW, HARRY, 1905-   , and DAVIS, RUTH, 1913-
Americans One and All (Harper, 1947). An anthology of twenty-three short stories, each about a different ethnic group. Among the authors are John Fante, Oliver La Farge, Nancy Hale, Ruth Suckow, Sinclair Lewis, Kathryn Forbes, and William Saroyan. Designed to show that "all people possess basic samenesses and essential differences," that all Americans have a common humanity.

SINCLAIR, UPTON B., 1878-
The Jungle (1906). The main characters are Lithuanian immigrants who work in the stockyards of Chicago and live in the slum district.

SONE, MONICA ITO, 1919-
Nisei Daughter (Atlantic-Little, 1953). A good-hearted little report on bi-cultural home life in Seattle and of existence in American concentration ("resettlement") camps after the bombing of Pearl Harbor. Apparently autobiographical, with fictionalized conversation.

SPITZER, ANTOINETTE
These Are My Children (Macaulay, 1935). Thoughtful, sympathetic treatment of the familiar theme of three generations in America. The first generation is Austrian immigrants.

STONG, PHILIP DUFFIELD, 1899-
Iron Mountain (Farrar, 1942). A story of a Minnesota mining town and the various immigrant workers, showing American attitudes toward various minority groups.

SUHL, YURI, 1908-
One Foot in America (Macmillan, 1950). This novel that reads like an autobiography deals with Polish Jews in the Williamsburg section of Brooklyn and a "greenhorn" who becomes a butcher's boy. Excellent for comedy and for contrasts of European background and American environment.
Cowboy on a Wooden Horse (Macmillan, 1953). Sequel to *One Foot in America*. In this story the main character becomes an upholsterer, a union member, and becomes engaged to an American Jewish girl. His "greenhorn" stupidities continue too long to be believable.

SYKES, HOPE WILLIAMS, 1901-
Second Hoeing (Putnam, 1935). Of a German-Russian family in the beet region of Colorado. Realistic.
The Joppa Door (Putnam, 1937). A quiet, understanding story of a German peasant woman transplanted to Utah.

THOMAS, NEWTON GEORGE
The Long Winter Ends (Macmillan, 1941). This faithfully represents the Cousin Jack—Cornishman—of the Michigan copper country on Keweenaw Peninsula. Competent writing, as in reproduction of the Cornish dialect, but more descriptive than narrative.

TOBENKIN, ELIAS, 1882-1963
Witte Arrives: A Novel (1916). Story of the Americanization of a
Russian Jewish boy who works his way through high school and uni-
versity, in Illinois, to become a Chicago reporter. He struggles in
New York and finally marries a Gentile girl. A sincere, liberal ac-
count of the interaction of American and immigrant.
The House of Conrad (1918). Pictures a German immigrant family in
New York through three generations. A story of European proletari-
ans becoming Americanized.

VARDOULAKIS, MARY
Gold in the Streets (Dodd, 1945). A good-humored presentation of immigrant peasants from Crete in a Massachusetts milltown. The author
shows Greek customs and also the slow Americanization of the group.

WARD, LEO RICHARD, 1893-
Holding Up the Hills (Sheed and Ward, 1941). Sketches of Catholic
Irish in Iowa who maintain old customs and phrases.

WEBER, LENORA (MATTINGLY), 1895-
Mr. Gold and Her Neighborhood House (Little, 1933). The story of a
settlement house worker who points a way toward constructive work
for democracy.

WHITE, GEORGIA (ATWOOD) (DASCOMB ATWOOD, pseud.), 1882-
Free as the Wind (Liveright, 1942). A chronicle novel of a Dutch family in Michigan from about 1850 to 1917.

WILLIAMS, WILLIAM CARLOS, 1883-1963
The Build-Up (Random, 1952). The story centers around a Norwegian
woman married to a German and their rise in American society in a
small New Jersey town in the years leading up to World War I.

WILLIAMSON, THAMES ROSS, 1894-
Hunky (Coward, 1929). A psychological study of a Slavonian laborer
who is passive and unskilled, and a social study of his bewildered existence in a big American city.

WINSTON, CLARA
The Hours Together (Lippincott, 1961). Of elderly refugees from
Austria, a psychiatrist and his wife, who try to make their way in New
York.

YEZIERSKA, ANZIA, 1885-
Hungry Hearts (Houghton, 1920). Ten stories of the immigrant's
struggles in the New York ghetto. Intense, vivid, and appealing.
Children of Loneliness: Stories of Immigrant Life in America (Funk,
1923). Full of feeling, of bread hunger, and hunger for people. Also
full of protest, disillusion, affection, and desire to co-operate.

MEXICO

In addition to the novels about Mexicans and those of Mexican descent in the U.S.A., there are now many novels in English with Mexican settings. Some of them include characters who have moved from the United States to Mexico or are visitors in our sister republic, but mainly they deal with the Mexican people and historic events in the republic of Mexico. The subjects range from stories of the Conquest in the early sixteenth century to explorations of daily life in the mid-twentieth century. The novels about the exploitation of the poor in the period before 1910 and about the revolution beginning in 1910 are the most numerous among those we have listed. Among other topics are the relationships between Indian, mestizo, and creole; business enterprise; religious beliefs, Spanish and Indian; the continuing misery of the poor, particularly some Indian groups, after the revolution; bull fighting; and the relationships between North Americans and Mexicans.

AZUELA, MARIANO, 1873-

The Underdogs (1916; translated by E. Munguia, Jr., Brentano, 1929). Earthy story of a revolutionary leader of the period 1910-1919, showing that the revolution became a way of life for some.

Marcela (published as *Mala Yerba* in Mexico, 1909; translated by Anita Brenner, Farrar, 1932). A pathetic story of the life of poor peasants on a large hacienda. The terrible treatment of the peons by their overlords helps the reader to see the conditions leading up to the revolutions of this century. An appealing, tragic picture.

Two Novels of Mexico: The Bosses (Los Caciques, 1917) and *The Flies (Las Moscas, 1918)*. (Translated by Lesley Byrd Simpson, University of California Press, 1956). Part of a trilogy with *The Underdogs*. *The Flies* is a satiric picture of the panic of ordinary people as they fear the coming of Obregón's troops. *The Bosses* is the story of a ruling family in a small town in western Mexico during the Madera regime and later.

BARTLETT, PAUL

When the Owl Cries (Macmillan, 1960). The story of one family and its large estate near Colima in 1910, at the beginning of the revolution. The son of the family tries to make the lot of the Indian peasants more bearable.

BEALS, CARLETON, 1893-

Black River (Lippincott, 1934). A picture of American oil companies in eastern Mexico. Contrasts the industrial pattern of the North American and the older Mexican pattern of life.

CAMPBELL, FRANCES
Men of the Enchantress (Bobbs, 1947). A story of Mexico, centering in an American-owned silver mine worked by Mexican laborers. Skillfully paced and sensitive.

CASTELLANOS, ROSARIO
Nine Guardians (Vanguard, 1960). An old family endures the revolution under Cárdenas and loses land and status.

COCCIOLI, CARLO
Manuel the Mexican (translated from French by Hans Koningsberger, Simon, 1958). Story of a boy who became a religious mystic, combining in himself the Mexican god Tepozteco and the Christian Jesus. The story centers about the area of Tepoztlán.

DE LA RUE, TREVINO, 1894-
Spanish Trails to California (Caxton, 1937). A romantic tale of an expedition from Spain to Old Mexico and on to California. Adds to the tradition of the dashing, romantic caballero.

FERNANDEZ DE LIZARDI, JOSÉ JOAQUÍN, 1776-1827
The Itching Parrot (1830; translated by Katherine Anne Porter, Doubleday, 1942). A picaresque story of a young man in the early nineteenth century in Mexico. Reminiscent in style of Fielding and other eighteenth-century writers. The protagonist has many adventures, finally becomes honest, settles down to rear a family.

FUENTES, CARLOS
Where the Air is Clear (Obolensky, 1960). Translated from *La Región Más Transparente*. A long novel about the revolution in Mexico from 1907 to 1951. Through the lives of many characters, the reader gets a full-length picture of society from aristocrat to the poorest of the poor. "Teje la multitud de vidas encontradas de una sociedad que aún no descubre su rostro auténtico."
The Good Conscience (Obolensky, 1961). A gently ironic story of a boy growing up in an influential family in Guanajuato. The theme is that it is easier to come to terms with a bad conscience than with a bad reputation, as the boy at the age of eighteen decides to live up to the code of the family, to remain respectable, and to forget his own mother and his Indian boy friend.
The Death of Artemio Cruz (translated by Sam Hileman, Farrar, 1964). Story of a successful businessman in Mexico, who rose from poverty to wealth by using ruthless methods.

GEROULD, KATHERINE F., 1879-1944
Conquistador (Scribner's, 1923). A story of an American (half-Mexican) who effects a reconciliation with his mother's alienated Mexican family, and himself becomes one of the conquistadores in spirit. A romantic tale hinging on the peculiar notions of the old high caste creole.

GREENE, GRAHAM, 1904-

The Power and the Glory (published by Viking under the title *The Labyrinthine Ways*, 1940). A dramatic story of one priest who tried desperately to escape from the government during the persecution of the church in the 1930's. He was a corrupt, wine-drinking man, the father of a child, but died a martyr, according to the book. Both government and church seem quite corrupt, in line with Greene's statement in the preface that he had "a distaste to Mexico."

GUZMÁN, MARTÍN LUIS, 1887-

The Eagle and the Serpent (Knopf, 1930). A novelized history of Pancho Villa and the Mexican revolution, combining exciting reporting by a participant, with analysis and historical summary. Covers the years 1913-1915.

HERGESHEIMER, JOSEPH, 1880-1954

Tampico (Knopf, 1926). A melodramatic story of American oil business in Tampico, Mexico. Of a roughneck who double-crosses his boss and gains control of a big business.

HOBART, ALICE TISDALE, 1882-

The Peacock Sheds His Tail (Bobbs, 1945). A romantic story of a North American learning to live in Mexico; and of his wife, an aristocratic Mexican, learning to live with the changes made by the Revolution of 1910 and following.

LAWRENCE, DAVID HERBERT, 1885-1930

The Plumed Serpent (Quetzalcoatl) (Knopf, 1926). A symbolic story of Mexicans returning to the god Quetzalcoatl. The leading character, an Irishwoman, marries a Mexican Indian and embraces the new cult. A speculative approach to the subject of a perfect marriage is a part of the story.

LEA, TOM, 1907-

The Brave Bulls (Little, 1949). Vivid story of two bullfighters, the older brother already known, and the younger beginning his career. Scenic rather than human in tone.

LÓPEZ Y FUENTES, GREGORIO, 1897-

El Indio (Edición Botas, 1937; translated by Anita Brenner, Bobbs, 1937). A good social novel, showing that the revolution didn't solve the Indian's problems, here presented with force and understanding.

MADARIAGA, SALVADOR DE, 1886-

Heart of Jade (Creative Age, 1944). An old-fashioned novel about an Indian princess and a cavalier serving under Cortez. Much detail about the Conquest.

MAGDALENO, MAURICIO, 1906-

Sunburst (translated by Anita Brenner from *Resplanor*, 1937; Viking,

1944). A novel of the Otomí Indians of Hidalgo, showing how the exploitation of the peasants continued under other leadership after the revolution. The misery and poverty of the Indians are vividly portrayed.

MENÉNDEZ-REYES, MIGUEL ANGEL, 1905-
Nayar (Farrar, 1942; translated by Angel Flores, 1940). Beautifully written story of the lives of Indians of Nayarit, their hardships, their relationships to the landowners and the government. Much on local customs, superstitions, etc.

MONDRAGÓN AGUIRRE, MAGDALENA, 1913-
Someday the Dream (Yo, Como Pobre, 1944; translated by Samuel Putnam, Dial, 1947). Of the poor living in the city dumps of Mexico City. They dream of the glories painted in the famous murals. Strong women characters.

NIGGLI, JOSEPHINA
Mexican Village (University of North Carolina Press, 1945). A story of a man half Mexican, half North American, and his life in a small village near Monterrey as he becomes thoroughly Mexicanized. Much on the class system and on folkways.
Step Down, Elder Brother (Rinehart, 1947). Of an old Monterrey family in 1947, beginning to succumb to the new middle-class mestizo group who begin to dominate the city. Interesting flashbacks to the period of the revolution and its leaders, 1910-1920.

NORDHOFF, WALTER (ANTONIO DE FIERRO BLANCO, pseud.), 1858-1947
Journey of the Flame (Houghton, 1933). A likable account of the trip of a boy of twelve through the two Californias during Spanish days. True to the Mexican spirit and psychology.

REVUELTAS, JOSÉ, 1915-
The Stone Knife (El Luto Humano, 1943; translated by H. R. Hays, Reynal, 1947). Poignant story of the last days of a small group of Mexican farmers in a flood. The story gives the background of each main character by recording his thoughts. The relation of the character to the revolution is clear.

ROMERO, JOSÉ RUBÉN, 1890-
The Useless Life of Pito Perez (translated by Joan Coyne from *La Vida Inútil de Pito Perez,* 1938, found in *Fiesta in November*). A picaresque story, in which the pícaro comments on society of his time, around the turn of the century. Ends with his satiric will found on his body.

RULFO, J.
Pedro Paramo (1955; translated by Lysander Kemp, Grove, 1959). Study of the owner of a vast estate, his many loves, his domineering attitudes, and his final downfall.

SPOTA, LUIS
The Wounds of Hunger (1949; translated by Barnaby Conrad, Houghton, 1957). A carefully drawn portrait of the relationship of a young bull-fighter to the "sport" or "racket," as it is actually carried on. An antidote to the romantic treatment.

The Enemy Blood (translated by Robert Molloy, Doubleday, 1961). An analytical story of a middle-aged impotent man and his teen-aged mistress. The insane jealousy and the sadism of the man and the pathetic struggles of the young girl to find happiness in life make up the story. A truly moving story of underprivileged people in a Mexican city.

STACTON, DAVID
A Signal Victory (Pantheon, 1960). The story of a young Spaniard ship-wrecked in Yucatan in 1511. After years of living with the Maya, he is so thoroughly one of them that he accepts their ideas about the destiny of their race and dies in their struggle with the Spanish.

STEINBECK, JOHN, 1902-
The Pearl (Viking, 1947). Beautifully written novel about a young couple living near La Paz. They discover a large pearl, but it seems to bring nothing except hard luck to them, so they finally throw it back into the sea. Good picturing of the life and attitudes of poor fisher-folk.

TRAVEN, BRUNO
The Rebellion of the Hanged (Knopf, 1952). A story of the inhuman exploitation of mahogany loggers in the latter days of the Díaz regime, and of their revolt.

YÁÑEZ, AGUSTÍN, 1904-
The Edge of the Storm (translated by Ethel Brinton, University of Texas Press, 1963). The life of a small priest-ridden village in Jalisco during eighteen months preceding the revolution of 1910.

INDEX OF AUTHORS